Bet...

WOMEN'S STUDIES PROGRAM
UNIVERSITY OF DAYTON
ST. JOSEPH 414

NANCY SHIPPEN
HER
JOURNAL BOOK

NANCY SHIPPEN
FROM THE ORIGINAL MINIATURE
ATTRIBUTED TO BENJAMIN TROTT
Courtesy of
Dr. and Mrs. Lloyd P. Shippen

NANCY SHIPPEN
HER JOURNAL BOOK

*THE INTERNATIONAL ROMANCE
OF A YOUNG LADY OF FASHION
OF COLONIAL PHILADELPHIA
WITH LETTERS TO HER AND
ABOUT HER*

COMPILED AND EDITED BY
ETHEL ARMES

BENJAMIN BLOM   New York/London   1968

First Published 1935
Reissued 1968
by Benjamin Blom, Inc. Bronx, New York 10452
and 56 Doughty Street London, W.C. 1

Library of Congress Catalog Card Number 68-21204

Printed in the United States of America

TO

CATHY

AND

DICK

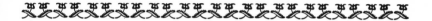

PREFACE

My discovery of the letters and journals which make up the major contents of this book was an accident. In doing research for the Robert E. Lee Memorial Foundation, Inc., my object was to secure records and information that might be of service in the restoration and furnishing of Stratford Hall, the national shrine in Westmoreland County, Virginia, commemorating the patriot Lees. Through Miss Elise Packard, Chairman of Lee Records Committee of the Foundation, I learned that Dr. and Mrs. Lloyd P. Shippen of Washington, D. C., had in the storeroom of their home several chests containing original letters, diaries and other documents which had never been examined in their entirety by any person now living. This in itself was a challenge to the student of Americana. For the records of the Shippens, like those of the Livingstons and the Lees, extend far back into the seventeenth century. These three families were foremost among those taking early root in the Province of Pennsylvania, the Province of New York and the Colony of Virginia, and their records are interwoven with every stage of the beginnings and early progress of the United States of America.

Accordingly I welcomed the opportunity to see and to study the Shippen collection. The major portion of the documents relating to the eighteenth century had been classified by Dr. and Mrs. Shippen, placed in letter books in chronological order and deposited in the Division of Manuscripts of the Library of Congress. The investigation of the collection in both places was begun in October, 1933, with the certainty of finding valuable material for Stratford. When the selection, classification and identification of the documents in the Shippens' storeroom was made, letters and documents of the early nineteenth century found there clarified many previously half-told events in the lives of the families concerned.

The collection as a whole proved to be far broader in scope than was at first surmised. Finding intact such a series of letters practically covering the lives of each member of an entire family: births, education, marriages, separations, deaths, was in itself an amazing circumstance. When considered against the late eighteenth century background of their lives, the historic events of which they were part, before, during and after the American Revolution, this collection contains a priceless record of the inner life, thought and psychology of the times. Nothing else like it has come to light.

In this volume, wherever possible, the full text of the original letters has been reproduced in chronological order and in its original form—with the exception of slight changes in punctuation or capitalization. The letters, notes and fragments written by the Comte de Mosloy appear precisely as in the originals. Only limitations of space prevent inclusion of the whole sheaf of them. Because almost all of his letters are without dates I have placed them where they seemed logically to belong.

At length the collection was ready for typed transcription. Both volumes of the Journal Book and the love letters of the French Diplomat and the other letters were transcribed directly from the original documents by Maud Kay Sites, assistant research worker attached to the Library of Congress. To her I wish to express appreciation for this important service. Miss Sites also assisted in collecting other records, including original letters, contemporary diaries and bibliographical source material. Florence Spofford, research worker at the Library of Congress, gave valuable service, especially during the early stages of the collection and organization of material.

To Roma Kaye Kauffman, who gave a critical reading of the entire manuscript, I am also particularly indebted. From Henry Lanier, who became deeply interested in the journals and letters as a "find" of importance to American history and literature, I have received gracious and practical coöperation.

For source materials I am indebted to Dr. and Mrs. Lloyd P. Shippen, Mrs. Edmund Jennings Lee, Miss Mildred Lee, Mr. I. Newton Lewis, Brigadier-General John Ross Delafield, Mrs. H. Sheldon Rosselle, Mrs. L. C. F. Hambley, Miss Margaret Suckley, Mr. Clifford Lewis, M. André Girodie, curator of the Musée de Blérancourt and Comte Louis de Crevecœur; to the Library of Congress and to Frick Art Reference Library.

For special aid in the location of additional materials or for points of technical information, grateful acknowledgment is given to: Charles Nagel, Jr., Curator of Decorative Arts, Yale University School of the Fine Arts; Fiske Kimball, Director of the Pennsylvania Museum of Art; Georgine Yeatman, Thomas Tileston Waterman, J. Donnell Tilghman, Lucy Hamilton Lamar, Charles E. Rush, Associate Librarian of Yale University Library; Miss Anne Pratt, Comte Pierre de Leusse, Secretary of the French Embassy to the United States; Howard Reinheimer, R. P. Tolman, Acting Director National Gallery of Art, Smithsonian Institution; Dr. E. G. Swem, Librarian of William and Mary College; Dr. John C. Fitzpatrick and Claus Bogel of the Library of Congress; E. Holliday, Editorial Secretary of Yale University Press, Elizabeth Hooper and Mr. and Mrs. George P. Coleman.

For their most generous and courteous coöperation in the

7

way of constructive criticism, I express my gratitude to Mrs. Orton Bishop Brown, Miss Florence Buckman, Mr. and Mrs. Richard William Millar, Mrs. Egbert Jones, Mrs. John P. B. Sinkler, Miss Marion H. Addington, Mrs. Pope Yeatman, Mrs. Alfred I. du Pont, Miss Frances J. Turner, Miss Ethel Newell, Peyton Hawes, Anne Sevier Carter, Helen Hunt West, Lois Buenzli, Byron West, Mr. and Mrs. William H. Fain, Dr. O. H. Huckel, Mr. and Mrs. John Henry King Burgwin, Mr. and Mrs. Harry Thayer, Mrs. Lois Umbsen, Mrs. Wilson Norfleet Felder, Mrs. Naudain Duer, Miss Lilian M. Small, Mrs. Nairn Koellmer, Mrs. William Glasgow, Mrs. H. Snowden Marshall, Mrs. David Roberts, Caroline Stiles Lovell, Mrs. Charles D. Lanier, President of the Robert E. Lee Memorial Foundation, Inc., and other directors in this organization, especially the members of its Committee on Research, of which Mrs. Emerson Root Newell is chairman.

Their enthusiasm over the discovery of the manuscript was delightful, and they have shared with me in the adventure of the research.

ETHEL ARMES

Acorn Club
Philadelphia

CONTENTS

Part One
TIME AND PLACE

Part Two
JOURNAL BOOK AND LETTERS

ILLUSTRATIONS

ILLUSTRATIONS

Part One

Time and Place

INTRODUCTION

Nancy Shippen was a belle and beauty of Philadelphia during the closing years of the American Revolution, when William Penn's "greene country towne" was the capital of the United Colonies. Her lovely Georgian home at Locust Street and South Fourth was then within the heart of this tree-embowered Court End of the little colonial city.

Through Nancy's mother, who was Alice Lee of Stratford Hall, the Shippen family were allied with the Colony of Virginia and devoted to their friends and kinsmen there. When Nancy was a little girl, she addressed a letter to her cousin Matilda Lee, "Miss Lee in dear Virginia." When she was grown up,—that is, as old as fifteen years!—her father was gratified and more than proud when she would "behave like a Virginian" as he expressed it, "like her mother."

In later years when her brother Thomas Lee Shippen was in London studying law at the Inner Temple, his thoughts ever turned towards Virginia . . . "Have you been since your return on a visit to James River?" he wrote his father. "When you go, say to the houses of Westover, Shirley, Hundred & Meade—How do ye in my name . . ."

The Shippen home is still standing, aloof and aristocratic in a neighborhood long since grown shabby and forlorn. It is quite as it was originally, with the exception of an annex put up in the first part of the nineteenth century in what was once the garden.

It is a three and one-half story corner house, built of red

15

brick interspersed with glazed black brick, and has white marble steps and trimmings like many of the other houses of the same Philadelphia colonial architecture in that once fashionable quarter. An iron railing of charming design extends around the areaways from the front door on Locust Street to the door of the annex—once the garden gate. The house presents its chimney side or gable end to the street so that the wall between is carried up in formidable solid mass, sheer from the stately entrance door to the steeply-pitched roof. Some of the ivory-toned, paneled shutters of the small-paned windows are almost hidden by English ivy. Well proportioned, simple in character and vigorous in scale, Shippen House expresses the quiet dignity and well-being of the life of the early American aristocracy.

The French legation was located but a few squares away from Shippen House, on Chestnut Street between Sixth and Seventh Streets. Not a trace of it remains.

At sunset shafts of light fall upon the glistening black and red walls of Nancy Shippen's house. The whole place becomes strangely alive and rich with warm, bright color until the twilight fades and the house turns to one great shadow. All the things of grave historic import that happened there during the last half of the eighteenth century, and the human joys and woes of birth, life, and death, have the vague outlines of shapes seen in dreams.

Through these very windows gazed the French Diplomat one hundred and fifty-five years ago, to see Nancy Shippen pouring tea and to mark for whom she poured. From the Fourth Street pavement—a footpath in 1779—a complete view could be had of the interior of the parlour of Shippen House just as it may be seen today, with the identical woodwork, doors and paneling of the old time, and the same charm of lofty ceiling and spacious proportions. Oddly enough in a

SHIPPEN HOUSE AS IT WAS IN THE EIGHTEENTH CENTURY
SKETCH ADAPTED FROM A PHOTOGRAPH

corner beyond the mantelpiece—which is a later acquisition—is the old hand-wrought iron fireback, bearing the arms of King George III, which was taken from that patriot hearth during the Revolution and thrown face down in the cellar!

This stately parlour, which might be termed Nancy's throne room, witnessed the procession of her beaux, her lovers and her suitors. One by one, each said his say in his own characteristic manner, took his part in the drama of her life, and passed on. There was "Mr. Archer." Nancy's mother termed him "well-bred and sensible" and admonished her daughter forthwith to "put on y^r best looks" when he waited upon her. There was Lord D——, whose actual initials were H. B. L. with whom Nancy flirted so outrageously that she found herself in a dilemma from which the French Diplomat showed her how to "disintigrate" herself, as he expressed it. His "Exercise in English," in reality a lesson in diplomacy for a young lady who is first introduced in the world, is quoted in full at its logical place in this narrative.

Third in that passing group was young Leftenant Thomas W. Moore, stationed at "Camp West Point, lingering out a most disagreeable campaign" with his detachment of troops of the Continental Army "compleating the works." In his letter of July 29, 1779, to Nancy, he said: "Most amiable Miss . . . All my pleasure is compos'd of wishes for the speedy arrival of the Month of November, which I look for with an impatient eye, and hopes for a return of that bliss which accompanied the auspicious moment I first enjoy'd in your presence, and stamp'd your pleasing image on my soul. I will not attempt (for the task will be unequal to me) to repeat the many professions of love that I have made to you let it suffice to assure you that they were the ofspring of Affection and founded upon honour and sincerity. Was I convinced that the flame to its

17

utmost extent was mutual, I should be the happiest mortal in existence. Please to make my humble respects to Mrs Shippen, (I hope soon with propriety to make use of a more tender epithet) . . ."

Nancy's fourth adorer was the law student, Bushrod Washington, Esq., of Bushfield, Westmoreland County, Virginia, General Washington's favorite nephew and, in future years, his heir and successor to Mount Vernon, and a Chief Justice of the Supreme Court. As a diffident youth he called on Nancy at the intervals prescribed by custom. Always reserved and correct in demeanor, this scholarly young Virginia gentleman hardly dared to presume to address "a female acquaintance." There is a wistful note in his letter to her: ". . . my regret on parting with you was not the effusion of a moment or from the peculiar happiness *of a Day*, but it was produced by a sincere and lasting attachment which dreaded a seperation. I have often wished that Philadelphia had fewer charms for me, or that Fortune had fixed me there for Life . . . I only lament that illiberal Custom should in this Country alone discountenance a correspondence between the Sexes . . . . . . The family beg to be remembered to you. My sister's compliments to you and will be much indebted to you for the Ballad of One Fond Kiss &c . . ."

Of sharply contrasting colour was the speech and deportment of Leftenant-Colonel Henry Beekman Livingston of the Continental Army, scion of the Lords of the Manor Livingston, one of the heirs of that family's great fortune, and the catch of the thirteen colonies. Colonel Harry Livingston was mad about women in general and Nancy in particular. On each successive Monday he made his gallant bow to the daughter of Shippen House, until the time when he projected himself into its parlour every afternoon and evening of the week. Once, at

18

half-past three in the morning he wrote to Nancy: "My Dearest Girl, , , to divert myself will Scrall a few Lines; the writing, which at Best [is] Bad, is now worse, from the Dimness of a Lonesome Taper, emblematical of your Lovers Situation with this Difference that it Burns at one End, I all over . . ."

On Tuesdays and Saturdays, so the chronicle records, the parlor of Shippen House witnessed the visits of the French Diplomat, sixth in number of those historic personages of Nancy's train. He it was who became known in later years as Comte de Mosloy; who made the Peace of Amiens; who became the interpreter of the young republic of America to many of the courts of Europe, and when ambassador to Vienna, negotiated the marriage of Napoleon to Marie-Louise. During the period of nearly twelve years that he was in America, he was secretary of the Chevalier de la Luzerne and successively attaché, first secretary and chargé d'affaires of the French legation. At the time of his arrival in Philadelphia in September, 1779, Nancy Shippen, having been formed and educated for the world of fashion, was taking her place in that world. Members of the Spanish, Dutch and South American legations, as well as those of the French legation, and certain of their distinguished guests, were intimates of Shippen House. Among them were Francisco de Miranda, the Marquis de Lafayette, the elegant Vicomte de Noailles, Marquis de Chastellux. It was the future Comte de Mosloy, the French Diplomat, who said to Nancy: "Surrounded with Lovers I could at first see you without great danger." He was handsome and only twenty-five, and Nancy was sixteen and a beauty! Soon he was saying to her: "When Nature had done all what was in her power to make a perfect Woman, when she had graced her work with all the beauty of youth—with all the charms of domestic virtue there was still something left—and that something was at last . . .

19

She gave her the tender heart . . ." Then, another moment he says, "Wit is entertaining but in the heart she must find the source of her happiness." A little later he warns her! "Nothing escaped my watchfull eye since I have the pleasure of knowing you! Lovers are very quick sighted; every little unmeaning favour is precious for them; this Evening I received my tea from your own hands whilst the rest of the Company was served by a black Servant. Perhaps you did not think on it, but I valued it more than any thing I ever received from another hand. But not withstanding I was foolish enough to leave you at 9. o'clock, when I could enjoy a delightfull *tête-à-tête*. That thought puts me in the most violent passion and nothing can cure me but telling you that I adore you more than ever. . . ." Again with all the fervor of his ardent nature he continues: "Your image is so entirely present to me, all my thoughts are so entirely directed towards you that I see or feel nothing in the world but you. . . . In another world I shall distinguish you before a million of your companions and love you in spite of the universe."

For Nancy was sweet to look upon, and sweeter yet to have and hold. Joseph Wright once painted her loveliness. Nancy said "he has dressed me in Leylock satin edged with gold, with a blue girdle. My hair is thrown back negligently & tied with pearls—ringlets in my neck—long sleeves with white satin cuffs and a cape." This portrait of Wright's is lost, but a miniature attributed to Benjamin Trott exists. It is delicately drawn in tender pastel tones, and is now in the possession of the Shippen family of the present generation. It shows Nancy a young lady of fashion, wearing the high-waisted frock of the period with short, puffed, shoulder sleeves, and diminutive ruffles clinging like flower petals to a white throat and bosom. A lavender-colored ribbon encircles her waist. A piquant white taffeta cap with a spreading bow is smartly set on her powdered hair, which falls in waves and ringlets almost to her sloping shoulders. Her features are distinguished: an aquiline nose with widespreading nostrils, rich and sensuous lips, thick, dark, curving eyebrows and deep blue eyes. The face of an intellectual, impulsive, emotional young woman—human in every fibre. Her sheer need of life and love fulfilled was a claim upon Destiny greater perhaps than that of many other women.

That Nancy Shippen had at the one time, a husband, a lover, and a beau, yet did not transgress, by so much as a hair's breadth, the moral standards or the proprieties of her day— nor a single tenet of the laws of love—seems a paradox. None the less such a conclusion is proven by the documentary evidence on which this book is builded from its first page to its last. But be it understood that "lover" is interpreted in its eighteenth century sense of worship from afar!

Every phase of Nancy's love story and her whole youth are set against the stormy background of the American Revolution. Viewed in perspective, each event and episode is inextricably interwoven with dramatic and heroic scenes of the nation's history. Yet because of her education and upbringing—like that of all girls of her time—she was personally untouched by this background and as remote from the great conflict as if she were living in another planet.

Nancy's uncle, Richard Henry Lee, went from the rooftree of Shippen House to the halls of the Continental Congress on that seventh day of June, 1776, to move "That these united Colonies are, and of right ought to be free and independent States; that they are absolved from all allegiance to the British crown; and that all political connection between them and the State of Great Britain is, and ought to be, totally dissolved." Yet Nancy, thirteen years old during that summer, was not impressed, and in writing to her brother Tommy at that very time, never even mentioned this stirring occurrence.

On the fourth day of July of that same year, her favorite uncle Francis Lightfoot Lee, whom Nancy termed "Thou sweetest of all the Lee race" united with his brother Richard Henry in signing the Declaration of Independence. Her mother's five brothers, the patriot Lees of Stratford Hall who took so significant a part in the making of the nation, appeared to Nancy only as beloved uncles, with or without pretty wives, intent upon business which did not interest her. Quite naturally the ode to her new hat which her uncle Arthur wrote for her would impress her far more than ever could the Treaty of Amity, Commerce and Alliance with France which he helped Benjamin Franklin and Silas Deane to make. Of course her mother's kinsmen would be patriots, soldiers, statesmen or diplomatists—every man was who came to their house! That did not keep them from being jolly and delightful.

Others of Nancy's kith and kin were not on the patriot side. The House of Shippen, like many another of that day in all the colonies, was divided against itself. Judge Edward Shippen, first cousin of Nancy's father, kept open house for Sir William Howe and his staff, Captain John André among them, from the day the British entered Philadelphia. So did the majority of the Shippen kinspeople, friends and associates—while General Washington and his Continental Army were being crucified at Valley Forge!

Nancy's pretty cousin, Peggy Shippen, was also but the product of her environment and the prevailing system for "female education." Nearly three years older than Nancy, she was a Philadelphia belle during Nancy's school period, from 1776 to 1778, when her marriage with Benedict Arnold was arranged, so it would appear, by her father. Peggy and her sisters were inordinately fond of dress and jewels and the extravagant silk and satin slippers of the period. Judge Shippen was driven almost to distraction by the demands of his luxury-loving wife and daughters. In vain did he protest his falling fortunes! The *Mischianza* was in the air!

Shippen House was closed during those quicksand days of the British occupation of Philadelphia. As the Philadelphia home and headquarters of the Lees of Stratford and of many of their colleagues from the colonies of Virginia and Maryland, it had been a patriot stronghold for a decade before the Revolution and during the first year of conflict. So it became again throughout the final period of the bitter struggle, and in the succeeding years when Philadelphia was the capital of the United States, the seat of official life and a centre of art, industry and wealth.

President Washington lodged there occasionally and, with his family frequently drank tea at Shippen House. Members of the First Cabinet with their ladies breakfast, dine and drink tea or "sentiments" there, again and again, among them, John Adams, the vice president; Thomas Jefferson, secretary of state; Alexander Hamilton, secretary of the treasury; General Henry Knox, secretary of war; Nancy's kinsmen, Attorney-General Charles Lee of Alexandria and his brother Light Horse Harry Lee, Richard Henry Lee, Arthur Lee and Francis Lightfoot Lee, with prominent members of each succeeding Congress, and Chancellor Livingston, first secretary of foreign affairs and members of the first foreign legations to the United States.

With the exception of these glimpses of parlour episodes of Shippen House, the chronicle presented here proceeds in more or less chronological order. Its contents fall logically into nine chapters. Events and letters of the period of Nancy's school

23

days, from 1777 to 1779, with a description of her mother's birthplace, Stratford Hall, Virginia, are followed by the record of the years from 1779 to 1783. The third and fourth chapters, in which the young French Diplomat is introduced, treat of the period during the closing years of the Revolution when Nancy Shippen shared with her cousin, Nancy Willing, the rôle of being Philadelphia's most popular and attractive belle. They carry one through her joyous youth to the day of her marriage, and draw the background for the tragic drama unfolded in her journal books.

The connecting link between Stratford Hall in Virginia and Shippen House in Philadelphia was forged through the marriage of Dr. William Shippen the Younger, of Philadelphia, and Alice Lee, daughter of the Honourable Colº Thomas Lee, acting governor of the Colony of Virginia, builder of Stratford Hall. Their children were Nancy Shippen and Thomas Lee Shippen. Tommy visited and also lived in Virginia at intervals during several years, at Williamsburg, and at the homes of his various kinspeople. His brief description of the gardens of Stratford Hall written in the year 1790 and originally published in Edmund Jennings Lee's "Lee of Virginia" helped to form the basis for the plan adopted in the year 1929 by the Garden Club of Virginia in its restoration of the Stratford gardens. Among the first of the unknown treasures revealed in one of the boxes at the Library of Congress was an autographed letter of Tommy's, dated December 30, 1783, written from Westover, Virginia, to his parents in Philadelphia, containing a description of the ancestral seat of the Byrd family with a crude diagram of the layout of the buildings, gardens and grounds.[1] On the off chance that Tom

---

[1] The first photostat copy of the original letter was made by the editor and given to Mrs. Luke Vincent Lockwood for publication in "Gardens of Colony and State." Dr. E. G. Swem said of it: "This letter contains the most ade-

Shippen might also have described Stratford in more detail and perhaps made a diagram similar to the Westover sketch, the editor concentrated on the Shippen box containing a number of Tommy's diaries, memorandum and account books.

Suddenly came a glimpse of a small book, in different binding from the others, and almost hidden by them. An odd, thin little volume that in itself diverted attention from everything else for the moment. The book is vellum-covered, in size 6¼ by 7¾ inches. Its parchment binding, sepia-toned with age, with a double box rule on both covers is stretched over cardboard and sewed with vellum bands. Compared with its contemporaries, usually dressed in ordinary paper or cardboard, cowhide or pigskin, it has an air of exclusiveness. It is smart, aristocratic. Sloping across the cover in an irregular line, printed by hand in neat, well-formed capitals in faded brown ink, is the following title: "Anne H. Livingston Journal Book First Volume."

"Ann Home Livingston" is repeated on the cover with the "e" omitted from Anne. "Anna Home Livingston" with a flowered initial "A" occurs in the lining-cover. The middle name is "Hume" on the title page reproduced at page 138. Although her mother's friend, for whom Nancy was named, was Anne Home, Nancy changes it at will.

Who was this variable young person? It was in the argument that she must be young. Up to that moment the editor knew only of Thomas Lee Shippen. Review of the Shippen genealogical chart proved that Tommy had an only sister, Anne Home, otherwise Nancy Shippen, who was born in Philadelphia February 24, 1763. In the family archives there is solely the record of her birth, marriage and death, according to the prescribed

quate, complete and detailed description that has ever been found of any one of the eighteenth century houses of Virginia." See *Supplementary Records*.

rule of the eighteenth and early nineteenth centuries for the female sex. Not another line, not another word about her! The probability that Nancy also wrote journals and letters had not been considered by the editor in delving into the wealth of her brother's voluminous papers. Here was news!

Closer study of the small treasure showed these lines inside the front cover: "Reciepts: Mrs. A. H[arriet] Shippen", with a pen scratch deleting them. This smart little volume was originally intended to be Alice Lee's cook-book. Appropriated by her daughter for a diary, it is stamped with that daughter's name in every way it was possible to spell it! The book contains 116 pages and the paper is the regular eighteenth century handmade linen, with the watermark of a helmeted Continental soldier in action, musket in hand, pointing to the legend *Pro Patria;* thus proving the paper to be of native manufacture and of the Revolutionary period. The ink, of the usual contemporary type, is sepia-brown with age and tones in with the rare, time-stained vellum, effectively preserving the record it may be for centuries to come. The penmanship as a whole is legible, though it has not the rhythmic quality and chiseled character of the handwriting of certain of Nancy's Virginia cousins and contemporaries. On some pages it is uneven as if hastily and carelessly written, or as if the writer were laboring under extreme emotional strain.

With what curiosity, eagerness, suspense, one stepped into the maze! How could one find the way in or out? The very first lines in the strange little book wafted the aroma of her place and time. But whatever was Nancy talking about? Who ". . . rode out with Lord Worthy?" or "had a conversation about Lord B. & dear Leander?" and found "His sentiments corresponding with mine made me extremely happy—wou'd to

God it was a happiness that wou'd last—but the die is cast—&
my life must be miserable!" Was this melodrama? Comedy?

Who were these titled and romantic personages? The first
and second reading answered many of these questions, solved a
number of problems, provided the key, and showed that Nancy,
true to her character and her period, was merely giving fanciful
names to everyday people and weaving about them and herself
the artificial glamour typical of her day. Where titles are not
used, the characters in her journal are referred to as The Old
Lady, Lord Worthy, Lady Worthy, Young Worthy; others
by initials, such as Mr. W., A. L., R. H. L., Mrs. M., etc.
Mr. W. is Mr. Bushrod Washington, A. L. is Arthur Lee,
R. H. L. is Richard Henry Lee, and Mrs. M. is Mrs. Janet
Livingston Montgomery, widow of General Richard Montgomery.

Volume II of the journal was found in the same box. It is
slightly larger than Volume I, 6½ by 8 inches in size and
bound in eighteenth century marbled paper on boards, with
a leather back. The hand-made paper and cover are typical of
colonial Pennsylvania. The dramatic narrative of volume one
is continued in logical sequence through one hundred and fifty
pages to its tragic conclusion.

In editing the journals, Nancy's quaint, arbitrary spelling
is kept precisely as it is in the original; also the usage of the
letter superior, the "&," "ye" and the apostrophe—all com-
ponent parts of eighteenth century form and custom. It is
to be regretted that the long "s" has to be sacrificed for clar-
ity's sake. For a like reason, some of Nancy's arbitrary dates
have to be corrected at times and punctuation and capitalization
occasionally altered, except when the episode told, or the
writer's emotional strain forbade, such a liberty. Practically all
entries in Volume I have been retained with the exception of

a few which record quite unimportant details and a number of quoted verses, so that this volume is almost a reproduction of the original. From Volume II many pages have been omitted. Nancy's laments at having to live alone with her mother in the country—a life which she found so dull—were likewise dull in the reading. Her final pages are omitted because they drift into transcripts from soporific sermons, distinctly burdensome. The letters Nancy Shippen received from her uncle Arthur Lee, her brother, her parents, from Mrs. Robert R. Livingston of Clermont, mother of the Chancellor, from Mrs. Theodorick Bland, General Knox, Bushrod Washington and especially those from the Comte de Mosloy—all give a striking historic value—an aspect of national and even international interest to these documents.

In this volume there is the same usage of names and initials, —therefore a bewildering task to solve the riddle of who was who! At length each character was snared and caught, labeled and set aside excepting one. The elusive "Leander," the hero "who was once . . . my lover" figures in the lines and between the lines throughout the volumes. He was the Man Mysterious! Who was he? Many readings revealed not one clue. Nor were any signs evident in the other letters or papers to point to his identity. Nor could any living descendant of the William Shippens or the Lees or Livingstons throw a gleam of light on the mystery. That Nancy called him "Leander" might possibly connote association in her mind with sharp difficulties for her lover like those vanquished by the youth of Abydos, mighty swimmer of the Hellespont, to reach his Lady, Hero, in the high tower.

Continued study of the manuscript, however, presented at last an intangible clue, in Nancy's entry of May 27 (1783): "Leander went past the window while we were at Tea—he

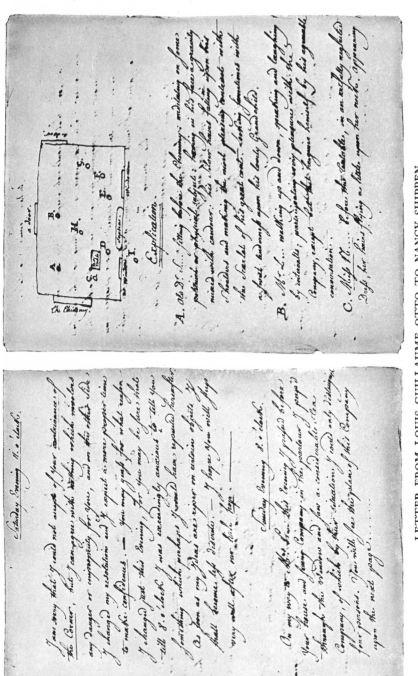

LETTER FROM LOUIS GUILLAUME OTTO TO NANCY SHIPPEN

(Pages 3 and 4 on the Reverse)

look'd in—and his Eyes told me he would be happy to join us—but I did not ask him—prudence forbid it."

Perhaps a mention of such an afternoon tea at Shippen House might be made in some of the unsigned, unidentified letters in the boxes. There was a sheaf of such mysterious letters in elegant penmanship, but without signature or address, which were put aside for later examination. Now miraculously—no other word can describe it—this reference caught the eye: "Sunday evening 8 o'clock. On my way to Mrs. P[owell] this evening I passed before your house and seeing company in the parlour I peeped through the window and saw a considerable Tea Company. . . . You will see the plan of this Company upon the next page. . . ." A neatly drawn diagram on the following page is an actual replica of the parlour floor plan of Shippen House, even to the exact placement of doors, windows and fireplace! The "Explication" describes briefly each person in the room: Nancy, her mother, her uncle and grandfather, the butler "Cyrus," and Leander himself "Mr. O"—the spy outside, looking in. This letter is reproduced in these pages both in the text and in a photostat copy of the original. For the editor it marked the gain of a salient point in the skirmish to capture Leander's identity—his name began with "O"!

The next logical move was to assemble and read every letter, verse, note and fragment in that same exquisite handwriting. They were amazing letters. A man of fashion, well bred, charming, and moving in Nancy's sphere, this correspondent was also obviously a young man of parts. He had good sense, intellect, fancy and even a certain literary grace and distinction of expression. That he was a foreigner—a Frenchman—was indicated by the letters. But the one point gained, that his name began with an "O", was lost as the scrutiny continued! The

29

majority of the letters were unsigned and undated, but several were signed with the initials "M" and "L", as well as "O." One was signed "Lewis"; others "Maria," "John-Wait-Too-Long," "Damon," "Mr. Venoni," "J Wait-Patiently," "Mr. Runaway," "Lewis Scriblerius," "Mr. Reciprocity!" Addresses on two letters proved to be "Patience Island in Elysium" and "In the Other World." The salutations, all in reality meant for Nancy, as proven by the context, were addressed to "Miss Runaway," "Dear Miss," "Miss Inconstant," "Amanda," "Julia," "Phyllis" and "Emilia"!

Here was a situation! There was still no clue whatsoever to the identity of this correspondent. Did the screen of fictitious names point to a clandestine affair? This question is answered by Nancy herself when she repeats the dictum of one of her beaux, Mr. Bushrod Washington: "Illiberal custom prevents a correspondence between the sexes." Yet here was a sheaf of Leander's letters proving how Love laughs at locksmiths and will have its way, while carefully protecting both principals from prying eyes and public censure.

Thus every path led to a cul-de-sac. It became advisable to turn elsewhere and examine letters written by Nancy's family. Surely Tom Shippen would speak of his sister's beaux. But Tommy was off at boarding school. Possibly Nancy's father might mention them in his correspondence with his son, who was his one confidant. A closer study of Dr. Shippen's letters brought surprisingly fruitful results: two letters which contained magic phrases. The first was in a letter dated November 9, 1780, . . . "Otto and Nancy playing harpsichord together"; the second, in a letter written from Philadelphia January 14, 1781, "Your sister has Otto and Livingston contending for her smiles."

His name was Otto!

There was but one Otto in the card index at the Library of Congress. "The Annual Report of the American Historical Association" describes him as L G O, Comte de Mosloy. "The State Papers of France," mention him as French chargé d'affaires. One brief letter from Charles Thomson, Secretary of the First Congress, gives his name. Every fact was compared and checked with dates and incidents connected with "Leander" mentioned by Nancy Shippen, and then with the happenings, descriptions, and phrases in the intriguing letters all in the same handwriting and signed by so many intriguing names.

Here was the myth become man! A comparison was made of the handwriting of all the unsigned undated letters to Nancy with Louis Otto's official papers in the Henry Adams Collection of French State Papers of Moustier, 1787-1789-1791, which are in their original form. The handwriting there is Louis Otto's and the documents bear his autographed signature. The memoirs of the French officers who came to the American Colonies with the Marquis de Lafayette and Rochambeau contain mention of him. As further corroboration, in the Marquis de Chastellux's "Travels in North-America in the Years 1780, 1781, and 1782" are references to Philadelphia and Otto [Ottaw by typographical error] with explicit reference to the incident when Nancy Shippen danced with Vicomte de Noailles, and the visit paid to Shippen House by Lafayette, Chastellux and all their group, shortly after the French fleet arrived off Newport. And further there came to light in the second volume of Nancy's journal an entry beginning: "My Friend Leander is arrived from France in the honorable character of Secretary to the Embassy & charge des affaires of France," under date of Sunday, September 6, 1785. This is quoted in full at the proper place in this volume. It was found almost smothered in Nancy's transcripts from old sermons.

31

Thus it was established by documentary evidence that the French Diplomat, Louis Guillaume Otto was the Comte de Mosloy, who in his youth was the mysterious "Leander" of Nancy Shippen's journal; further, that he was her first love and her last, and the author of the series of love letters by an unknown person preserved in the Shippen Papers for a century and a half.

Later researches of the editor extending to France, were enhanced by information received directly from Comte de Mosloy's great-great-nephew, M. le Comte Louis de Crevecœur, now living in Paris, and from M. André Girodie, the courteous curator of the Musée de Blérancourt, both of whom are authorities on Otto's history. M. Louis Salanson's collection of de Mosloy portraits, relics, documents and souvenirs is now in the Musée de Blérancourt. At the Palace of Versailles there is a great portrait of this French Diplomat, who, some years after leaving the United States, took such significant part in the diplomatic history of France and in world events. This portrait was painted in M. Otto's old age. With him is his son-in-law, Joseph Claremont Pelet de la Lozère. There is also a portrait of Comte de Mosloy done by Trumbull, miniatures on ivory by Vieth and Jukes, and an engraving in profile made at the time of the American Revolution. The picture that appears in this book, by courtesy of M. le Comte de Crevecœur, is from the original miniature by Jukes. It was painted in London in the year 1801, the time when M. Otto was initiating and directing negotiations for the Treaty of Amiens. It is the face and figure of an aristocrat, a statesman and a poet. The artist has shown as vigorously the gracious inner life and honourable character of the man as he has the strongly modeled, handsome features. They prove him resolute and courageous, adamant of will yet gentle by reason of strength, with

32

LOUIS GUILLAUME OTTO, COMTE DE MOSLOY
FROM THE ORIGINAL MINIATURE BY JUKES. PAINTED IN LONDON 1801
Courtesy of M. le Comte L. de Crevecœur

a pleasant humor to grace intelligence. But in every lineament of his face there is a depth of melancholy unfathomable.

His secret letters to Nancy Shippen, so miraculously preserved, enrich American literature. Of all the tender contributions, to say nothing of the heroic gifts, made to young America by the Frenchmen who came here with Lafayette and Rochambeau at the birth of the Republic, these letters written by Louis Otto straight from his heart to his Beloved Friend have perhaps the most precious human quality of documents of that age. His chivalrous devotion to the daughter of a patriot house filled her youth with beauty, fragrance, and poetic charm.

A cursory reading of the "Journal Book" and the love letters might make them seem but a young girl's illusions and vagaries, a young man's passing fancies and emotions—half fiction, the stuff of dreams—but unexpectedly they turn into bright historic fact. Every word is true. Every experience and event actually happened; every emotion came in reality to pass. These ancient fragments of torn parchment recording their secret love still bear the tear stains of the long heartbreak that was theirs. They quiver in our hands today like white birds with broken wings lost in an alien world far from their home— the Land of dear Romance. In these pages I try to return them there.

CHAPTER I

1777

[Addressed:] Mrs Alicia Shippen
                    in
                  Virginia

                                    Trenton, January 2^d 1777

My more than ever dear Mamma,

Once more I take up my pen to write to the one I love. O! Mamma though short to some, the interval of time since I had the pleasure of seeing you, to me it seems an age! and when I reflect how many such I am doomed to bear, in the absence of the best of parents, I am inconsolable! and if it were possible that nature could subsist on sleep alone, I could with pleasure renounce every amusement, & make the silent pillow my retreat. I am affraid by my not hearing from you that the distance has prevented your receiving my letters, the number being five. I hope soon to hear of your safe arival in dear Virginia & possessing a greater share of health than when I left you. Mrs Roger & the young Ladies present their compliments I cant express their kindness to me.

God bless you my dear Mamma & make me a deserving daughter of so good a mother.

                                                Anne Shippen

At the moment Nancy was writing from Mistress Rogers' School for Young Ladies in Trenton, New Jersey, Lord Cornwallis with eight thousand British infantry was wheeling back on the town, bent upon retrieving his lost stronghold. For on Christmas night, during that holiday week, General Washington with his single division of troops of the Continental Army had crossed the Delaware, surprised and overthrown the Hessians and flung his challenge to the enemy. Overnight the American

35

artillery had shorn the little city of its strength as a British centre, and this unforeseen triumph for the patriot cause turned the tide of the American Revolution.

Almost at the doorstep of Nancy's school, during that closing week of 1776 and through the first fourteen days of 1777, was wrought the miracle of victory out of defeat. Through Washington's rally of his broken, despairing army, and its gallant fight, the state of New Jersey was wrested from the grasp of the British and heart and hope were put into the crippled patriot troops.

Through the battle zone moved Nancy's father, William Shippen, the Doctor of Physick and Surgery. Chief physician of the flying camp of the Continental Army, he was a stalwart, tireless, invincible figure, now at headquarters, now on the march, in camp or at home in Philadelphia, improvising out of the very air, hospitals, staff, medicines, equipment. He directed the care of the sick, the wounded and the dying under the greatest difficulties. Yet between his unwearying labors and those savage engagements with the enemy at Trenton, Princeton, Brandywine, Germantown, he would find a way to procure for his little daughter the "canvass" her mother said she must have. For Nancy was making a mat "with the Towns worked in marking stitch." Perhaps he provided, too, the "book muslin," the bits of cambric, satin, cotton and dimity and the needles— all that she required for her tambour work, sewing and embroidery. His letters to her and to his son Tommy, also placed in a safe boarding school during those perilous years, were written on the wing: "My dear Nancy . . . was pleased with your french letter which was much better spelt than your English one, in which I was sorry to see four of five words wrong. Take care my dear girl of your spelling and your teeth. Present

36

DR. WILLIAM SHIPPEN THE YOUNGER
FROM THE ORIGINAL PORTRAIT BY GILBERT STUART
Courtesy of Dr. and Mrs. Lloyd P. Shippen

my compliments to Mrs Roger & Miss Jones . . . your loving Father."

While her father was drawing up for presentation to the Continental Congress his plan for the organization of a hospital department, Nancy was making, at his request, "a p^{rr} of ruffles for General Washington." During that very spring Dr. Shippen's plan, which formed the groundwork for the future Medical Corps of the United States Army, was adopted by the Congress and he was unanimously elected "Director General of all the military hospitals of the Armies of the United States." But there was doubtless no question as to which enterprise was the more momentous to the Shippen family—the p^{rr} of ruffles would stand first!

Whether or not the enemy forced Washington from the Brandywine and occupied the city of Philadelphia, Nancy must learn to curtsy with her head and shoulders held high! She must play the harpsichord, sing, dance, study French and speak the tongue with flavor. She must read Young's "Night Thoughts," Milton, Dryden, Pope, Cowper, *The Spectator*, and Goldsmith. Her penmanship must be elegant; her needlework and embroidery perfection. Her manners and her behavior, within and without, must be set in a pattern outlined by her "tutresses" and her parents. All this, when Philadelphia was a charnel house, when the "sick, and wounded" of the patriot army were being brought from camps and battlefields to the Court End of the city close to Nancy's home . . . "alas! our Philadelphia is not as it used to be. One can scarce walk a square without seeing the shocking sight of a Cart with five or six coffins in it. Oh! it is too dreadful a scene to Attempt to describe. The poor Creatures die without number. Large pits are dug in the negroes ground,—and

37

forty or fifty coffins are put in the same hole . . . The well soldiers are Quartered on private families." [1]

In one house converted overnight into a hospital there was an incredible death toll of the soldiers. Little Nancy Shippen knew this place as Carpenter's Mansion or The Old Graeme House, on Chestnut Street above Sixth. It was first occupied by Governor Thomas and his Lady. Dr. Graeme and his wife, who was a daughter of Sir William Keith, also a Governor of the Province of Pennsylvania, had lived there with their daughter the poetess, Mrs. Ferguson. It was the home of Colonel John Dickinson during the first sessions of the Continental Congress. Vacant during the winter and spring of 1777, it was turned to the needs of the moment. The sick infantry of the Virginia and Pennsylvania line who were stricken by the scourge of camp fever were quartered there. They died by the hundreds. Such medical care as could be given did not avail, and in vain did the neighbours bring nourishing food and General Washington send the huge cask of Madeira which he had received as a gift from Robert Morris. [2] The ancient house became a dormitory of the dead, its once lovely orchards, gardens and courtyard and the green beyond its doorstep a ghastly sepulchre.

The spectre of plague was shuddering over the city, when, on the dark, low horizon beyond the Delaware, like the ominous sound of distant guns, came rumor of the British advance. The patriot families of Philadelphia were small in number by comparison with those who openly supported the British cause. They made ready to flee the place. Dr. Shippen's cousin, Mr. Thomas Willing, received a letter from the British commander

[1] Letter written Jan. 27, 1777, by Deborah Norris (Mrs. George Logan of Stenton) published in Sally Wistar's "Journal," p. 190.
[2] Watson: *Annals of Philadelphia*.

Sir William Howe, requesting him to inform the inhabitants to remain quietly and peaceably in their own dwellings and they should not be molested.[3] But Nancy's home, Shippen House, was among those instantly vacated. On September 26, 1777, the British troops, under command of General Sir William Howe, took possession of the capital of the thirteen colonies.

With Nancy's father in the field, her mother, like many another wife of the Continental soldier, became a refugee. Tossed by the changing seas of conflict, she was sometimes close to the enemy's lines in Pennsylvania and New Jersey, and again in Maryland or Virginia. She could not have Nancy and Tommy with her, for she was too ill and frail since the birth in August, 1776, of a son, William Arthur Lee Shippen, who died soon after. Furthermore, the two children were better cared for and more secure in their respective schools. With New Jersey British ground, Mistress Rogers' School seemed a haven of safety for Nancy and her companions, daughters of both patriot and Tory families, and Tommy was being well trained at The Forest of Needwood Academy near Frederick Town, Maryland. In her mother's eyes the subject of Nancy's "improvements" transcended all else except Tommy's welfare:

My dear Nancy

Your Papa has not time to write & I am scarcely able but I am pleased with your letter. . . . Tell me in your next how you spend your time. Ask M[rs] Roger where she supplys herself with materials for Japaning, Crowning, Painting & if they can be got you shall have them for I would willingly do anything in my power that would assist in your improvement. Much depends on your being improved. Neglect nothing that will make you agreable to M[rs] Roger & your school-fellows; never make mischief but rather when any of them fall into a scrape try, if you can see

[3] Diary of Robert Morton, *Pennsylvania Magazine of History*, Vol. VI, 1877, p. 7.

any opening, to do so, to bring them off. I have sent you a little thread & three p^r of sleeves to make for yourself, in a few days I will send you a good asortment of needles, & you must let me know what sort of thread you want.

I am my dear Girl

Your Affec^e Mother

31st August 1777.

If you can get anybody where you are to take the lock off y^r Pian[a]forte do & send it & a key shall be made. I have sent you but one p^r of sleeves because I am not sure they will fit as I had nothing to cut them by. Do you want any more of y^r silk? Y^r matress not ready yet. You must alter y^r calash. Be a good Girl & give my Comp^ts to Mrs Roger. Y^r desk shall come when the matress comes.

My dear Nancy

I was extremely surprized when the waggon return'd the other evening without one line from you after I had been at the trouble & expence of sending for you as soon as I was inform'd 4000 troops were landed in Elizabeth-Town. Surely you should not omit any opportunity of writing to me, but to neglect such a one was inexcusable, but I shall say the less to you now, because you have been taught your duty & I take it for granted Mrs Rogers has already reproved you for so great an omission, but do remember my dear how much of the beauty & usefulness of life depends on a proper conduct in the several relations in life, & the sweet peace that flows from the consideration of doing our duty to all with whom we are conected. I am sorry it is not in my power to get you the things I promised. It was late before I got to Philadelphia the afternoon I left you & the shops were shut the next day. I have looked all over this place but no muslin, satin or dimity can be got. However your Uncle Joe says he has a whole suit of dimity very fine & that you may have what you want. Get enough for two work bags one for me & the other for yourself.

Your Pappa thinks you had better work a p^r of ruffles for General Washington if you can get proper muslin. Write to me as soon as you receive this & send your letter to your Pappa. Tell me how you improve in your work. Needle work is a most important branch of a female education, & tell me how you have improved in holding your head & sholders, in making a curtsy, in going out or coming into a room, in giving & receiving, holding your knife & fork, walking & seting. These things contribute so much to a good appearance that they are of great consequence. Perhaps you will be at a loss how to judge wether you improve or not, take this rule therefore for your assistance. You may be sure you improve in proportion to the degree of ease with which you do any thing as you have been taught to do it, & as you may be partial to yourself as to your appearance of ease (for you must not only feel easy but appear so) ask Mrs Rogers opinion as a friend who now acts for you in my place & you must look upon her as your parent as well as your Governess as you are at this time wholy in her care & you may depend upon it if you treat her with the duty & affection of a child she will have the feelings of a parent for you. Give my compliments to her & tell her I thank her for the care she takes of you. Give my compliments to the young Ladies. I am sorry Miss Stevens has left you. Dont offend Miss Jones by speaking against the Quakers. Tell Polly I shall remember her when I return. There is an alarm here the enemy are said to be coming this way, tis lucky you are not with me. Your Uncle F. Lee & his Lady & M^r & Mrs Haywood are with me in the same house. They set out today for Lancaster & I for Maryland. I believe I will write to you as soon as I get settled. Farewell my dear. Be good & you will surely be happy which will contribute very much to the happiness of

Reding 22 Sept. 1777. Your Affect. Mother
  Miss Shippen A Shippen
    at Mrs Roger's

My dear Nancy

Why don't you write to me & tell me how you do & how you improve in your work, in writing & drawing, in your address, in holding yourself & in the Graces. These are absolutely necessary to make you shine, but above all let me know how you improve in humility, patience & love, these will make my dear Girl shine

41

to all eternity. These are the inheritance that fadeth not away. I was pleased with your last & only letter I received since I left you. I say it pleased me because it inform'd me your good Mrs Rogers has found out a way of encourageing you in your work & pays great attention to your improvement & by way of joining her in encourageing you to be industrious, which makes so great a part of a female character. I have sent to Carolina for Tambour cotton, silk & needles, & that I may be prepared to reward you if Mrs Rogers shou'd write me you are much improved & are a very good Girl I have sent for some very pretty things which I can either bestow upon you or dispose of in another way if you should not answer my expectations. I have sent you silk for a bonnet & cloak which you must take great care of, not only because a young Lady should not dirty her cloathes but because they cost your Papa so much money. I wou'd have had them made here but that they wou'd have been spoil'd in coming to you. No trimmings of any sort can be got therefore you must make your squirell skin do. I have sent flanel to line it which is genteel & very warm & that I know you like. I wou'd have sent you black silk for a bib & apron but can't get any in this place. but I have desired your Papa to look out. Don't leave off y^r Vandikes till December, y^r Collar is at Bethlehem, your Papa I hope will remember to bring it you for I am sure it is absolutely necessary for you. I send you a yard of cambrick which you may give as much as you please of to your Polly for caps. The book muslin I send is to work a p^{rr} of ruffles for General Washington. I should like them grownded like the Apron Mrs Rogers shew'd me & I am sure if you do them well they will be taken for lace, but it is impossible for me to get thread. You need not make Bobins for me I shall not want them. Has your Uncle Joe given you the dimity? he promised me he wou'd. I have some thoughts of going to Virginia when I return with your dear Brother. If I shou'd I will bring Mrs Rogers a pupil, one of your pretty Cousins. Present my Compliments to Mrs Rogers & that you may so improve as to do her credit & make Your Papa & me happy is the **Prayer** of

Your very Aff^e Mother

A. Shippen

Redding. 8th November. 1777.

If Mrs Rogers has no objection I'd like you to work a map. it is not grounded the Towns only are worked in marking stitch. Y^r Papa will try to get the canvass.

Letters to Nancy from her twelve year old brother Tommy show the striking contrast between the education of the boy and the girl. His, in tune with the times and events, related to the world in which they lived. The very motto on his seal was "America possessed of liberty!"

Forest of Needwood Decem^r 2^d 1777

My Dear Sister,

Nothing but affection could induce me to write you a second letter, since you did not answer my first, nor even sent your love to your dear Brother, who loves you dearly, and wishes to see you shine. Our Dear Mamma left me the other day, so that I am now here alone, in a worse situation than you, for Papa comes (I suppose) to see you very often, and I never see anybody of my acquaintance, I am now reading Terence, in the first Class, also Geography. I am pretty far advanced in both. My Dear Nancy, pray answer this short epistle by the first opportunity. Please to give my best Compliments to your good Governess Mrs Rogers, and your school fellows. I hope that mutual amity subsists between you. Time, Pen, and Paper, I hope will be a sufficient excuse to my Dear Sister. I am my Dearest Sister

Your very loving & affectionate brother
Thom^s Lee Shippen

On verso: Lest you should mistake, my seal is America possessed of Liberty

Manheim May 11th 1777

My Dear Sister,

It is now near a twelvemonth since I had the pleasure of seeing you, but hope in a fortnight to have a Conversation with you I

have so long wish'd for. I will bring you some paper with me
when I come as you stand so much in need of it. What do you
think of Lewis the 16th King of France's Conduct? Dont you
think the Curtain is drawn, and the ball finished? Pray toast him
in whatever you drink. I have heard that the Enemy are leaving
Philadelphia very fast when we (I hope) shall live in uninterrupted peace and tranquility.

Do give my Compliments to your good Mistress Mrs Roger.
Mr Spencer who favours me with his care of this waits, So that I
have only time to assure you that,

 I am, my Dear *little* Girl
     Your ever affectionate and loving brother
        THOMAS LEE SHIPPEN

Please to excuse my Scrawl as I have
a very bad pen and no time.
We had walking illuminations.

Addressed: Miss Shippen

The entire Shippen family, father, mother and brother, were
united in the desire to see their Nancy shine! The school, like
a little tranquil island untouched by even the spray of the
tempestuous waves raging around it, held Nancy from all harm.
But how different was the situation for her mother! For, with
the British occupying Philadelphia, her home would be abandoned for no one knew how long. Her children were far from
her, and their letters lost in the passing. Her husband was bur-
dened with the heroic tasks in which she could no longer share.
Her own arms were empty and she yearned for her lost baby.
Then, too, her England which she once so loved had turned
tiger in the night. Sick in body and in mind, Alice Lee Shippen
turned to the southward—toward one place deep in her heart
and far then from range of the enemy's guns. This was her
birthplace, Stratford Hall "in dear Virginia," the home which
she had not seen for more than seventeen years.

INTERLUDE

1777-1778

THE warmth and glow of Indian summer lay upon Stratford Hall. Long and low, close to the earth, the Great House with its breast-high garden walls and brooding out-buildings seemed planted in England itself, rooted in the ground of ages past. The tall watchtowers made by the groups of huge chimneys in each wide-spreading wing were like the massive trunks of virgin forest trees growing out of the bastions of some ancient fortification. The high-pitched hipped roof of the Great House was moss-grey. The ever-changing colors of the Virginia brick blended softly in dull gold and crimson, bronze and purple, like the fresh fallen leaves in the vast plantation woods, the faded grasses of its highland meadows and low marsh hollows, and the tree-tops misty against the rim of sky and river at its northern edge. The smell of old box was in the air,—just as it used to be—the pungent odor of crumbling leaves and the fragrant aroma of pines. The wind whispering or rising to a roar in the enclosing forest was like the sound of waterfalls, now far, now near.

Into the wide-open doors of the south entrance of the house mounted the front steps steep and high like those of the Castle at old Green Spring on the River James, the Tudor home of Alice Lee's mother, Hannah Ludwell. On those rich autumn afternoons the very stones of this high stoop were warm to the touch, so that the Great House and all that belonged to it and came forth from it seemed united with the sun. Stratford Hall

45

was welcoming its daughter home out of the teeth of war.

The dancing feet of two little girls were all about the place when Alice Lee came home. The daughters of her dead brother, Philip, Matilda and Flora Lee were grown so tall! Matilda was the same age as Alice's own child, Nancy Shippen, just fourteen. The baby and heir of Stratford was Philip Ludwell Lee II, who was born in February, 1775, the day after his father died.

In the long interval since Alice Lee had seen her old home and its gardens, how little they had changed! But how many changes had come in the lives and circumstances of each member of the Stratford family! Long ago it seemed—that May day of the year 1760—when she had said good-bye to Stratford and had set sail for England, never dreaming to come back to dear Virginia. Yet the house was the same as when her father's hand had put on the last touch. The same as when her brother Richard Henry Lee was born and after him Francis Lightfoot, herself, and then William and Arthur. There was the Great Chamber—unchanged—her mother's room where they all were born.

This was the large south room in the east wing of the Great House. Two of its deep-recessed windows looked out upon the eastern prospect: the grove of English beech trees and the walled garden beyond, with its descending terraces, box-bordered paths, parterres of flowers and shrubs and beds of fragrant herbs; its grapes, figs and pomegranates ripening in the sun—all the flowers, fruits, and shades that her father had planted. The other two windows opened to the southward full upon the pleasant lawn with the sun-dial lifting its head like a flower stalk above the ha-ha wall, and far ranging lawns and pastures through which the oak and cedar-shaded entrance drive wound nearly two miles to the King's Highway.

46

STRATFORD HALL, VIRGINIA, THE HOME OF THE LEES
FROM AN OLD PRINT

The warmest, sunniest room in the Great House—her mother's room! She could lift again the very latch her mother's hand had touched each day—the latch on the richly paneled door with the butterfly hinge. How softly it drifted shut when the baby was asleep! Here was the wide fireplace that warmed them all—the parent fireplace. And in the nursery into which the Great Chamber opened was the baby fireplace with the wrought iron cherub heads on its fireback that guarded them while they slept, when they were little. . . . She would open again each many-paned window that had felt her mother's hand. She would walk again every wide floor board on which that gentle foot had stepped from day to day for many a year. Perhaps on the bureau there might still be the little triangular pin-cushion her mother had fashioned in autumn colors. Perhaps in the huge oak chest or the lowboy there still might be the milk-white christening gown made and embroidered by her mother, and worn by each child in turn on the day of christening. The very act of seeing it and touching it would make it seem perhaps as if her own baby who had died were in her arms again. The delicate stitches were as perfect as the day when Hannah Ludwell Lee had set them—filaments fragile and sweet as the stamens of the pale anemones that blossomed in the shade by Stratford Spring. Coming back to Stratford, for Hannah Lee's daughter, was like coming back to her.

Those memories were like dim strands and threads of shining daylight seen through the closed shutters of a long-darkened but once familiar room. Alice Lee never wrote of them but some she told to her children, and through their journals and letters the mist-like breath of Stratford Hall is wafted down the centuries.

The long vista to their River Potowmack from the north door of the Great Hall must also have quickened heart and

47

mind for Alice Lee. Under the light of the moon when she was a girl the broad reaches of that river had showed the friendly ships that came and went between the Colony of Virginia and Mother England, when Britain was in truth their mother. By day the air was so clear that every branch and twig and leaf of the trees in the foreground was etched in tremulous lines against the sky and water. Every pinnace, barge and yacht afloat there off Stratford Landing looked near, and old St. Mary's on the Maryland shore across from them seemed close as a friend.

CHAPTER II

1744-1778

I

ONCE in Alice Lee's childhood there had come a spring day, May 17, 1744, when the vista to the river reached farther than the boundaries of Maryland,—up the vast sweep of Chesapeake Bay into the stranger Province of Pennsylvania and unknown lands beyond. This was the time when her father, the Honourable Col⁰ Thomas Lee Esq., and her brother Philip Ludwell Lee, and other men took a long journey on the yacht *Margaret*. They went to meet the Indians of the Six Nations in council at Lancaster and to treat with them for the opening of new lands beyond the Alleghanies for English settlement. It was a great journey, and all the family of Stratford and the neighbors went down to Stratford Landing to see the *Margaret* off, "One Jack Ensign and Pennon flying."

Alice Lee had no means of knowing then—not until nearly a generation later, that curiously coincident with the year of her father's visit to Philadelphia was the gift of a land grant from Thomas and Richard Penn, proprietaries of Pennsylvania, to William and Joseph Shippen. This grant comprised the entire square between Spruce Street and Locust—then called Prune—bounded by Fourth and Fifth. The square became the site of Shippen House built in the following decade by the Elder William Shippen and made a gift to his only son William Shippen the Younger, the man whom Alice Lee was to marry. Through that marriage Shippen House was destined to become the northern headquarters of the Virginia patriots of the Revolution, among whom the five brothers Lee were foremost—and to be dedicated to the cause of Liberty just as Stratford had been.

When Thomas Lee, with his companions of the Commission, had signed and sealed the Treaty of Lancaster which gave to America so vast a territory in the name of his majesty George III, he returned to Stratford. Besides the Treaty duplicate, he brought back from the Province of Pennsylvania a history of England inscribed with the honored name of William Penn, and for the beloved gardens of his home a few slips of Lombardy poplars and weeping willow trees from Woodlands.

This was another place in Philadelphia town associated with his memorable journey. For he had spent a day or more at Woodlands, the country seat of Andrew Hamilton on the west bank of the River Schuylkill. Its nursery gardens, like those of John Bartram the botanist further up the river, were a mother place of rare trees, shrubs, vegetables and flowers. For three successive generations sons of the Hamilton family imported these treasures from England, the Continent and the Far East. The first weeping willows and the first Lombardy poplars in the Colonies grew there. So the grounds of Stratford Hall and the little garden of Shippen House derived many of their beauties from Woodlands.

Five years passed by and Alice Lee reached the age of fourteen. It was January, 1749. Her mother died. Over the long rough roads to her father's birthplace, Matholic, nearly twenty miles away, her body was borne in the drear cold and the snows. There, near the blackened ruins of the home to which Hannah Ludwell had come as a bride twenty-seven years before, she was buried in the family graveyard which took its name from the fire that destroyed the place, "Burnt House Fields." The grave beside her was for her husband. Less than a year later

Alice Lee's dear father passed away. The little girl and her brothers were thus doubly bereft!

The oldest brother Philip, succeeding to the ownership of their home, was the executor of their father's will and guardian of the younger children. The older sister Hannah had long since been married to Gawin Corbin, and was living at the great house Peckatone on the Potowmac, twenty miles from Stratford. Richard Henry was at school in England. Arthur, the youngest of the family, was only nine years old. Philip Lee, now master of Stratford, was also a member of the King's Council. Turning haughty and pompous under his new fortunes and responsibilities, he became alien to them all. Little Arthur and, it may have been, William too—was put to live, eat and work with the slaves, until at length it was arranged that he should go to England and be educated at Eton. Sharp divisions arose in the family as time went on; legal complications and contests between the heir-at-law and his brothers.

All of this must have weighed heavily upon Alice Lee's peace-loving spirit and darkened her entire youth. Stratford, where they had all been so happy and so well cared for, became a place of misery. Even the indentured servants ran away when they could. Should a hungry slave break into the full storehouses for food, his hand would be branded with a red hot iron. If Alice Lee had any of the Virginia girl's usual gaiety there is no record of it. When she reached her twenty-fourth year she came to a momentous decision—to renounce all right and title to her father's legacies for a settled annuity of forty pounds sterling, and to leave her once beloved home forever. She empowered her brother William to look after her interests. She got together all her belongings, and in May of 1760 she left Stratford and took passage to England.

A short time before, her mother's only brother, Philip Ludwell III, with his two motherless daughters Hannah Phillipa and Lucy Grymes Ludwell, had left Green Spring and gone to live in London. William Lee joined Alice and Arthur there afterwards. The Ludwell family was well established. Their circle of friends, who were also the intimates of young Arthur Lee, included Dr. Samuel Johnson, Boswell, Fanny Burney and John Paradise. The well-known surgeons, Sir John Hunter and Dr. Home with his daughter Anne, were also among them, and one American besides themselves, "a student in the medical art," William Shippen the Younger of Philadelphia.

An amazing array of marriages occurred in this group within the next few years. Alice Lee, who had reached spinster's age living at remote Stratford, became engaged to her fellow countryman William Shippen. Her cousin Lucy Grymes Ludwell married John Paradise and afterwards went to live in Williamsburg, Virginia, bearing with her the dining table which had been so often graced by the Great Lexicographer. Lucy's sister, Hannah Phillipa Ludwell, married Alice's brother William Lee and through this marriage the Castle at Green Spring and the other vast Ludwell estates on the lower James River, and in Jamestown and Williamsburg, came into the ownership of the Lees. Arthur Lee alone seems to have been left without a partner. Dr. Home's daughter Anne who became the wife of Sir John Hunter was Alice Lee's closest friend. There was an understanding between them that each would name her first born daughter for the other.[1]

Young William Shippen had been sent abroad by his father "to be perfected in the medical art." Of him the Elder Shippen said: "My son had his education in the best college in this part of the country, [College of New Jersey, later Princeton University] and has been studying physick with me, besides which

[1] Letter Jan. 15, 1786, Dr. William Shippen to his son.

THE GOVERNOR'S HOUSE, THE FIRST GREAT HOUSE OF PHILADELPHIA
SEVENTEENTH CENTURY HOME OF THE CITY'S FIRST MAYOR, EDWARD SHIPPEN, FOUNDER OF
THE SHIPPEN FAMILY IN AMERICA
Courtesy of Dr. and Mrs. Lloyd P. Shippen

he had the opportunity of seeing the practice of every gentleman of note in our city. But for want of that variety of operations and those frequent dissections which are common in older countries, I must send him to Europe. His scheme is to gain all the knowledge he can in anatomy, physick and surgery. He will stay in London for the winter, etc." He was attending Dr. Hunter's anatomical lectures and was also a student in Guy's hospital. His marriage to Alice Lee took place April 3, 1762, at the Church of St. Mary Le Strand, Middlesex, in the presence of Alice's uncle Philip and her brother William Lee. Returning to America to Philadelphia after the wedding, they went to live at Shippen House.

The little capital city of the United Colonies was still of the early eighteenth century in appearance and temper. Almost every house with its outbuildings and stables stood in the center of grounds planted with fruit and shade trees, shrubs and flowers. Near by, close to the Delaware River, was "the princely place" of young William Shippen's great-grandfather Edward Shippen, the first mayor of Philadelphia. It was a byword that the old gentleman "had the biggest person, the biggest house and the biggest coach in the city!"

The plan of their own house, small and simple by comparison, was unusual and peculiarly adapted to a physician's needs and uses. The kitchen, a separate building with bedrooms above, was connected with the house by a covered passage which enclosed the stairway. The dining-room, parlour and office all opened into the wide entrance hall. Each room was of spacious, beautiful proportions with high ceilings, wide, deep windows and interesting woodwork, mantel and open fireplace. The gardens in the rear and on the upper side of the house extended to Fifth Street and the stable and coach house. Young Dr. Shippen put up a lecture room in the yard on the Prune

53

[misspelled Pruune on the map of 1762] Street side and advertised: "Dr. William Shippen's anatomical lectures will begin tomorrow evening at his father's house in Fourth Street. Tickets for course at five pistoles each. Gentlemen who incline to see the subject prepared for the lectures and to learn the art of dissecting, injecting etc are to pay five pistoles additional." A group of ten students came. Thus was inaugurated the first course of lectures on medical subjects ever given by any American physician. Out of the equipment of his crude classroom, later transferred to the College of Philadelphia, grew the first medical school of the American colonies.

Shippen kinsfolk and family connections lived in practically every neighboring house, Willing, Powel, Byrd, Bingham, Stamper, Story and Blackwell. To Alice Lee the situation was curiously reminiscent of her home in Virginia, where through the intermarriages of six or eight generations between Lees, Carters, Balls, Fitzhughs, McCartys, Washingtons, Stuarts, Tayloes, Ludwells, Grymes, Corbins,—all eventually became kinspeople. They were literally one great family. In Philadelphia the situation was practically duplicated.

The home of Dr. Shippen's cousin Edward Shippen, namesake of the first mayor, was also on Fourth Street, close by. Of his houseful of daughters, Peggy Shippen was then the baby. Directly across the street from Shippen House, in the midst of a large acreage of ground still shaded by virgin forest oaks, was the group of beautiful houses built by "Aunt" Willing and Uncle Charles, for themselves and several of their children.[2] On the Third Street frontage of their grounds lived

---

[2] "Aunt" Willing was Anne Shippen, only sister of the Elder Dr. William Shippen. Through her marriage to Charles Willing, shortly after he came from England to Philadelphia, was founded this family which for more than two centuries has had a significant part in the social, political and commercial life not only of Pennsylvania and Virginia but also of the United Colo-

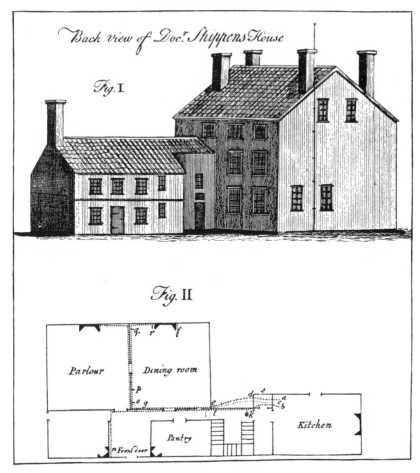

REAR VIEW OF DOC^R SHIPPEN'S HOUSE WITH FLOOR PLAN, 1781
From Illustration in Letter from Arthur Lee in "Memoirs of the
American Academy of Arts and Sciences," Vol. I, July 29, 1781
Courtesy of Clifford Lewis, Esq.

their daughter Elizabeth, wife of Samuel Powel, another early mayor of the city. Elizabeth Powel was the most intimate friend Martha Washington had in Philadelphia and her house was ever a beacon of hospitality in the nation's first capital. Next door to Elizabeth at 110 Third Street was the winter home of her sister Mary, wife of Colonel William Byrd III, of West-over, Virginia. Their house too, a stately Georgian type, was a marriage gift from Mary's parents.[3]

Among other Philadelphians important in the city's history with whom the Shippens had been friends and intimates for several generations, were the families, Hamilton, Logan, Pemberton, Waln, Hill, Moore, Norris, Wynne, Lloyd, Morris, Pennington, Allen, Chew, Tilghman, Bayard and Wistar.

At Shippen House on February 24, 1763, Alice bore her first child, a daughter. Remembering the promise to her friend in far-off London, she gave the baby the name of Anne Home Shippen, soon shortened to Nancy. Two years later their second child—a son—was born and received the name of his wise and "philosophic" grandfather, Thomas Lee. Another baby born August 21, 1776, named William Arthur Lee for his

nies and the United States. Thomas Willing, son of Charles and Anne Shippen Willing was president of the Provincial Congress, delegate to the Congress of the Confederation, president of the first chartered bank in America and a partner with Robert Morris in the financing of the country during the Revolution. His daughter, Nancy Willing who married William Bingham in 1780, was one of the most celebrated beauties of her day in America, England and France. Their Philadelphia home, also located in this group of Willing houses, was grand and elaborate.

[3] Both the Powel and Byrd Mansions are standing today in almost their original state. Each bears a bronze marker designating certain points of their historic association with Philadelphia's past. The Powel house is an historic shrine and part of its original garden has been reclaimed from the surrounding tenements. The house of Colonel William Byrd of Westover, Virginia, and Mary Willing his wife, was occupied for some years by descendants of William Penn. After the Revolution it passed into the occupancy and possession of the Chew family, of Maryland.

55

mother's younger and favorite brothers, died a few months after birth. Of a family, ultimately eight in number, Nancy and Tommy were the only children of Dr. and Mrs. Shippen to survive infancy. They became to their parents and kinspeople the objects of an almost idolatrous devotion and the center around which the world of Shippen House revolved.

Their first playground was the entrancing maze of the grape-vines, jessamine and roses, and the weeping willows of the little garden at the rear of their house. On the Fourth Street side, its flowers, vines and shrubbery ran riot to the very base of the fort-like brick walls of St. Mary's Catholic Church. In this church during Nancy's youth worshipped the entire personnel of the French, Spanish and South American legations and visiting delegations, as well as the Catholic soldiers of the Continental Army when it was in Philadelphia. It was built within the grounds of Shippen House on a part of the original Penn grant sold by Dr. Shippen's father and uncle to the Jesuit Order, when the parent chapel of St. Joseph's in Willing Alley became too small for the ever increasing number of parishioners.

The first mention of Nancy Shippen aside from the record of her birth is in a letter written Jan. 1, 1766, by Anne Home in London to Mrs. Doct^r Shippen in Philadelphia.

London Jan 1st 1766

. . . I beg my comp^{ts} to M^r (I believe I shou'd say Doct^r Shipen; [ )] & my love to my little namesake, & I wish I may ever have it in my Power to make it of any use to her. I am heartily sorry for the disturbances which now reign in the Colonies & I hope the Doct^r & yourself will be no sufferers from them . . . I shall expect to hear from you by the first opportunety as I have a good right, having taken the first in my power to inquire after you & to asure my dear Mrs Shipen that I am unalterably her friend & Servt

Anne Home

Miss Home

P.S. Your Friends the Miss Browns are the Miss Browns still; & if the men think as I do will remain so as long as they live. . . . I hope the Great Wigg has not rob'd your husband of that vivacity [illegible]

By this time "my little namesake" of the letter was three years old and her father was successfully launched upon his medical career.

During that period the continuing protests of the colonists against Great Britain's tyranny and oppression, "the disturbances in the Colonies," were about to culminate in revolution. Alice Lee's brothers in Virginia, Richard Henry, Thomas Ludwell, and Francis Lightfoot, and William and Arthur abroad, were turning every force at their command to the cause of Liberty. Shippen House became their rallying place in Philadelphia and the meeting ground of their friends and compatriots. Shortly before the opening of the First Continental Congress John Adams wrote in his diary, 1774, September 3, Saturday:

Breakfasted at Dr. Shippen's: Dr. Witherspoon was there. Col. R. H. Lee lodges there; he is a masterly man. This Mr. Lee is a brother of the sheriff of London, and of Dr. Arthur Lee, and of Mrs. Shippen; they are all sensible and deep thinkers. Lee is for making the repeal of every revenue law,—the Boston Port Bill, the bill for altering the Massachusetts constitution, and the Quebec Bill, and the removal of all the troops, the end of the Congress, and an abstinence from all dutied articles, the means,—rum, molasses, sugar, tea, wine, fruits, &c. He is absolutely certain that the same ship which carries home the resolution will bring back the redress. . . .

Mrs. Shippen is a religious and a reasoning lady. She said she had often thought that the people of Boston could not have behaved through their trials with so much prudence and firmness at the same time, if they had not been influenced by a superior power. . . .

57

On the following day George Washington arrived in Philadelphia and was a guest at Shippen House. In his *Diaries* under the caption "where, how or with whom my Time is spent" he records that on September 4, 1774, he "lodged at Dr. Shippen's in Philadelphia after supping at the New Tavern." And, on September 5: "Breakfasted and Dined at Doc'r Shippens spent the Evng at Tavern. In Congress all day."

Time alone can uncover all the history made during the next two years at the Shippen breakfasts, the Shippen dinners and teas in that house on Fourth and Prune Streets.

Nancy's own letters chronicle only those matters in which she was herself concerned. A few weeks after her uncle Richard Henry Lee "spoke an Empire into birth," Nancy wrote to her brother:

Wednesday 27 august 1776

My dear Tommy

I thank you for the picture you was so kind to send me, Mamma has sent you a box of fruit, which will probably be the last as the season of fruit is almost over. I have no news to tell you only that my Uncle R. H. Lee & his Lady are come to Town: Mamma thinks My Aunt very pretty. Mamma thinks your books & gun had better not be sent till your stay at colledge is determined.

If Mr Springer goes to Virginia it is more than probable you will leave the colledge. However in a short time Mamma will be able to send you something very clever in return for the comfort you have given her in studying so diligently and applying yourself so close to your learning, our dear brother is well and our dear Mamma is on the recovery. Mamma says you are a great darling and she loves you dearly, & loves every body that is kind to you & takes notice of you & I am my dear Brother

your affec^t Sister

Shortly afterward little William Arthur Lee Shippen died and Nancy was entered at Mistress Roger's School in Trenton.

58

Tommy stayed on at The Forest of Needwood Academy near Frederick, Maryland.

As the bitter conflict drew nearer and nearer, and the sharp cleavages of political opinion, philosophy or religion severed ties between countless houses in Philadelphia and throughout the colonies, a tragedy came to pass within that other neighborhood family allied as closely as the Shippens were with the colony of Virginia—the House of Westover. At the outbreak of the Revolution, Dr. Shippen's cousin, Mary Willing, ever a staunch patriot herself, suffered at the Tory convictions of her beloved husband, Colonel William Byrd. When, however, he became stirred by the violent acts of Lord Dunmore to a realization of the wrongs and injustice inflicted by England upon the colonies, he suddenly and ardently took up the patriot cause. He was back in Philadelphia in late December of 1776 at the time a group of his friends in the Convention of Virginia proposed him for the command of the state line with rank of major general. He was rejected. The difficulties about him seemed insurmountable—a veritable phalanx of obligations, debts, anxieties and, at length, the shock of this last humiliation and defeat. On the first day of the New Year of 1777 he killed himself. People were transfixed with horror and dismay. Mary Willing honored her dead with incomparable courage. She was left with eight children to rear and protect; with a vast estate on the brink of the precipice to recover; with a curiously persistent misunderstanding of her own patriot principles and acts to controvert and the never ending agony of heart and spirit over her husband's tragic end. But he had died a patriot! And in his death and in her life and the lives of their children the House of Westover was again united with Virginia in its alliance with the patriot cause.

· · · · · · ·

59

Many of these events of the past years touching Alice Lee's life and the lives of others near to her must have passed through her mind in the still and quiet of Stratford.

II

As the long evenings of the late fall and winter days stretched their interminable length across the threshold of Stratford, the bright gladness of being once more in her old home faded from Alice Lee's heart. For no letters came from Nancy, Tommy or her husband. Added to childish thoughtlessness, there were in that time of peril and disorganization frequent obstacles to regular mail delivery between the Virginia post-office at Leedstown on the Rappahannock and points in the north.

Like icicles sharp against the cheery comfort of the hearth fires of the old Virginia homestead were the tragic scenes of Valley Forge, the heroism and suffering of Washington, the Continental soldiers . . . and of her husband! While she was fed and warm, he was riding in the bitter cold from camp to camp, half-starved no doubt, fighting to keep the breath of life in dying men. She thought, too, of a possible turn of the enemy's objectives toward the schools where her children at first had seemed secure. Perhaps, still worse, Tommy might be attacked by the deadly camp fever! Her besetting fears unendurable, at last she wrote to her husband:

My dear Mʳ Shippen,
What is become of you & my dear Tommy—it is almost 3 months since I left my dear Mʳ Shippen & I have received but one short letter with my gown & apron but you are harried with business your good for nothing Doctors & commisarys give you

all the Trouble. O! when shall I have you all to myself? & it is now two months since I parted with our dear our only son, the pledge of our love & have not heard once from him—surely if he was well he wou'd contrive a letter to me, he is certainly ill or dead of that vile feaver Crags son had, my fears render me so miserable it is impossible for me to stay here where I find I cannot hear from those I love most. I shall return to Frederick-Town where you must my dear Mr Shippen get a lodging for me. Mrs Gates & Mr Plato have both empty houses there which they will not want soon, & I shou'd suppose they will be glad to let them by the month, we agreeing to let them have them at any time if they shou'd want them, if you will write to my B^r Frank he will speak to Mr Gates at York & Col. Loyd will speak to Mr Plato for you. I mention these houses because I know of no other in Frederick, I shall be at Frederick the first of March unless you will contrive to meet me here before that time. If I cou'd correspond with you at this distance it would be some thing, but when I set down to write I feel myself tied up [with] the uncertainty of what I write getting to you only, I cou'd now fill a volume but no matter you shall know all when we meet. Perhaps it will be in' the world of spirits & then we can convey our Ideas with delightful ease & certainty.

Are you sorry for the Ladies in Philadelphia? Had they taken my advice they wou'd now have breathed in free air as I do. O! how good it is to do right, My dear Mr Shippen tho' we are loosing thousands having loved (our) country and its interests invariably more than supports me under every difficulty. I feel I love in my very heart the true liberty of America the liberty of saying & doing every thing that is beautiful & proper. Adieu my dear faithful husband, direct for me at the Post Office at Leedstown & believe for it is really true that I am intirely & unalterably

Yours

Stratford 17 Jan^{ry} 1778.

Do let me know if you have received a letter from me directed by our B^r Richard & one from Frederick. Give my comp^{ts} to any body you think will be pleased at being remember'd by me & tell me if you think our dear Girl improves by being with Mrs Rogers. I don't think she improves in her writing, I mean the manner & pray don't let her wear a ribbon on her shoulders it will certainly make her crooked. My anxienty to know how Tommy does has already induced me to do what my reason w^d have forbid. I sent the man I hired at York back to Mr Booths from Dumfries on Tommy's horse Stark & have not heard of him since & it is now six weeks; if he go to our Army Dr Cutting knows the man & you can describe the horse, but no doubt he will part with him, for Mr Thornton Washington says he knows the man, that he is a great horse Jockey & rogue. He described him exactly says he was a few miles from his Fathers & has promised to inquire after him & endeavour to get the horse for me, but I tho't it best to mention it to you lest he s^d come y^r way. You must not be angry, if you knew my feelings I am sure you wou'd not.

Addressed: Dr. Shippen, Director General
         at Bethlehem.
         By Post

Dr. Shippen made immediate arrangements for his wife to leave Stratford and come to Maryland to live near Tommy's school. Thus her terrors were dispelled and her mind was at rest about her family. Although she was in communication with Nancy, it was evidently not possible for her to make the journey to Trenton. On February 9, 1778, Dr. Shippen wrote to his daughter:

My d^r Girl
    I am always pleased to hear of your health & good conduct— Your dear Mamma & brother were well 10 days agoe. I enclose a letter from Tommy to you—Your Mamma desires you will never wear a ribband on your Shoulder because it is apt to make the person crooked—I have spoken to Mr Barclay about Genl

Pulaski & am in hopes no more Troops or horses will be quartered on Mrs Roger.

Present my compliments to Mrs Roger & Miss Jones
Your loving Father
W. Shippen jr.

--Philadelphia, still occupied by the British, was gay as it had not been for years. The Byrd mansion, 110 South Third street, served as their military headquarters. All the Tory families in town vied with one another in showering courtesies and attentions upon General Sir William Howe, his successor, Sir Henry Clinton, and the officers of their staffs. In the foreground of that seething whirl of dinners, dances, theatre parties stood a group of young women of Philadelphia's first families. Among them was Nancy's cousin Peggy, daughter of Edward Shippen. Peggy was then sixteen, the age when the young ladies of the colonies entered the world of fashion. She had been finished at a school like Nancy's. That she and the handsome Captain John André, General Howe's popular young officer, were in love with each other might readily have been surmised by Philadelphia gossips. Had not the Captain cast Peggy in a leading rôle in the *Mischianza*, the festival which he conceived and produced just before the British evacuation?

For the William Shippens it must have been a source of acute regret, anger and grief that so many of their own kinspeople and old friends and neighbors kept open house to the enemy, and shared with them their fêtes and favors.

However if Nancy's kith and kin within the city were thus welcoming the British to their hearths and homes, another of her kinsmen was harassing them by day and night from without the town—young Captain Harry Lee of the Light Horse! Closely allied to the Stratford line of Lees he had at the very outset of the struggle for independence offered his sword, his

63

men and his horses to the Continental Army. Placed by General Washington on detached service from 1776 to 1780, he kept on the heels of the enemy—or at their very heads—in surprise attacks throughout that battle zone of Jersey, Pennsylvania and Delaware. What dust he threw in the eyes of the army so futilely entrenched in Philadelphia, giving to them entirely erroneous ideas of strength and the pitiful resources of the Continentals! With his flying dragoons, like himself no more than boys, daring and invincible, Captain Harry Lee crippled the British outer lines, "straitened communications in and out of Philadelphia, cut off their light parties, intercepted their supplies, forage, and droves of cattle on the marshes of the Delaware and over and over again diverted the live stock to Valley Forge." With food supplies, medicines, clothing, equipment and ammunition just outside the reach of the fighting Continentals, the failure of the Army's commissary department to function wrought disaster that might have been far more deadly, had it not been for the aid and support given by Captain Harry Lee and his Light Horse. The week Nancy's mother left Stratford Hall, General Washington wrote to Captain Lee commending his gallant behavior in the field. Had not word come of the sailing of the French fleet his tactics doubtless would have been in time a dominant factor in bringing about the British evacuation of Philadelphia.

The first intimation of such a prospect received by little Nancy Shippen was the following letter from her father:

Headquarters June 7, 1778

My dear Nancy

An expectation of being in Philadelphia very soon has prevented your Mamma's & my visiting you at Trenton which we are very desirous of doing, ever since we have heard you behaved so well. The enemy are preparing to leave Philadelphia and 'tis thought here they will go tomorrow. If so, you may expect to see us in a few days. Many people from the city say all the ships are gone down below the Cheveaux de Frize, & that many of the inhabitants are gone with them. Your Mamma has bought you many clever things for yᵉ summer & longs to see you much.

Another comment on the evacuation, which also emphasizes the fact that Nancy's cousin Captain Harry Lee and his Light Horse frightened the Philadelphians more than did the British, appears in an entry of Elizabeth Drinker's journal, under the date of June 18, 1778:

Last night it was said there were 9000 of ye British Troops left in Town: 11,000 in ye Jerseys. This morning when we arose there was not one Red-Coat to be seen in Town, and ye encampment in the Jerseys also vanished. Col. Gordon and some others had not been gone a quarter of an hour before ye American Light-Horse entered ye city—not many of them, but they were in and out all day. A Bellman went about this evening, by order of one Col. Morgan to desire the inhabitants to stay within doors after night, and that if any were found in ye streets by ye Patrols, they should be punished. Ye few that came in to day had drawn swords in their Hands; they gallopped about ye streets in a great hurry Many were much frightened at their appearance

Sally Wistar's journal records two days later:

Our brave, our heroic General Washington was escorted by fifty of the Life Guard, with drawn swords. Each day he acquires an addition to his goodness. We have been very anxious to hear how the inhabitants have far'd. I understand the Gen'l Arnold, who bears a good character, has the command of the city, and the soldiers conducted with great decorum. . . . I now think of nothing but returning to Philadelphia.

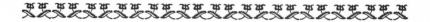

CHAPTER III

1778-1779

I

Camp White Plains
August [?], 1778.

My dear Friend Tom:

I have been much tempted to go to Rhode Island to see the Count D'Estaing & his fleet & am only prevented by a desire to see your dear mamma. You are blessed with capacity & it will be your own fault if you dont make a great & useful man— We have daily flattering accounts from R. I. & expect to hear of the reduction of that place in 3 or 4 days. Your mama shall have the most early intimation of it by express agreeable to our promise. Tell her I love her dearly—Duly present my compliments to Mr Brackinridge duty to Grandpappa

Je suis mon très chere
Fils votre ami fidele et père amant.

So Dr. Shippen wrote his son when the first French fleet, bearing four thousand troops and cannon larger and heavier than any the British had, anchored off Rhode Island's shores. Now indeed was France keeping faith with America! Her treaty of alliance which Nancy's uncle Arthur had helped to make six months before was at last being translated into terms of the genuine aid and support which it had promised and which the colonies so needed: ships and men and guns. Everyone was so happy that all America was speaking French!

No longer were they facing the enemy single-handed. A strong ally had come to them to help them fight by land and sea. Now was France close by their side, united with them as

66

she had not been before in the struggle to establish American independence. The Congress returned from York to Philadelphia to open diplomatic relations with the new ally. In itself this act acknowledged before the world the alliance that gave to the Continental Congress the character in Europe of a national assembly and to the people of the United States the dignity of a sovereign people.[1] The character of the war was changed and the status of the nation was changed. The United Colonies received a new title to recognition among the nations of Europe. The United States of America was introduced to the world by France. The French soldiers and sailors were trained to salute and fight for the American flag as for the flag of France.

The new feeling of security in the nation—of gratification and of triumph—are shown in this letter written by Richard Henry Lee from Philadelphia July 20, 1778, to Thomas Jefferson:

DEAR SIR—The condition of our affairs is much changed, since last I had the pleasure of writing to you, as by the favour of his most Christian majesty, we now are become masters of the sea, and our own coast at least. Ten days ago arrived in the Delaware, a French squadron commanded by Count D'Estaing, of twelve sail of the line and four frigates, having of seamen and land troops eleven thousand men on board. There is one ship of 90 guns, one of 80, six of 74, three of 64, and four frigates. Having missed the English here, they proceeded to New York in quest of them, and are now before that harbour, the depth of water being unfortunately insufficient to admit such large ships. The English, whose fleet is inferior, are well contented to remain within the honours, and suffer Monsieur, the count, to intercept every vessel coming to New York. He has already taken fifteen sail. But the French admiral being an officer of great activity and spirit, seems not con-

[1] "The Marquis de La Fayette in the American Revolution," Tower, Vol. II, p. 25.

tent with this small work, and therefore, I believe, he will go immediately to Rhode Island, where he can easily destroy the ships, and with the assistance of our force there make prisoners of two thousand British troops on that island. With this squadron came Le Sieur Girard, minister plenipotentiary from his most Christian majesty. He is a sensible well bred man, and perfectly well acquainted with the politics of Europe. From him I learn, that the court of France considers the message of the King of England to his Parliament, and their answer upon the Count Noaille's notification of our alliance, as a denunciation of war, on the part of Great Britain, and that they mean to act accordingly, without an express declaration, leaving this last to England. We are busied now in settling the ceremonials for the reception of foreign ministers of every denomination, and I assure you it is a work of no small difficulty.[2]

The center of British power and operations was now transferred to New York where, supported by American Tories, it was daily growing in strength. Philadelphia, so long occupied by the enemy, was again an American town and under the command of General Benedict Arnold, then so active in the cause of liberty. His sword, effective in compassing the defeat of Burgoyne, thus had its part in rallying the French to America's aid. All the colonies acclaimed him. Having shared honors with the noble Montgomery, as one of the heroes of Quebec, and covered himself with glory at Ticonderoga and Saratoga, General Arnold was high in the confidence of his commander-in-chief and of his country. Serving by Washington's appointment as military governor of Philadelphia, he converted the former British headquarters at 110 South Third Street into that of the American Army. This stately Georgian house—the Byrd house—marriage gift of Charles and Anne Shippen Will-

[2] "Memoir of the Life of Richard Henry Lee, and his correspondence" . . . By his grandson Richard H. Lee . . . In two volumes. Philadelphia, H. C. Cary and I. Lea, 1825. Vol. II, p. 42.

ing to their daughter Mary and their Virginia son-in-law, the late Colonel William Byrd of Westover, became once more a center of patriot activity. As the American headquarters and likewise a home of comfort and luxury, it seemed fitting that the Frenchman who had signed the Treaty of Alliance, who was the first diplomatic agent to the United States from any foreign country, and the first French minister—Conrad Alexander Gérard—and his staff should be received and hospitably entertained here. General Arnold accordingly proffered for the use of Sieur Gérard a suite of rooms in his military household.

Upon M. Gérard's arrival aboard the frigate *La Chimère*, he was received with great ceremony by a deputation of members of Congress and escorted from the boat landing on the Delaware into Philadelphia:

Upon his approach to the city, the troops were drawn up on each side of the streets through which he passed, and salutes were fired by the artillery during his progress. He was escorted to the residence of General Arnold, at that time the commanding officer in the city, and was invited to lodge with him until proper accommodations could be provided for him elsewhere. The reception given him delighted Gérard, who wrote home with enthusiasm of the attentions shown most freely by all classes of the community; and no doubt his reports had an important effect upon the relations between the United States and France.[3]

Nancy Shippen's uncle Richard Henry Lee was appointed by Congress one of the Committee to conduct M. Gérard to the audience-chamber in Independence Hall where his formal presentation as the first minister plenipotentiary to the United States was to take place according to a special ceremonial prescribed by Congress.

[3] "Lafayette in the Revolution," Tower, Vol. I, p. 408.

According to the plans agreed upon, therefore, everything being in readiness, Mr. Richard Henry Lee and Mr. Samuel Adams . . . arrived at the residence of the minister toward noon on the 6th of August, in a state coach drawn by six horses. M. Gérard entered the coach immediately, accompanied by the committee, Mr. Lee taking the seat at his left, and Mr. Adams sitting in front of him, whilst his secretary of legation and the French naval agent followed in the minister's private carriage. Having arrived at Independence Hall, the guard stationed there presented arms as they alighted, and the committee advanced immediately to announce the presence of the minister; whereupon they were informed that Congress was ready to receive him. . . .[4]

. . . After entering the chamber, M. Gérard was conducted by the committee to the chair provided for him, whereupon he sent forward his secretary of legation to present to Congress his letter of credence from the King of France. The President, having received this letter, opened it, and then handed it to the Secretary of Congress, who stood upon the steps leading to the platform and read it aloud. The letter was addressed "A nos très chers, grands amis et alliés, les président et membres du Congrès général des Etats-Unis," and ended, "Nous prions Dieu, qu'il vous ait, très chers, grands amis et alliés, en sa sainte et digne garde. Votre bon ami et allié, Louis."

It was read by the Secretary first in the original and afterward in English. It announced to Congress that the King had nominated the Sieur Gérard to reside as minister plenipotentiary in the United States. Immediately after the reading, Mr. Lee arose and presented the minister to the President of Congress, who also arose; whereupon the President and the minister saluted each other. M. Gérard remained standing whilst he delivered his address.[5]

Taking an important part in this ceremonial and in the subsequent events of M. Gérard's official operations in the nation was that patriot and able statesman, the country's first secretary of

[4] "Lafayette in the Revolution," Tower, Vol. II, p. 27.
[5] "Lafayette in the Revolution," Tower, Vol. II, p. 30.

RICHARD HENRY LEE
FROM THE ENGRAVING BY ALONZO CHAPPEL
Courtesy of Cazenove G. Lee, Jr.

foreign affairs, Robert R. Livingston of Livingston and Clermont Manors, New York, later "the Chancellor" and America's Ambassador to France. His younger brother, Leftenant-Colonel Henry Beekman Livingston, was also in Philadelphia at this time. As a friend and former companion-in-arms of General Arnold, Colonel Harry, as he was termed, frequented the American and French headquarters at 110 South Third Street.

. . . .

Before the New Year of 1779 the doors of Shippen House were opened once again. Its windows were bright with the light of many silver candelabra; fires crackled merrily in every room and, in the parlour, threw caressing shadows over the rows of sombre-toned books from floor to ceiling—ancient classics, poems, history, law philosophy, *materia medica.*[6] The huge Spanish chair of Nancy's grandfather Shippen was placed again before the parlour hearth where he always sat in his great scarlet coat. The tea-table was again drawn out and set with Alice Lee's Queensware china, and the shining silver, the tea-urn bowl and pitcher of the Shippens inscribed with their motto, *Vigilans,* and the Squirrel spoons of the Lees with their motto, *Non incautus futuri,*

Although Nancy's father was yet in the field and Tommy at boarding school, her mother at last was back in her own home. For the first time in more than two long years, Alice Lee and her little daughter were reunited and her beloved Virginia kinspeople could come to them again.

All was set for harmony—save Daughter!

Nancy, being fifteen and therefore grown up, must have her way in all things at all times, and, to use her own phrase . . . she "had high words" with her Mamma! Possibly she objected

[6] This eighteenth century library is still intact and is in the possession of Dr. and Mrs. Lloyd P. Shippen.

to being cast in the set mould fashioned for her by her parents and her "tutresses." Undoubtedly she rebelled—perhaps even flatly refused—to wear the headgear her mother prescribed for the country: "The cap-hat is proper to wear in the country & will save caps I have sent you a cap of Mrs Shaws making. It is very ugly but will serve to put on of a morning as no person appears now without a cap at any time."

Her gentle mother must have been distracted and her father greatly exercised for he wrote: "My dear Nancy . . . Have you persuaded yourself that your dear Mamma knows better than you & that it is your duty to obey her cheerfully always, altho it may sometimes seem hard. She loves you & wishes to make you one of the finest women in Philadelphia this should excite your love & gratitude & I flatter myself does."

To her brother Tommy, Nancy, being so completely finished for a young female, must have been a paragon of perfection! She could sing and play on the harpsichord and "guittar"; she knew some French and many English poems and essays; she could do tambour work and every form of sewing and embroidery, and even other domestic arts such as pickling and preserving and clear starching. How she could curtsy and dance the minuet and assume the grace of mien and stately demeanor of a tall lady! According to the standards of her day, at fifteen she was grown up and ready to take her place in the world of fashion and to charm all men.

With the parlour of Shippen House her stage, Nancy made ready for the play. It was all great fun. Who would be her first beaux?

Her Tory cousin Peggy Shippen, whom she scarcely ever saw, was getting a little passé—being then almost nineteen years old. Although Peggy had been a reigning beauty much admired by the young English officers during the British occupation, she was still beautiful in spite of her advanced age! And the military commander of Philadelphia, General Arnold, fell head over heels in love with her. Was Peggy herself in love with Captain André? Arnold was a widower, more than twice Peggy's age, with sons as tall as she. From his standpoint the field may have appeared promising, in that Peggy's father had lost his fortune in the decline of currency, and her British admirer was gone, perhaps forever, from the scene. It might be his suit would prosper . . .

Arnold's friend and brother officer, Colonel Harry Livingston, was equally in love with a girl many years younger than himself. The girl was Nancy Shippen! In fact Colonel Livingston resigned from active service to pursue his suit . . . either for that reason or because he had not been made a brigadier-general. He was among the first of the beaux to step upon Nancy's stage, a dominating and sinister figure. Yet from the beginning Nancy's father favored his suit. Not only was he a son of the house of Livingston, that wealthy, loyal and famous New York family, but he was also a distinguished officer of the Continental Army. Having raised his own company for the Canadian campaign of 1775, Colonel Harry Livingston had joined forces with his brother-in-law General Montgomery and General Arnold in the ill-fated attack on Quebec. When Montgomery was killed and Arnold severely wounded, Livingston was beside them in the thick of the fight. In the capture of Chambly he performed such valorous feats that the Continental Congress, on December 12, 1775, resolved, "That this Congress will make a present of a sword of the value of $100 to Captain Henry B. Livingston as a testimony of his services at Chambly Canada to this country and that they will embrace the first opportunity of promoting him in the Army." Transferred then to the Continental Army, he served as aide-de-camp to General

73

Schuyler. In the engagement at Quaker Hill, R. I., he performed meritorious services. That he was selfish, imperious, licentious,—the black sheep of his family—were circumstances that in Philadelphia faded into oblivion before his wealth and his high social station and his distinguished military career.

But in dealing with Nancy her father must be astute! In one of his letters to her from headquarters, Dr. Shippen said of Livingston: "Yesterday I dined at General Greenes & at 3 oClock who should come in, guess. He looks mighty well & I never will consent unless you try to be very clever too & deserve him. I wont tell you what he said neither till your Mamma writes me you are a good Girl—Your affect. Papa"

·   ·   ·   ·   ·   ·   ·

On the eighteenth of April, 1779, the marriage of Nancy's cousin Peggy Shippen to Benedict Arnold took place at her father's home on Fourth Street. The wedding immediately followed the execution of a deed for Peggy to Mount Pleasant, one of the most imposing houses and property in the city. Her father and John and Samuel Powel were appointed trustees, thus assuring Peggy the valuable estate in the event of her husband's death and securing her future.

II

A new French Minister to the United States, the Chevalier de la Luzerne, was coming to succeed the Sieur Gérard, who had asked to be recalled because his health had failed in the climate of Philadelphia. With him were the first Secretary of the Legation, Barbé de Marbois, and the Chevalier's personal secretary, M. Louis Guillaume Otto, who was an attaché. Carpenter's Mansion, also known as the "Old Graeme Place" and "John Dickinson's House," was selected for their American home and headquarters.

At this time, September, 1779, no trace remained of its use two years before as a military hospital and graveyard. Closed during the British occupation, it had continued empty after the enemy left, and stood silent, dilapidated and forlorn. Grass grew over the innumerable graves of the Continental soldiers who had died there and were buried in its grounds and in the spacious green beyond its courtyard, later named Washington Square for the commander-in-chief.

Nancy Shippen's grandfather knew the house when he was young, as his father did before him. Her own father could remember the long range of fine cherry trees in its front courtyard on Chestnut Street, when he was a boy, and how Governor Thomas's Lady would invite all the boys in the neighborhood to help themselves. He remembered too that every May Day the little girls were given bouquets and nosegays from its gardens. Then during the period of the First Continental Congress it became the home of that Friend who was "The Penman of the Revolution," Honourable Mr. John Dickinson. He added to the house a new front "of modern construction" facing Chestnut Street. A number of historic documents, among them the Declaration of Rights of the Stamp Act Congress, the First and Second Petitions to the King, and the first draft of the Articles of Confederation, were undoubtedly outlined and prepared within its walls. Another memory of the old house in Nancy's own time was a strange story of how a mother came to seek her son who was of the Pennsylvania line, dead at the "Old Graeme House." She found him there stark and cold just before he was to be buried. But she ministered unto him in faith, prayer and hope, and a miracle came to pass. In her arms her son woke from the dead and lived! So the place appointed for the nation's first French Legation, and indeed the first foreign legation in the United States, had its memories rooted in the city's earliest colonial days and also in the time of the Revolution.

Now the house was being changed inside and out, repaired, remodeled, fitted up and furnished for the "splendid mansion of the Chevalier de la Luzerne" and his suite. From the day the Frenchmen set foot in Philadelphia, these friendly strangers from America's beloved ally came into the hearts of the people.

The pattern of diplomacy devised by Luzerne for those critical and perilous times for the Colonies and for France is described by the Marquis de Chastellux:

The conduct of the Chevalier de la Luzerne in America justified every idea that has been formed of the superior skill and address of the French nation on embassies, and in the cabinet, He not only conformed to the manners, and customs of the country, but he studied the character of every individual of the least importance. He rose early in the morning, and watched the hour that best suited their convenience, to wait on the Members of Congress, and the leading men of state: at dinner he received company of all political complexions . . . He paid his court particularly to the ladies in the suspected families, an evidently wise policy; in this class, he was supposed to have a very agreeable, as well as

76

useful acquaintance, in the two Miss C——'s, who put no restraint upon their tongues, but were well informed of all the transactions of their party.

Whenever he could not himself be present, Mr. Marbois, and Mr. Ottaw, [Otto] the Secretaries were distributed, so that you could not make an afternoon's visit to a *whig* or *tory* family in the city, without being sure to meet with this political General or one of his Aides de Camp. When he made a public entertainment, and the presence of the tory ladies gave offense to those of the patriotic party, he always pleaded ignorance, contrived to shift the blame from himself, and throw it on the Secretaries, who were left to fight the battle in the best way they could over the tea table; but all this was carried on with undescribable address, and so managed as to keep all parties in good humour with him. He indulged every man's peculiarities, and bestowed the *petites attentions* on all. It is thus the French maintain their ascendency in the cabinet, which is worth a thousand victories, and their superiority in the Courts of Europe, under every varied form of Government, from Holland to Constantinople. . . .

In such a school of diplomacy under tutelage of the master diplomat Luzerne,—for to the young attaché it was a school,—Louis Otto brought his own resources of inheritance, education and character. He had come to serve Luzerne as secretary in 1776, while still a student of public law at Strasbourg. Of an ancient family of distinction, originally from Alsace, Louis Guillaume Otto was born at Kork, in the Grand Duchy of Baden, August 7, 1754. His brother Jacques was also in the French diplomatic service. Their father, Jacques Guillaume Otto, was confidential counsellor of the Landgrave of Hesse Darmstadt, and his father before him had occupied the same office to the court of Hesse Darmstadt. With such a background and a certain natural finesse, it was not surprising that M. Otto was very soon termed with M. Marbois "the two petit ministeres of france."

Speaking of the first legation in America, the Marquis de Chastellux said he could not desire any more agreeable quarters for refreshment than the house of the Chevalier de la Luzerne where "our Minister maintains a considerable state and gives frequently great dinners."

The popular Philadelphia hostess Mrs. Theodorick Bland, who was Martha Dangerfield of Virginia and one of Nancy's friends, said of the Chevalier de la Luzerne, "he is one of the most amiable, the politest easiest behav'd Men I ever knew— I may be partial perhaps and give my opinion in too high a strane, as he has been particularly attentive and even friendly to us since I first knew him."

Thus the old house of melancholy ghosts and stirring memories became once more a center of pleasant hospitality and a place of beauty, within and without. The first secretary, Marbois, was a student of botany and much interested in the strange plants, shrubs, nut trees, and flowering trees of America. In an incredibly short time he nursed the vanished gardens back, healed the jagged and broken fruit trees, and planted magnolias, sassafras and tulip trees, new vines and flowers throughout the legation grounds. He dug, sowed and planted with his own hands and took pleasure, as he said, "in seeing the progress of my family." For him it took the place of concerts, operas, comedies, hunting, promenade or picture galleries of which there was such dearth in Philadelphia. In drawing a picture of this first French Legation and its surrounding neighborhood, M. Marbois says: ". . . imagine a square surrounded by four streets and covered with a fine lawn like those in England, and in the middle of it a large house open to the air on all sides. This mansion is at the western edge of the city, almost opposite that in which the State and Congress of Pennsylvania hold their sessions and spend their days in blessing France and cursing

THE FRENCH LEGATION, PHILADELPHIA. THE FIRST FOREIGN LEGATION IN THE UNITED STATES

From Watson's "Annals of Philadelphia"

England, while they contemplate forcing the latter power to become reasonable. On one side we have a view of the city, on the other, of the new prisons, the hospital and the poorhouse . . ."

All of the surrounding buildings were alike, dull brick with white marble trim, regular, symmetrical, monotonous, with the streets straight as strings. Only in the legation grounds were there little footpaths that wound through the trees and flowers. From Shippen House a corner of the odd irregular Swedish-fashioned second story of the legation could be seen when the leaves were off the trees. By the Maytime following the coming of the Frenchmen, the gardens of the legation were in full bloom. The very air about it was rich and sweet with the perfume of fruit and flowering trees. This gay unexpected toss of apple and cherry blossoms was a swinging sign in the wind proclaiming a new sort of tavern put up in the town! And at evening, especially on Sundays when Quaker Philadelphia frowned and brooded in a deadly silence, there at the home of the friendly strangers it was smiling and every window blazed with light. The sound of talk and laughter came from its halls and sometimes strains of classic music as Louis Otto played his harp.

To Nancy Shippen the French Legation became the seat of Romance itself.

CHAPTER IV

1779-1781

I

"I made today a very pleasant discovery in our parlour," so Monsieur Louis Otto wrote Nancy from the French Legation. "I can see there two of your windows and one chimney. . . . I assure you never was a chimney so interesting for me!"

This may have been several weeks after they met. Or perhaps it was but several days. There is no mention of their first meeting in the letters or the journals. It undoubtedly came about shortly after the young diplomat's arrival in Philadelphia when, according to Chastellux, as Luzerne's aides-de-camp, Otto and Marbois, were "distributed" in the houses of the leading families of the capital city. Though his position with the French Legation was a minor one, when he first appeared in Philadelphia and in the life of Nancy Shippen, Louis Otto was even then distinctly a personage.

Soon he was composing music for her. One afternoon when he called and found her out, he left the MS. of his *Menuet of Strasburg* with this message: "Mr. Runaway presents his compliments to Miss Nancy Shippen, and is very sorry he had not the pleasure to see her at home. He wrote his *Strasburg Menuet* as well as he could and Miss Runaway knows that nobody is obliged to do [mutilated] A very fine evening indeed, I am not surprised people runs [mutilated]"

An exchange of poems next appears. M. Otto entitled his endearing verses "Address to Miss A. S."

MENUET OF STRASBURG: ONE OF OTTO'S GIFTS TO NANCY
Courtesy of Dr. and Mrs. Lloyd P. Shippen

My Nancy, Y^e Shepards, is fair as young Light
In her mind Nature, Sience and Sweet temper unite
The Smiles of Complesence, the candour of Youth
The Rosebuds of inocence, Virtue, and truth.

She blends them with dignity, elegance, grace
Which glow in her manners and charm in her face
She is the joy of my Eyes, she is the pride of ye place
Within my fond Heart shall her dear Image reign.

For beautyes like hers ne^r fade nor decay
But blooms in Life's Automn as purelly as May
Hence Reason and Pashion both bow at her Shrine
And she captivates Hearts, or at least has wone mine.

Nancy named her verses "A Poem on the Birth of the Dauphin," subtly concealing her tribute to Louis Otto.

An Infant muse attempts an Infants praise
Angelic Choirs assist my votive lays
A [u] spicious be the day that gave thee birth
To bring fresh joy to half the polish'd Earth
Propitious Omen! of thy happy reign
Which no unroyal act shall ever stain
See joy triumphant gladens every face
That one is added to the princely race
Where magnanimity & wisdom join
To make the name of Lewis half divine
A S

In response to these graceful lines Louis wrote:

To Amanda.

Notwithstanding your suspect behaviour of last Evening, I can not believe that I am the object of those beautiful verses. Their merit therefore consists more in the verses themselves, than in their application, but particularly in the proof you gave me of your Friendship in gratifying my curiosity.—Last evening offerd me some of those happy moments which compensat for all the miseries and disappointments of human life and give us a taste of heaven. I am not vain enough to believe that you felt it with me, but at least let me be sure that you was not *quite* unhappy, and that amongst all your *indifferent* acquaintances I am the less disagreeable. You do not write me *because You have nothing to say*, and I write not so often as I would *because I am affraid to say too much;* and though the first is not very flattering for me, I admire even that candour, with which you own it.

P.S. I am sorry to see that your verses are very good, because according to my principles a *Lover* is a bad *Poet.*

Friday morning.

Lewis.

Presently it became M. Otto's custom to take his daily walk down to Fourth and Prune Streets and saunter along, from there to Spruce Street, "to reconnoitre her house" as he phrased it, and survey the parlour windows. Precisely when or how Nancy suggested "the contrivance of the corner" does not appear. Possibly her Mamma did not approve a tête-à-tête within doors! The French Diplomat had the delicacy and discretion to unite subtly with Mrs. Shippen, frowning upon even so much as a gesture on her daughter's part that might have placed the young girl in a disadvantageous light.

Accordingly he wrote on a "Saturday evening 11 o'clock" the following:

I am sorry that I could not accept of your *contrivance of the Corner,* but I can agree with nothing which involves any danger or impropriety for you, and on the other side I changed my resolution and I expect a more proper time to make *confidences.* You may guess for what reason I changed just this Evening, for you may be sure that till 8. o'clock I was exceedingly anxious to tell you something which perhaps I would have repented hereafter. As soon as my Ideas are riper on certain objects I shall become less discrete. I hope you will sleep very well after our little *hop.*

On the following day, "Sunday evening 8 o'clock," he passed as usual by her house . . . "I peep'd through the window and saw a considerable Tea Company," he said, "of which by their situation I could only distinguish four persons. You will see the plan of this Company upon the next page. . . ."

Explication

A. Old D^r S^hippen sitting before the Chimney; meditating on some political or physical subject: having in his face a gravity mixed with candour: his Silver hairs falling upon his Shoulders and making the most pleasing contrast with the Scarlet of his great coat. Looking sometimes with a sweet tenderness upon his lovely Grandchild.

B. M^r L^ee walking up and down, speaking and laughing by intervalls; participating every pleasure with the Company, except but that he gives himself by his agreeable conversation.

C. Miss N^ancy before the teatable, in an artfully neglected Dress, her hairs flying a little upon her neck, appearing sometimes to be *absent,* sometimes forcing a laughter by a soft inclination of her back and head, and by hiding her face with her hands, probably in order to shew them without being suspected of vanity; changing her Seat several times, but allways pretty far from the candel: and looking however *as lovely as an Angel.*

    Nota. This last expression is not designed to make up for the others, it is really founded, and is by no body felt in so high a degree as by the Spy who stands before the window.

D. M^rs S^hippen lost in sweet meditations. Probably thinking—"Where can he Stay so long?—this evening he must be arrived "at 'Trenton,' and then I may see him tomorrow at least after "tomorrow. Dear Brother when shall I clasp thee in my arms! "When shall I repeat thee that after William thou has the first "place in my heart." &c. &c. These anxious thoughts do not prevent M^{rs} S . . . from expressing upon all her features that heavenly mildness, which is the Characteristick of her Soul. She smiles sometimes in order to conceal her grief and this complaisance gives a new luster to her Sensibility.

E. F. G. Some Strangers which the Spy could not distinguish.

H. Cyrus, [the negro butler] standing in the middle of the room. —half asleep.

I. M^r O^{tto} standing before the window and looking very distressed that the Almanack does not allow him to walk in: his Eyes Fix'd at the letter C. he wishes that he may be the happy object of the *absence* which he observes.

After having taken this inspection I went on to my ceremonious visites where I made but a little Stay, in order to give you sooner this account of my indiscretions and submit it to your indulgence. I hope you will pardon the Spy for the good use he made of his Discoveries, and for his sincerity in telling them.

Nancy had as gay a humour as his and a fancy equally as delicate, and the same verve! "You are a lady what would make a great noise in France," M. Otto said: "I studied your conduct since I have the pleasure of knowing you, nothing escaped my watchfull eye. Lovers are very quick sighted; every little unmeaning favour is precious for them; this Evening I received my tea from your own hands whilst the rest of the Company was served by a black Servant. Perhaps you did not think on it, but I valued it more than any thing I ever received from another hand. But not withstanding I was foolish enough to leave you at 9. o'clock, when I could enjoy a delightfull tete a tete. That thought puts me in the most violent passion and nothing can cure me but telling you that I adore you more than ever."

Nancy's harpsichord became an instrument through which each might find expression for that which could not be written or spoken. In her father's letters to Tommy, several times throughout that winter he mentions— ". . . Otto and Nancy playing harpsichord together . . ."

The "joys of a simple modest life" for a lady were drawn, in vigorous strokes, by M. Otto ". . . a pretty good library, leisure to improve herself in her studies and be able to practice Musick . . . a Spinet and Guittar . . ." and in another letter: "Is there any greater Blessing in the world than that which love affords?"

Through the wilderness of false values, silly affectations and provincialisms that made so large a part of Nancy's world her foreign lover cut a wide swath; gave her a view of horizons far beyond Philadelphia's ken. "I will take a ride on my Fancy," he said, "it will carry me far."

The increasing tenderness of their friendship became still further accentuated as the months went by. When Nancy left the city for a few days' visit to friends in the country Louis wrote her:

Thursday morning.

To Phillis.

The City is dead for me since you left it, the finest houses appear to be mere cottages, and the largest company is become a Sollitude to your Friend. I have *some reasons* to believe that you think sometimes on me—but never enough to be a compensation of a long absence, and 3. or 4. days are an eternity. I will allways remember what you told me Tuesday evening and what you do not like to hear me repeat. I will not go to see you this evening and I am vain enough to believe that you will sooner return in town, when you can not see . . . I hope you will easily guess what I mean and—*tell me if I am right.* I am very unhappy that I must write you in a language that is not my own and even in my own language I should be at a loss to express my feelings. Be indulgent, my dear friend, and think that in your company I may soon acquire more facility.

85

Friday morning.

I spent last evening in the Garden of my beautifull neighbour. She was just gathering some roses that she offer'd me with the greatest simplicity. I was sorry to be not able to see them die on that Bossom, which I wish to see palpitating for Damon.—Than I meditated in Moonlight and I never found that luminary so interesting. I thought that you may possibly look at it in the same moment and I began to be jealous. I am ashamed of my wishes. I desired that you may be in so a disagreeable Company that you may be obliged to return tomorrow. I am too selfish indeed.

I hope my dear Friend you will correct my bad Stile. I believe I ought to write not at all, but—I have no other pleasure when you are absent.

I may guess whether you gave me leave the other Day or not; this is very hieroglyphic and I read in vain a thousand times your dear *note;* I can not guess what is the meaning of that expression:—may I believe that it was *Leave?*—no answer?

Your Mama will take a ride this Evening to see you; she was so kind to write me but I believe I shall not go. She told me *Absence is the taste* [test] *of Love,* and so I prefer to have that taste and oblige you to return tomorrow. Could you be cruel enough to disappoint me?—What a delightfull evening I shall spend tomorrow. Never speak of your journey to Virginia; it distresses me.

With Nancy's arch reply—a copy of which was attached to her lover's letter, the enigma grows!

To Damon—

If you are guilty of a great offence, I would not contradict you for the world, but I will not frown this Evening, tho' your apology is a very *poor* one: I do not give you Leave, & you may guess whether I did the other Evening or not. You are the most agreeable questioner in the world, but I cant immagine what you Dilemma can be. I have not been taught to return Evil for evil.

And Louis Otto, being Damon, replied:

I am very much obliged for your kind answer, which I believe could only be understood by me and by no body else. The delightful Evening I spent, left so a soft impression in my breast, that I think I will sleep but very little this night. Very often I think I understand you when you look at me or when you press my hand in yours, and notwithstanding I wish every moment to be more certain of your Sentiments. If your heart is not very troublesome to me till to morrow Evening, I hope you will leave it in my possession; you can not trust it to a more faithful care than mine . . .

It must have been a charming note from Nancy which made Louis declare:

Never was pleasure equal to mine when I read the few flattering lines, which are more than I *expected,* but not more than I deserved.—Your kindness can only be paralleld by my gratitude, which is boundless.—I have so much to *feel* and *think* for myself that I can not do much for others, but I am determined to *live* for you.—I would write volums on this Subject if I could follow my inclinations, but being afraid of tiring you by a long letter I am obliged to tell you in a few words, how much I am

Your best Friend
& humble Servant.

II

. . . a scene of yᵉ blackest villany had been just disclosed; that Arnold was gone off to the enemy; that Col. Andre, General Clinton's aid and confidant was apprehended in disguise in camp; that West Point (where Arnold commanded) was to be the sacrifice, and that all the dispositions were made for delivering it up last Monday, the 25ᵗʰ ult. at night.

It is further said that G. Washington arrived at West-Point just after yᵉ Plot was discovered. He lodged there that night, and was to have been given up with the Fort. G. Arnold was, by his orders, pursued, but without effect. Col. Andre 'tis said is condemned to be hanged.

On seventh day last, ye 30th ult^e was exhibited and paraded through the streets of this City, a ridiculous figure of Gen [1] Arnold, with two faces, and the Devil standing behind him pushing him with a pitchfork. At ye front of ye cart was a very large lanthorn of green paper, with a number of inscriptions setting forth his crime &c. &c. Several hundred men and boys with candles in their hands —all ranks; many Officers, ye Infantry, men with Guns and Bayonets, Tag, Rag &c, somewhere near ye Coffee-House. They burnt ye Effigy (instead of ye Body, as was said in ye Papers).

This grim news broke rudely upon the tender intimacies of the two young lovers. West Point had all but been delivered over to the enemy by Benedict Arnold and the very existence of the new republic threatened with collapse. In Philadelphia the citizens burned the man in effigy, and when his wife returned to the city they would have none of her. She was ostracised.

At that very time, early in September, 1780, Louis Otto's chief, the Chevalier de la Luzerne, was absent, in Hartford, Connecticut, with the Marquis de Lafayette, leaving Marbois acting chargé d'affaires. Marbois says they were attending a conference with General Washington and his staff, to outline and determine the future operations of the war, and to arrange for the disposition of the troops of the second French expedition under the Comte de Rochambeau, which had arrived off Rhode Island a few weeks before.

In the face of Arnold's treason and the narrowly averted disaster to the Revolution, each member of the French Legation was on guard, and the Tory ladies of Philadelphia cultivated, doubtless, every hour of the day and evening. Marbois and Otto worked with Luzerne and Lafayette as a single unit in a new survey of the American situation, and recommenda-

[1] Extract of a Letter to Congress: *Journal of Elizabeth Drinker*, pp. 128-129.

tions to Congress for more effective aid to Washington in his plans for the reconstruction and rehabilament of the Continental armies.

The troops of the army of Róchambeau, four regiments strong—swung off the boats anchored off Rhode Island. They wore cocked hats or grenadier caps with white and rose-colored plumes. Each man's hair was carefully done in a queue. Their fresh uniforms were white; white and green, or white with rose-colored facings . . . a bow of promise to the stricken land! And very soon, the nation forgot the storm of the night before and woke to greet with lifted hearts this new rainbow arching the ocean from France.

The officers in command of these four dashing regiments were of the illustrious families of France, members of noble houses renowned in history for centuries past. All Philadelphia was thrilled at the news that these noble-born young men of the staff of Rochambeau were coming with their own Lafayette to visit the capital city! Among them would be Lafayette's brother-in-law "the elegant leftenant-colonel of the Soissonnais, Comte de Noailles" and the Chevalier de Chastellux, major-general of the expedition, M. de Damas, the Comte de Darnes and the Duke de Lauzan, commander of the Legionary Corps. Already a favorite in Philadelphia, where he was convalescing from his wounds, was Colonel Dubysson, Lafayette's former companion, now aid to the Baron de Kalb. Henri de la Motte, too, was another one of the Frenchmen of distinction who had come some time before to live among them and remained.

The French Legation was placed at the disposal of the gallant young French visitors. The Chevalier de la Luzerne with his aids, Marquis de Marbois and M. Otto, arranged every detail for their comfort and entertainment.

While Lafayette intended to make a military reconnaissance

89

of the former battlefields and of the lines thrown up by the British in the earlier days of the Revolution, nevertheless there were other considerations, as Lafayette himself would be the first to know! As soon as possible after their arrival in Philadelphia, Major General, the Chevalier de Chastellux,*—went forth to reconnoitre . . . It was ladies he saw . . . among whom he marks Nancy Shippen as "distinctive." He tells about it himself, thus:

At the end of this morning's walk I was like a bee, so laden with honey that he can hardly regain his hive. I returned to the Chevalier de la Luzerne's, with my memory well stored, and after taking food for the body as well as mind, I dedicated my evening to society. I was invited to drink tea at Colonel Bland's, that is to say, to attend a sort of assembly pretty much like the conversazzioni of Italy; for tea here, is the substitute for the *rinfresco*. Mr. *Howley*, Governor of Georgia, Mr. *Izard*, Mr. *Arthur Lee*, (the two last lately arrived from Europe) M. de la Fayette, M. de Noailles, M. de Damas, &c. were of the party. The scene was decorated by several married and unmarried ladies, among whom, Miss *Shippen*, daughter of Dr. Shippen, and cousin of Mrs. *Arnold*, claimed particular distinction. Thus we see that in America the crimes of individuals are not reflected on their family; not only had Dr. Shippen's brother given his daughter to the traitor Arnold, a short time before his desertion, but it is generally believed, that being himself a tory, he had inspired his daughter with the same sentiments, and that the charms of this handsome woman contributed not a little to hasten to criminality a mind corrupted by avarice, before it felt the power of love. . . .

The assembly, or subscription ball, of which I must give an account, may here be properly introduced. At Philadelphia, as at London, Bath, Spa, &c. there are places appropriated for the young people to dance in, and where those whom that amusement does not suit, play at different games of cards; but at Philadelphia, games of commerce are alone allowed. A *manager*, or master of ceremonies presides at these methodical amusements: He presents

* Chastellux's "Travels in North-America," Vol. I, page 234.

to the gentlemen and ladies, dancers, billets folded up containing each a number; thus fate decides the male or female partner for the whole evening. All the dances are previously arranged, and the dancers are called in their turns. These dances, like the *toasts* we drink at table, have some relation to politics: one is called the *success of the campaign,* another, *the defeat of Burgoyne,* and a third, *Clinton's retreat.* The managers are generally chosen from amongst the most distinguished officers of the army; this important place is at present held by Colonel Wilkinson, who is also clothier general of the army. . . .

. . . at Philadelphia, as in London, it is the custom to dine at five, and frequently at six. I should have liked it as well had the company been not so numerous, as to oblige me to make acquaintance with a part of the town; but our minister maintains a considerable state, and gives frequently great dinners, so that it is difficult not to fall into this sort of ambuscade. . . .

Another interesting observation of customs made then by the Duke de la Rochefoucauld Liancourt, is:

The Young women here enjoy a liberty, which to French manners would appear disorderly, they go out alone; walk with young men, and depart with them from the rest of the company in large assemblies; in short, they enjoy the same degree of liberty which married women do in France, and which married women here do not take. But they are far from abusing it; they endeavor to please, they desire to obtain husbands, and they know that they shall not succeed if their conduct becomes suspected. Sometimes they are abused by the men, who deceive them, but then they add not to the misfortune of having engaged their hearts to a cruel man the regret of deserving it, which might give them remorse. When they have obtained a husband, they love him because he is their husband; and because they have not an idea that they can do otherwise; they revere custom by a kind of state religion which never varies . . .

Of all "the most pretty young ladies of Philadelphia," Nancy Shippen was the one elected to dance with Vicomte de Noailles

at a ball at the legation after the marriage to William Bingham
of Nancy's cousin Nancy Willing. In his letter to Tommy of
November 10, 1780, Dr. Shippen has this reference to the
wedding and to the part his daughter took:

> . . . Mr. Bingham & Nancy Willing married two weeks ago.
> . . . Nancy [was] Bridesmaid & dressed off in all her Plumes &
> [name illegible] said she cut out ye Bride which did not please her
> a little . . . Your Cousin Ludwell will tell you all the news, politi-
> cal & domestic he is a very clever youth . . .

It is probably this wedding to which Marquis de Chastellux
refers when he again speaks of Nancy Shippen in his record of
a ball at the French Legation at this time:

> I knew there was to be a ball at the Chevalier de la Luzerne's,
> which made me less in a hurry to return thither: it was, however, a
> very agreeable assembly, for it was given to a private society, on
> the occasion of a marriage. There were near twenty women, twelve
> or fourteen of whom were dancers; each of them having her part-
> ner, as is the custom in America. Dancing is said to be at once the
> emblem of gaiety and of love; here it seems to be the emblem of
> legislation, and of marriage; of legislation inasmuch, as places
> are marked out, the country dances named, and every pro-
> ceeding provided for, calculated and submitted to regulation;
> of marriage, as it furnishes each lady with a partner, with whom
> she dances the whole evening, without being allowed to take
> another. It is true that every severe law requires mitigation,
> and that it often happens, that a young lady after dancing the
> two or three first dances with her partner, may make a fresh
> choice, or accept of the invitation she has received; but still the
> comparison holds good, for it is a marriage in the *European
> fashion*. Strangers have generally the privilege of being compli-
> mented with the handsomest women. The Comte de Darnes had
> Mrs. Bingham for his partner, and the Vicomte de Noailles, Miss
> Shippen. Both of them, like true philosophers, testified a great re-
> spect for the manners of the country, by not quitting their hand-
> some partners the whole evening; in other respects they were the

admiration of all the assembly, from the grace and nobleness with which they danced./. . . I may even assert, to the honour of my country, that they surpassed a Chief Justice of Carolina (Mr. Pendleton) and two members of Congress, one of whom (Mr. Duane) passed however for being by ten per cent more lively than all the other dancers. The ball was suspended, towards midnight, by a supper, served in the manner of coffee, on several different tables. On passing into the dining room, the Chevalier de la Luzerne presented his hand to Mrs. Morris, and gave her the precedence, an honour pretty generally bestowed on her, as she is the richest woman in the city, and all ranks here being equal, men follow their natural bent, by giving the preference to riches . . .

In one of Martha Bland's letters describing this entrancing period of the French occupation of Philadelphia—beside which the British occupation fades into dull drab tone!—she says: . . . "for I well remember the Balls at the french minister and particularizing a petit maître—oh my dear such a swarm of french beaus, Counts, Viscounts, Barons & Chevaliers, . . . and your old acquaintance Col. Dubysson aid de Camp to the Baron de Kalb figures away here amazingly among the Gallants of the Season—he has recovered from his wounds—and as an acquaintance of my Charming Sister (yr. Ladyship) visits me regularly every day . . ." [2]

In the gay rounds of tea-drinking dinners, balls, assemblies, Nancy Shippen became the center of the Frenchmen's hearts and eyes and must have "shone" to her family's full content and to Louis Otto's delight! At Shippen House was spent in pleasant informality the last afternoon before the French officers rejoined their regiments at Newport for the long period of arduous preparation preceding the operations around New York and their eventual march to the southward, to Virginia. Arthur

[2] *The Virginia Magazine of History and Biography*, January, 1935, p. 42.

93

Lee was one of the family of Shippen House at this time, happily reunited with them after many years. There was a large gathering of the Lee clan there to welcome him, among them his sister Hannah Lee Corbin of Peckatone, and their nephews young Thomas and Ludwell Lee of Chantilly, sons of Richard Henry Lee. Possibly Arthur and his two sisters were the "grave personages" the Marquis de Chastellux refers to in his description of their last visit to a Philadelphia home:

M. de la Fayette had made a party with the Vicomte de Noailles and the Comte de Damas, to go the next morning, first to German-Town (which the two latter had not seen) and from thence to the old camp at *Whitemarsh*. . . . Having taken our view, we returned briskly to the Chevalier de la Luzerne's, where dinner came very a propos, after being eight hours on horseback, and riding six and thirty miles. In the afternoon we drank tea with Miss Shippen. This was the first time, since my arrival in America, that I had seen music introduced into society, and mix with its amusements. *Miss Rutledge* played on the harpsichord, and played very well. Miss Shippen sung with timidity, but with a pretty voice. Mr. Ottaw, [Otto], Secretary to M. de la Luzerne, sent for his harp, he accompanied Miss Shippen, and played several pieces. Music naturally leads to dancing: the Vicomte de Noailles took down a violin, which was mounted with harp strings, and he made the young ladies dance, whilst their mothers and other grave personages chatted in another room. When music, and the fine arts come to prosper at Philadelphia; when society once becomes easy and gay there, and they learn to accept of pleasure when it presents itself, without a formal invitation, then may foreigners enjoy all the advantages peculiar to their manners and government, without envying any thing in Europe.

III

[Addressed] Mr Thomas Lee Shippen
   at Mr Booths Academy
    near Frederick Town, Maryland
      Philadelphia
       Thursday evening
        Nov. 9, 1780

My dear Son:

 . . . Your Mamma is highly delighted with her brother & 3 nephews about her; Otto & Nancy playing Harpsichord together.

 Your Mamma is well & expects the next letter. Nancy will write by the first private opportunity & both send much love. Mr Otto visits Tuesday & Saturday—Col. Harry Livingston often. I intend to visit ye army & my hospitals in 3 or 4 days & be absent perhaps 3 or 4 weeks.

 God bless you my dr Son.

         W. Shippen, Jr.

Nancy's father was describing the scene at Shippen House. While Louis Otto was acutely aware of Colonel Livingston's position there he did not sense the actual peril impending, because perhaps his heart and mind were so at one with Nancy's.

Nancy had been cajoled by her father into accepting Henry Livingston as a suitor. Possibly talk of the town was also a factor, for was not a match with a Livingston of New York of far more *emprise* than with, say, a Bingham? The young girl soon found that her vanity and "coquettery" had led her into a cul-de-sac . . . and could Monsieur Otto please show her how to get out? M. Otto could! Was he not in the diplomatic service of France? Summoning fancy and humor to his aid, he engaged to dispose of his rival in the following "Exercise in English":

Monday evening.

Being anxious on what subject I should exercise my English Correspondence I fell upon our last conversation and I contrived to write the following letter which I have the honour of submitting to your indulging eye.

"Letter of Milady Old-fashion to Miss Inconstant."

Dear Friend,

You acquaint me in your last letter with a Deficiency, which is to common in our Sex as to look upon it as a crime when it is kept in its proper boundaries—I mean *vanity* and Coquetterie.—I thank you that you made me the Confident of your feelings before they were carried too far and I shall reward this complyance with the most tender reception and with answering your questions with the greatest Sincerity. You tell me that you encouraged several months the addresses of Lord D.... though you did not feel any inclination for him and that you did it only in order to gratify your vanity, that you did not think on the consequences of your Behaviour and that you feel yourself in a great perplexity how to disintrigate yourself. I *love you too much*, my dear, to look with Severity at your conduct and I shall only endeavour to acquaint you with all the dreadfull consequences which may attend it.

I A Young Lady, who is first introduced in the world ought to act with the greatest precaution. Every one of her Steps lays a foundation to the opinion which the publick will have of her for the future. She ought particularly to respect all those, who honnour her by their addresses and never to play with their feelings. There is something so humiliating for a man in seeing himself deluded by a Lady that he will never forgive her; he will find means of ridiculing the object of his Love as soon as he sees himself despised and there is allmost no man capable of resisting in this case to the sweet temptations of revenge. Your heart is too pure and you have too little experience of the world to know how easy it is to injure the Caracter of a Lady and how will you expect mercy from a man whom you offended in the most cruel manner? You are the aggressor and you ought to expect all that disappointment vanity and revenge can inspire to an incensed lover. I

96

Without encouraging the addresses of those which we despise, there is an art of getting rid of their persecutions by a cold, indifferent, though polite, Behaviour. But when we have been vain enough to incourage feelings which we can not participate, the means of disengaging us are very difficult. It is mortifying for a young Lady to appear insignificant or thoughtless, however this is the only measure to be taken in the case you mention. If you tell Lord D.... that you deluded him, he will despise you as much as he loved you. If you show any preference to another he will be much more incensed and acquaint every body with your Coquetterie. But if you endeavour to be of an inconsistent, disagreeable, contradicting, even extravagant humour in his presence, if you affirm in one moment what you denied in another, if you appear to him to be quite insensible and indifferent for every thing except for pleasure, if you conceal with art the advantages of a liberal education, he will soon be more moderate in his feelings and at last be astonished that he ever was in love with so an extraordinary Being as you. I own that it will be very difficult for you to act this part, but necessity will probably make it easy. Perhaps he will mention your extravagances in publick, but nobody will believe him, because you will endeavour to appear to all, except him, as prudent, as modest, as reserved, as consistent, as well bred as you are.—I have too good an opinion my dear Friend of your heart as to believe, you would injure it for the sake of your vanity.

You will think Milady Old fashion a very old fashioned Caracter, but notwithstanding there may be some truth in her observations and as she has a great deal of experience I should follow her principles If I was a Lady.—I own that she knows exceedingly well the dispositions of our Sex and that she has probably been a very great coquette herself *a forty years ago.*—Those Ladies are like old Soldiers who after having lost their limbs in a hundred different expeditions are the more proper to give good instructions to a young Warrior.

Lewis Scriblerus.

97

How Nancy took the French Diplomat's advice is told in another chapter of this narrative. Very soon Louis's own love took precedence over advice.

Thursday Evening at 9. o'clock.

I never felt so disagreeable as in this moment. Leaving you in so abrupt a manner I was persuaded it must be very late. But how great was my astonishment when I heard it is only 9. o'clock, and how sorry must I not be that I did not take this opportunity of entertaining you of those objects which I mention in my last note. I was so uneasy the whole evening to see Company in your house at a time, where I could possibly speak alone with you, that I thought it at least midnight when Mr B . . . took his hat, though I flattered myself by your Smile when I took leave that you would not be sorry to see me stay. I am so distressed that I had run back immediately, when there was not an impropriety in it. I have now no other ressource than my pen, though I feel so unhappy, that I can not write one tollerable Sentiment. You will forgive me, dear Friend, I was never less master of my feelings. Perhaps I rely too much upon your indulgence—but how can you indulge too much a man who lives only for you.

I am allways at a loss how to express myself with you. There is something so heavenly in my soul when I begin to write that I should not be able of expressing it even in my own language. I had never so great a desire to please and never I felt so much my inferiority. Read in my Eyes, dear Miss, when I look on you, when I swallow with the utmost eagerness all the poison, when I examine with admiration those charming proportions of your person, the Symbole of the most perfect mind, when I press my lipps upon your hand from which I would never be separated, or in that happy moment when you told me that *you would rather die a hundred times than* . . . O why could not you read in the same time in my heart, every one of its fibres starting at the sweet . . . not *declaration*, because you would never tell me such a thing . . . not *information*, because you can not inform me of what I know allready . . . I do not know how to call it, but it was the most heavenly Music I ever heard in my life. It allways sounds in my Ear and I shall only forget it when I will be no more.—Or should I have put an ill construction upon your words,—should I have misunderstood your looks, should I be vain enough to flatter myself with an imaginary happiness:—Speak Miss,—and plunge me in one moment in an abyss of misery and disappointment.—*Misunderstand you?*—I should as well misunderstand my own feelings.

One hour after dispatching this letter to Shippen House, Louis Otto took his courage in his two hands and spoke his mind again quite plain. With all his courtesy and chivalry, the Frenchman had a keen sense of fair play between a man and woman in love—"For to recyue this Saynt with honour dew."

Thursday Evening, 10. o'clock.

I can not forbear writing a second letter though I am afraid you may allready be tired with the first.—Mr L . . . . mentioned this Evening some Verses and *Billets doux* which you shewed him. I am sure you did never reflect on the indelicacy of it, otherwise you are too good, too generous to indulge so an improper fit of vanity. Don't think my dear Friend that I am afraid for the fate of my own letters, I am too sure of your esteem to presume it, and too proud of loving you to fear that anybody should know it.— Forgive my sincerity, I am so anxious of seeing you entirely perfect that the least Deficiency in your Caracter offends me. My fondness for you is boundless, but I should think myself unworthy of your Friendship if I could spoil your temper by the least flattery. I expect from you the same candour in my behalf and I shall be happy in conforming myself entirely to your wishes. When this is the material advantage of Friendship, why shall it not be the same in Love?—I hope you will believe me that it is extravagant to think we can admire the faults of our intiment Friends when our connexion is founded upon virtue, we ought even sooner to discover them by their contrast with those perfections which induced us to love, to cherish, to admire.—I shall allways be an attentive observer of your actions but gratitude obliges you to do the same in my favour, and contribute to mutual happiness, which in my

99

opinion consists only in *moral perfection,*—I am too sure of the purity of your heart as to think this extraordinary topic will astonish you; it would be ridiculed by a thousand other Ladies but those Ladies are not *Nancy.*

My Philosophy went on with my pen in such a hurry, that my heart which is a very poor philosopher did not chuse to follow her, and as I am a greater Friend of the latter, I left Madam Philosophy with her frowning Eyebrows, and came back to my darling. It tells me a thousand things about you, which are so tender and so pleasing that I promise him never to make any Phylosophical excursion without its Company. It is so fond of you that it is afraid you may turn diffident and reserv'd after having read those little observations. I confess that I am myself a little uneasy about it, though I use all the dissimulation which is in my power to appear perfectly quiet.

Friday morning 7. o'clock.

I awaked with the thought on you, and when the admiration of creatures is the most perfect Worship of the creator, I never honoured him—I never adored him with more fervour. I can not tell you my Prayer, but you may guess it,—and if you feel *pleasure* in guessing it, a great part of it is allready fulfilled,—but if you are *indifferent* I shall only repeat the latter part and wish you as happy as you can possibly be,—and if the thought on it is quite *disagreeable* to you (heaven forbid) I shall pray that you may never feel the thousand[th] part of the anxiety, the agitations, the torments of

Your devoted Lewis.

P.S. I have only a *small* collection of *Small* notes, written on very *small* paper and sometimes with a very *small* degree of Sensibility. These notes send you an humble petition for some sisters to keep them Company. Would you be so cruel as to refuse your own Children?—

IV

Philadelphia
Jan'y 27, 1781

[Addressed:] Mr Thomas Lee Shippen
at Dr Booths Academy
Frederick County, Maryland
favor'd by
M^r McPherson.

. . . Nancy is much puzzled between Otto & Livingston. She loves ye first & only esteems the last. On Monday she likes L— & his fortune. On Tuesday even^g when O— comes he is the angel. L— will consummate immediately. O— not these 2 years. L— has solicited the Father & Mother. O— is afraid of a denial. In short, we are all much puzzled. L— has 12 or 15,000 hard. O— has nothing now, but honorable expectations hereafter. A Bird in hand is worth 2 in a bush. They are both sensible. O— handsome. What do you think of it?

Dont forget your French, be diligent, & improve & make happy
Your affectionate friend & father
My fingers are so cold I can
scarcely hold ye pen.

So Dr. Shippen wrote to his son after the Christmas festivities at Shippen House, when Tommy had gone back to school and Uncle Arthur Lee and Cousin Tom to Virginia. While the reply from sixteen-year-old Tommy is not available, it may be taken for granted that he advocated "the Bird in hand!"

Dr. Shippen, convinced that his daughter's material advantage was at stake, set himself astutely to the business of bringing about her marriage to Livingston. He did not immediately curtail her attendance at the series of entertainments at the French Legation when Louis Otto was her escort. Martha

101

Bland describes the two in a letter to her sister-in-law in Williamsburg:

> You judge right my dear In supposing that I am taken up by the Gay Scenes of Philadelphia . . . we had an oratorio at the Minister's last Tuesday, it was very clever—he gives a Ball one week, a concert the next—the Minister sacrifices his time to the policy of the french Court—he dislikes Music, never dances and is a domestick Man yet he has a Ball or a Concert every week and his house full to dinner every day—We had a Play performed by the Students in the College a few weeks ago—when there was the greatest crowd I ever saw. I went accompany'd by Mr. Marboys & Mr. Otto, the two petit ministers of france, Don Francisco the Spanish Minister and Miss Shippen we went at 5 o'clock but found several hundred people in the Yard waiting for the opening of the dores—they were shut & we were not inclined to join the crowd so drove round two or more squares of the City—when we returned we found the dores open'd and the people climbing up the Walls to get in—Some mounted upon the heads of others and in short, such a mob that it is impossible to describe if Garrick had been to perform it could not have been greater—Mr. Marboy took hold of one of my arms don francisco of the other—Mis Shippin of his and Mr. Otto of hers—in this manner we attempted to get through the crowd—They forced us about half way the passage but I was all most suffocated and declared I would not go up the Stairs a large woman broke our chain by forcing Mr. Marboy's hand from mine—our little party retired to a room in the College untill the Hurly Burly was over—. . .[3]

Nancy's mother approved of Louis Otto and her daughter's union with him. She wrote a tender and sympathetic letter to him, favorably responding to his letter asking consent for their

[3] *The Virginia Magazine of History and Biography*, January, 1935, pp. 41-44. Randolph and Tucker Letters. Letter from Martha Dangerfield Bland (Mrs. Theodorick Bland the Younger of Cawsons) to Frances Bland Tucker (Mrs. St. George Tucker). Loaned by courtesy of Mr. and Mrs. George P. Coleman.

marriage. On the other hand, Dr. Shippen, while not openly refusing his consent, at once took measures to restrict the visits of the French Diplomat to twice a week, after Louis had "acquired the custom" of calling almost daily on Nancy. How disturbed was the young Frenchman is shown in his letter of "Monday 10. o'clock in the Evening."

During Nancy's enforced seclusion, Otto would not have failed to remind her of his sympathy and devotion—though it would seem that the Philadelphia post forbade their writing oftener than twice a week, as this first letter indicates:

Monday 10. o'clock in the Evening

After having reconnoitred your house I spent the most disagreeable evening in Company with two Ladies of your acquaintance. My heart was allways running about with my witt and all the faculties of my mind, and did not suffer me to say one single word of consequence. I told them that I *think* Miss A., Miss B., Miss C., and Miss D. *very handsome*, they agreed with me and observed with great judgment that Miss E., Miss F., Miss G., and Miss H. *are very pretty*, and that *they think* Miss I. sings very well, and Miss K. has a very fine person, that Miss L. is very affected in her manners, that Mrs M. has a very bad cold, that Miss N. is gone in the country and that Miss Y. is to be married with Mr X. a very fine young man. After having settled all those important matters, I told them in confidence—that it was very warm today—much warmer than in France in Germany or—in *Venice*.

You see my dear friend what I loose by being obliged to keep days like the post which arrives *only twice a week;* but on the other side I am convinced with you of the necessity of it and I beg you only to read those foolish things which I intend to write down in the hours which were entirely devoted to you. This correspondence will be sometimes very comical, sometimes very serious, but—I wish—never tedious to you and when you adopt a depreciation of five for one I shall be very happy to receive one letter for five letters *papermoney*. I suppose you are too good a *Whig* to refuse my request.

103

I shall never forget that M^r L . . . was the cause of an explanation, which made me the happiest man in the world, I shall love him for that, though I have no other reason for it, and though I had none at all a few days ago. I am extremely glad of all that happened, and even the tears which I saw drop from your Eyes afford me an agreeable remembrance, when I reflect on their motive. You was so kind last Evening to beg me to come tomorrow, a pleasure—which you never did me before. Why am I not able to express my feelings in a better language—Ah! there is no language for it, read it in my Eyes, in my whole conduct, or if it is possible,—read it in your heart—

Tomorrow Evening—(18 hours more which will be filled with thoughts on you) I shall see you again, I shall tell you so often how much I love you that you will be found to answer; *and I too, I love you, my dear Friend!* No harmony in the world could equal these words flowing from your Lipps. When shall I hear them? I am full of expectations. My whole Life will be entirely devoted to you, and all my happiness shall consist in giving you proofs of my tender attachment; but I am afraid you will never pronounce those fatal words, and I shall be unhappy for ever.

Please to tell me which words you did not approve of in your Mamma's letter. Good night.

Nancy was either being coquettish or temperamental, for she gave no encouraging response to this ardent letter from her lover. Disconsolate and bewildered, Louis Otto resorted to the tactics of diplomacy. He left the city for a little while and wrote to his adored one:

Dear Friend

You was allways so reserved with me that I have [no] reason to believe, you felt any of those sentiments y[ou] inspired me, and so unhappy is my situation, that I must wish you never did. I understood so well the sentiments of your Mama, that I should think myself unworthy of your Friendship if I could alter the harmony of a Family (which I wish to be the happiest in the world) but in the same time I should be very distressed to be wittness of the prerogatives granted to a person, whom I can not think worthier of them, then me. Therefore I am obliged to use the only means, which may cure me of my presumtion—*time* and *absence*. I hope that reason, pride and particularly the consideration of your own [happi]ness as much as it depends from the good understanding with your family, will give me in some months that tranquillity of mind, which will enable me to see you without danger and to enjoy all the Blessings of Friendship without feeling the torments of a disappointed Love.

Time and *absence* apparently had the effect Louis Otto so desired. Seeing Nancy upon his return during the second week of March, 1781, he won her consent to marry him, only to have his triumphant joy clouded immediately thereafter— possibly that very evening. For Nancy's mother, acting under her husband's instructions, requested Louis not to see Nancy for a period of four days. On Tuesday evening he wrote to her:

Was it a dream, my dear Nancy? or did I really hear you pronounce that heavenly *yes!* which I never shall forget?—but your whole behaviour tells me that you love me more than a common friend!—forgive my mentioning it, my heart is so full, I am so extremely happy,—no tongue can express it, I feel it in so high a degree that every word appears to me weak, low, improper. I shall ever adore you, ever love you more than myself,—I have the approbation of your parents, and I think I feel the approbation of heaven.— Why must I now be four days without seeing you! Every Day will appear an age; it is true I may write you, but I must confess My dear Friend, that I am allways afraid to appear in my letters to a great disadvantage, however it is my only pleasure when I can not see you and you will indulge my stile for the motif. Good night Lovely Nancy, may Angels surround your bed and entertain you with delightful dreams.

How mistaken was Louis Otto—how misled with delusions of a woman's constancy and family commendation—was proven very soon. Wednesday, the beginning of his enforced absence, was a day of misery for him. He was utterly unaware of the lightning-like preparations at Shippen House for rushing Nancy into immediate marriage with Colonel Livingston. Forbidden to see Nancy in her home, Louis called on one of their mutual friends, in the vain hope of seeing his beloved there. That evening, with the first doubts stirring in his mind, he wrote her:

M^r W . . . told me that his Ladys are not at home and so I could not go there, where I had probably met you. One of those long days is passed; I am afraid I may to morrow Evening forget your Mama's comand. What is your opinion? Shall I . . .

Did you once think on me today, or did you write me one single line. It is true I proposed you five for one, but I expected your generosity will change the bargain at least in two for one. If you think that question ought to be answered I shall allways contrive some, in order to receive one of your—*notes.*—I send you here some of my favourite questions.

1. May a Lady say *No* when she once said *yes.*
2. Is there no equality in Love as much as in Friendship?
3. Is there any greater Blessing in the world, than that which Love affords?

There was no answer. Thursday must have been an intolerable day. Thoroughly alarmed, and racked with suspicion, he walks slowly by the parlour windows of Shippen House. There, unconscious of his gaze, are Nancy and Livingston. Can this be his own Beloved who smiles upon another? Later in the evening he writes to her:

I had not the courage this Evening of seeing you, for fear of acting against the command of your Mama, but I walk'd close by your house, as I do every Day. I pass'd just when M^r L . . . happened to hold one of your hands and to look very happy; you seem'd to be very happy yourself and this unhappy Discoverie mad[e] me, for one moment, the most miserable creature in the world; I felt in the same time every torments of jealousy and all my old suspicions were revived. But after having reflected on all what happened between us Tuesday evening, I was ashamed of my suspicions and I resolved to confess it to you with my usual sincerity. One word of my dear Friend could cure me of all these fears, but you seem to be affraid of making me perfectly happy: can you doubt one moment of the Sincerity of my Sentiments, speak, the most difficult sacrifice will appear nothing to me, when the possession of Nancy is the reward.

Indeed Miss, four days are too long, it is cruel to desire it.

You changed my whole caracter, all my gayety is gone, I am dead for company and afraid to see any body. I spend my time only with Books, and even these old Friends of mine, often appear to me stupid.

Answer me, dear Friend, or you will make me unhappy—It is 10. o'clock, I hope M^r L . . . . is gone.—Adieu.

Twenty-four hours later Nancy writes him the truth at last. It is not until Sunday that he can reply:

Dear Friend.

Your Confidence of Friday Evening encreased so much my ill State of health that I was not able to see you yesterday. I was in a kind of Dejection, which I never felt before, taking a thousand resolutions and changing them again till I was a little better this morning and resolved to write you.

You mention my making proposals to your P[appa] and which proposals?—I have no others than those mentioned in my letter to your Mama. he read that unhappy letter which first betray'd my intentions and made me enjoy a few months the delightful thought of possessing in you all the treasures of heaven.—Vain dreams of Blessing which I shall pay with years of grief!—Your P[appa] knows that my Fortune can not be compared with that of [Livingston] therefore he prefers him; perhaps true wisdom would distinguish happiness and riches, but I dont intend to censure, only to

107

Complain.—How can you believe that he will be more attentive to the remonstrations of a Stranger than he is to the feelings of his beloved daughter?—Your tender M[ama] consulting nothing else than her own Sensibility and finding something in her heart which told her that there is no happiness without Love answer'd me by a letter which I shall preserve as a pattern of magnanimity and which shews that she perfectly knows our Caracter's. I shall never forget her kindness and engrave her name in that heart, where yours will eternally reign.

I do not see for what reason in this *free* Country a Lady of Sixteen years who is handsome enough to find as many admirers, and who had all the advantages of a good education must be married in a hurry and given up to a man whom she dislikes; this observation is not at all calculated to make you oppose the desires of your parents and I am sure that Your principles will lead you to sacrifice your inclinations to your Duty.

In the first months of our acquaintance you was surrounded with a number of Lovers one of which I thought to be the favour'd one. Your exterior charms which were then the only I could admire made therefore less impression upon me and I saw you without great danger. By and by the polite attention of your parents, your candour, your pleasing behaviour and your complaisance in listening to my broken language made me feel something for you which I was ignorant enough to call Friendship. I observed then a total Desertion of your admirers and was surprised to spend allmost every Evening alone in your Company. But seeing no probability of establishing myself in this Country I was amazed to hear some of my acquaintances tell me that both D^r and Mrs S...... would be happy in a Connection with me. . . . *Jaques M. . . .* after having mention'd to me all the advantages of being married in this Country added *that if I had such intentions he recommended me his Cousin Nancy.*—You know my dear Friend that it wanted no recommendation, but these and a thousand other circumstances encouraged me to indulge that growing passion, which only Death will Cure. I was extravagant enough to believe that the Behaviour of your Family was entirely owing to their particular Friendship for me; and unhappily I discovered only a few months ago the Stories which a fool contriv'd without thinking on the Consequences, but which are the Commentary of the sudden change of some minds.—Though I could never suppose you would refuse an advantageous establishment for my Sake, yet I thought that being myself of a Family, worthy to be Connected with any one in the Continent and in such circumstances as to be entitled in a few years to an honorable appointment, I might expect silent the happy hour which should connect us to your advantage. The thought on a beloved mother and two Sisters, who expect my return with the utmost anxiety encreased my precautious Behaviour till that Day of explanations with your M[ama], which shewing me the danger of loosing you, made me forget all other Considerations. Since that time you seem'd to rely upon the approbation of your P[appa] and being less reserv'd than before, you shew'd me all the perfections of your heart and all the Softness of your dispositions. Since that time your image is so entirely present to me, all my thoughts are so entirely directed towards you that I see or feel nothing in the world but you.—If we must separate (*cruel* thought) but if we *must* separate, let us not follow common souls that know only the transition from Love to indifference. Be my Friend as you was before and let me believe that I occupy allways a part of your heart as much as religion and decency will allow you.—I promised you a thousand times that I will adore you for ever and that shall be my only Comfort in a life that will grow painfull by the remembrance of my disappointment, but probably much shorter than nature intended. In another world I shall distinguish you between a million of your Companions and love you in Spite of the Universe.—May you allow me a pityful tear from those Eyes where I am used to read my happiness and think that I am only miserable and not guilty. My own tears begin to mix with my inck, and forbid me to Continue.

I am yours for ever; though perhaps you will never be mind.

P.S. I shall attempt to see you this Evening.

Dr. Shippen must have known that the situation was too critical to leave his daughter unguarded on the eve of her wedding. He could not risk having her see Louis Otto! And if Otto tried to see her, he failed. As for Nancy, the excitement of a trousseau, brought suddenly, as if by magic, served to distract her attention as her father planned. Undoubtedly Colonel Livingston put in his appearance hourly.

Dr. Shippen was convinced that it was to his daughter's inestimable advantage to make an alliance with the Livingston family, whose vast estates and proverbially unlimited fortunes were scarcely touched by war's exigencies. And . . . after all . . . in comparison with a Livingston, who and what was an obscure young attaché of a foreign legation, even though it was that of France? Furthermore, his own financial affairs, like those of almost all Philadelphia families, were demoralized by the war. Depreciation of currency was then, as Louis Otto had observed, "five to one." Because of his own service in the war, so largely gratuitous, his practice at home had gone. Nancy's education had been a heavy expense and Tommy's promised to be heavier, for he was about to be sent to Williamsburg and then abroad.

From Dr. Shippen's viewpoint, therefore, his plans for his daughter's marriage seemed unquestionably the best! On the day before the wedding, March 13, 1781, he wrote to Tommy:

. . . Your Sister thanks you for your good wishes & is much pleased that her choice meets your approbation; wishes much for your company tomorrow night & the succeeding week of Festivity; so do we all.

She insists on my going with her to the North River to see her fixed in her own Mansion, as soon as I return which I suppose will be about the 20th of April. Your Mamma proposes we shall meet you at Baltimore & all proceed together to Chantilly [4] &c. How do you like this scheme? . . .

Your affectᵉ friend & Father

[4] Chantilly, a part of Stratford Plantation in Virginia was the home of Richard Henry Lee.

Next morning Nancy woke to still more excitement and to the romantic idea of being a bride! Not a moment, perhaps, for her to consider the agony of Louis Otto, to foresee that which she herself was soon to suffer, or to recall her broken troth. Her father, usually so indulgent, so kind to her, approved of Colonel Livingston as a husband, and perhaps he would know best.

At least he had brought her to see that it was best. Then too, he had agreed to go with her on her bridal journey to the North River, and to help her arrange her new house. It would not really have been possible, she may have reflected, to marry Colonel Livingston at all unless her dear Pappa could be with her!

So the wedding took place: On the fourteenth day of March at Shippen House in Philadelphia Anne Home Shippen, only daughter of William Shippen, Jr., and Alice Lee his wife, was married to Henry Beekman Livingston, third son of Robert R. Livingston III and Margaret Beekman his wife.

CHAPTER V

1781-1783

I

F OR Nancy the seat of the Lords of the Manor Livingston must have seemed another world, cold and austere—and dull perhaps—by contrast with the Virginian informality of Shippen House and the gaieties and gossip of Philadelphia. Then too, in the twinkling of an eye, her position and her status had entirely changed. No more was she Nancy, the spoiled darling and center of a home more southern than Philadelphian in its ease and warmth of life; she was instead Mrs. Henry Beekman Livingston—Henry's wife, mistress of a mansion of her own—or more truly speaking, of her husband's house.

Barely eighteen years of age, gay, vivacious, trained to the art of pleasing men—could she become all at once a staid matron and a grave personage? Having her father beside her at the first meeting with her husband's family must have been a relief. But when he left little Rhinebeck on the Hudson, where Henry Beekman Livingston had a house, and Nancy was alone with this strange, unreasonable and unreasoning man she had married, with only his relatives living near, the situation had its difficulties. And it was such a far, far journey to Philadelphia.

The Manor Livingston, a landed estate of one hundred and sixty-three thousand acres, was one of the largest in the Colonial Province of New York. It extended for fifteen miles along the North River, from a point near Tivoli to the borders of Connecticut and Massachusetts. In itself it was a kingdom, actually a feudal stronghold. Like the Dutch patroons, Livingston's ancestors were not only rich landowners but patriarchs of great families comprised of their children, grandchildren, an army of servants and their children, tenant farmers and laborers.

As far back as 1688, the grant of the Manor of Livingston had been given to the stalwart young Scotch pioneer settler, Robert R. Livingston, founder of the family in America. This grant was enlarged and confirmed some twenty-seven years later by Royal Charter from George I and the Manor and Lordship of Livingston formally erected. Livingston Manor thus became the mother place of innumerable estates and a group of little towns along the Hudson River. Practically all of these estates and villages were owned and occupied by members of this one family, their connections, tenants or servants. In Rhinebeck were the homes of many Livingstons. Through their alliances for over five generations with the Dutch patroons, Schuyler, Ten Broeck, Van Rensselaer, Beekman and others, and with the Jay family, the Livingstons' vast holdings had been increased, consolidated and strengthened.

When the Revolution came and the Livingstons stood almost alone on the side of the people, rather than with the Tory aristocracy, they presented a formidable front. Of all the citizens of New York, they were the most influential and effective in preparing the people for the change from a British Colonial Province into the new State of New York. What the Lees were to the Colony of Virginia and the Adamses to Massachusetts, the Livingstons were to New York, with the added power of almost fabulous wealth.

For more than a century and a half the Livingstons had dwelt in the security, comfort and majestic solitude of their North River kingdom. A certain serene simplicity, integrity, and dignified reserve distinguished them as a family. When staying in New York City or in Philadelphia, they seemed in a sense a people apart. That is, as a family they seldom entered into the petty gossip, scandal, intrigue of the small town-atmosphere of these Colonial cities, nor adopted the affectations, false values and standards of the times. With place and power for their birthright, their cultural standards and experiences were of a different calibre.

And yet, perhaps Nancy found, fancy was not bred in their family! Nancy saw that here at Rhinebeck and at Clermont were Livingstons everywhere: Livingstons only. In every house for miles and miles, up the river, down the river, across the river, lived the relatives of her husband. Although in Philadelphia everyone was related or connected, it was nothing like this. For there new people came, and, with Congress and the foreign legations as incentive, the social season was gay. So many tea-parties, weddings, balls, assemblies, lectures, dinners, concerts! Here, nothing went on.

Clermont, in itself an estate of thirteen thousand acres, was the home of Nancy's widowed mother-in-law Madam Livingston. A woman of personal force and distinction, she was a great lady of her day, and the wife of a man of exceptional worth, integrity and achievement. She was to the Province of New York what Henrietta Maria Lloyd in an earlier generation was to the Province of Maryland; and what Nancy's own grandmother, Hannah Ludwell Lee, was to the colony of Virginia—a great progenitress, mother of sons who did much to shape the political, legal and economic aspects of the world in which they lived.

Had Nancy Shippen come to Clermont first as a guest, a visitor—not as Henry's wife—her sensitive perceptions would no doubt have caught the spirit of sincerity, the actual hidden beauty and sweetness at the heart of this family's life: "My

MRS. ROBERT R. LIVINGSTON (MARGARET BEEKMAN)
FROM THE ORIGINAL PORTRAIT BY GILBERT STUART
Courtesy of Frick Art Reference Library and Brigadier General John Ross
Delafield

house is peace and Love," Madam Livingston said once to her in a letter written in later years. "This character is ever proverbial where [my family] are known. Never did 3 estimable Brothers and six Sister's Love each other better than they do." In reality there were four brothers. Not even in this chance ex-

CLERMONT
By Courtesy of Brigadier General John Ross Delafield

pression would Madam Livingston's innate honesty permit her to call estimable her son Henry Beekman. the man whom Nancy married.

It was from Clermont that Madam Livingston laid down the law to all her family, except to Henry, unfortunately the only son who needed it. Before her marriage, she had been Margaret Beekman, the one child of Henry Beekman, judge of Ulster County and a member of the Provincial Legislature. Her husband Robert R. Livingston III, like his father before him, was a strong believer in the independence of the Colonies. He was a Colonial Supreme Court judge, and a member of the

115

Stamp Act Congress which drafted the address to the King. He died just before the outbreak of hostilities, leaving six daughters and four sons, of whom Nancy's husband was next to the youngest.

As the seat of the two men termed by Britain "the arch rebels of New York," Robert R. Livingston and his son Robert, later the "Chancellor," and American Ambassador to France, Clermont was one of the first American homes to be attacked by the British at the beginning of the Revolution. Earlier in the conflict, Madam Livingston had given shelter and care at Clermont to a wounded British officer, a kinsman of her son-in-law General Montgomery, husband of her daughter Janet. Therefore, when, in October, 1777, the British ship *Vulture* was ordered to proceed from New York up the Hudson to destroy the villages, houses, properties and homes of the late Robert R. Livingston and his son, conciliatory word was sent to Madam Livingston that, because of her aid to this British officer, Clermont would be spared. Madam Livingston scorned this overture. She would not permit her hospitality to a family connection to be construed into the price paid by her to the British for the saving of her home. She therefore refused the favor, packed her furniture and personal belongings into wagons, buried the silver, and departed. As she sought refuge in a neighboring farmhouse her stately home went up in flames. The giant old locust trees alone remained. Later she rebuilt the house, using the old stone walls which stood firm after the fire.

Notwithstanding Madam Livingston's Spartan qualities and her well-poised and wisely-directed training and education of her large family, she appears to have been curiously unwise and indulgent in the bringing up of her idolized son. From his youth, Henry had been a problem. Subject to ungovernable fits of rage, he could not or would not brook restraint or correction in any form. Arrogant, self-willed, self-indulgent, temperamental, he sowed an early and luxurious crop of wild oats. The freedom and license of the soldier's life, which he had entered in his twenty-fifth year when he joined his brother-in-law in the ill-fated expedition to Quebec, accentuated his profligacy. Ever through the camps and the long marches to the far Canadian frontier and to the very field of battle, his over-fond mother's anxieties followed, in constant letters of inquiry and solicitude to General Montgomery. In the last letter Montgomery wrote to his wife was this tempered assurance to Madam Livingston about her spoiled son: "Present my affectionate duty to her and make her easy respecting Harry. He has by no means given any offense, though some uneasiness, by some little imprudence."

After the tragic events of that Canadian campaign, Henry received a transfer to the Continental Army. A few years later came his resignation; then, quite suddenly, probably even before his mother heard, his marriage to Nancy Shippen.

As the daughter of a patriot house and one to the manor born, Nancy Shippen found a formal welcome among the Livingstons and held her new and difficult position with a dignity that brought their high esteem and regard. But her husband's sister, Mrs. Richard Montgomery, widow of the hero of Quebec, always called her "Madam"! And all of the Colonel's other sisters and brothers and their husbands and wives met her in a Livingston way. That was not at all a Lee or Shippen way. Between herself and Madam Livingston, whom Nancy called in the affectionately respectful eighteenth century way "The Old Lady," a pleasant and tender intimacy was eventually established, and Nancy stayed at Clermont for weeks at a time. Her husband, who was the namesake of The Old Lady's father, being his mother's favorite son, his wife was evidently approved from the day The Old Lady first saw her.

It could not have been long after Dr. Shippen's departure from his daughter's new home at Rhinebeck, that Nancy came face to face with the realities of her husband's nature. His mind, like his temper, was quick to heat. His frequent and ungovernable fits of rage shocked and terrified her. He spared neither her, his mother, nor the servants.

Although it never occurred to Nancy to see or write Louis Otto, and the two had no communication by visit, sign or letter, her husband became malevolently suspicious of them both. Henry Livingston had known from the time he first thrust his suit upon Nancy that her heart was in Louis Otto's keeping. More than any other, he knew by what sinister connivance between himself and Nancy's father the young girl's consent to marry him had been brought about. Nancy held fast to the standards of her race and time, and her father's precepts. Louis Otto never spoke or wrote a single word to change her view or influence her act. But now that she was left alone in the power of a husband who misconstrued her every thought and act, the young wife was bewildered and tormented almost out of her senses. If she so much as smiled in greeting upon any man it was an amour she was contemplating, an adultery she was avid to commit. Colonel Livingston believed the worst of her as, in fact, he did of all women. He gave her no credit for any sense of honor, loyalty or decency. Added to this strain and misery was the circumstance that Nancy became pregnant almost immediately following her marriage.

There was not an inch of common ground between herself and her husband. Meeting with no response or sympathetic understanding, it must have been impossible for her to even talk with him. He said to her when she protested against his continual misconstruction of her feelings and actions: "But you will not wonder if I should judge erroneously when you recollect that I have always been kept a Stranger to your Motives and Views."

In a very few months after they settled in Rhinebeck, Nancy's gaiety was extinguished and her spirit put into eclipse. The idyl of her brief happiness with Otto's love was ended. That which was between them must have seemed to pass into the night. The clouds began to gather swift and dark.

II

Mrs. Col. H. B. Livingston   Sunday, July 8, 1781
Rhineback
on the North River
My Dr Nancy; . . .
How much more cool & happy you are, I am sure may be under your venerable Locusts. I conjure you to use all your endeavours to be yourself & make all around you happy. Much is now in your own power & conduct. Remember too my d^r Girl that the happiness of ye best of mothers & your affectionate Father, of all your friends in Philadelphia & at ye Manor depend in some measure on you.

Your uncle [R.] H. Lee desires his love to you & Comp^{ts} to the Col to whom present my affectionate compliments. In much haste, Dr Nancy

Your loving Father

W. Shippen jr.

In this letter there is hint of the ill wind brewing, and he puts it to his daughter to temper its currents.

From his next letter of July 25, it is evident that Nancy is doing her best to live up to his expectations and to observe his admonitions that the great duty of woman is to contribute daily to the comfort of her husband.

119

My dear Nancy

Your last letters are very pleasing, & our most fervent wishes are that you may not only continue but increase your happiness from day to day. Many friends rejoice with us at the prospect of seeing you in the winter. We insist on yᵉ Colonels accompanying you and staying here as long as he can consistent with his business; my affectionate compliments to him & tell him I insist on his coming if he can stay but a week. Many things make this necessary besides the pleasure I shall have in seeing you happy together. Your Mamma sends you a pound of fine Tea & sealing wax.

Have you returned the visits you owe to your kind neighbours. I shall be much disappointed if you are not called one of the most polite, affable, good-humor'd Ladys on the Hudson, and one of the most notable, careful & affectionate wives. You never look half so well as when you smile. If you encourage your natural good temper, tis calculated to make every body happy around you & love you. Never forget that it should be your first care to please & make your husband happy. You must take much pains to make your servants *love* & fear you.

Show the world you have all the good qualities of a Shippen & of a Lee without one of their bad ones. God bless you my dear child & direct you in the perfect way prays

Your affectionate Father

Love & compliments to
all your friends.
Addressed: Mʳˢ Henry B. Livingston
           Reinbeck
           Honor'd by The Chancellor

At approximately the same time, Nancy's brother Tommy, grown vastly patronizing in his sixteenth year under the ceaseless indulgence and over-praises of his father and mother, draws a naïve picture of his sister's pleasures and occupations as the Bride of Clermont:

My very dear Sister,

. . . If I do not hear from you, if your household affairs are so pressing as to deny you an hour now and then to communicate your sentiments to your brother, I shall paint to myself the most pleasing scenes, I shall with pleasure view my dear Sister at one time walking or fishing with her dear husband on the banks of the *Hudson* at another conversing with him about domestic or foreign affairs or playing with him at Draughts or Chess. At another time I shall behold you traversing the Orchard or some *plain* as agreeable with Mrs Montgomery or some other of your valuable and amiable sisters whose company I flatter myself you will always enjoy in some degree—these and similar reflections, they will always give me pleasure yet it would be an additional one to see your descriptive talent (which by the bye you ought most certainly to cultivate as you have a good turn for it) employ'd in describing the beauties et les agrémens of your situation etc.

We have received letters from our Uncle Richard who sends love and good wishes to you.

. . . Ludwell Lee has distinguish'd himself lately to the southward The Marquis writes very much in his favor. . . . Be pleas'd to make acceptable my most respectful compliments and best wishes to your good mother, Col Livingston, the Ladies and Gentlemen of your family and accept those of your Philadelphia friends who join me in wishing you every kind of happiness.

I am my dearest Sister with the most lively sentiments of regard & affection your loving brother & faithful friend

Thomas Lee Shippen

The reserve and brevity of Nancy's reply tell more perhaps of the stark realities she is confronting than would a folio of laments:

Manor Living^n A[u]gust 1781

My dear Tommy,

I received your letter by Mr B. Livingston, & thank you for your goodness in remembering me. . . . I am happy to hear you are improving yourself in your studies; I have no doubt but you will

121

continue, & be an honor to your connections; nothing gives me so great pleasure as recieving letters from my friends, therefore if you will spend every leisure hour in writing to me, you will oblige one who thinks it a happiness to call herself

Your affection[t] Sister
Ann, Hume, Livingston

The first intimation her parents seem to have had of the actual state of affairs for their daughter, and her own dread of the long rough journey in her condition, appears in this agitated letter from her mother written September 25, 1781:

My dearest Child

Make yourself perfectly easy. Your dear Papa as well as myself are determined you shall visit us the last of next month, tho' I s[d] like best if you cou'd come with the Chancellor & his Lady, . . . & thus & thus shall we do [.] Y[r] Papa will write to Col. L again & the old Lady & M[r] Duer will write to the Chancellor, & if all this will not prevail on the Col. to come with you or bring you half way, then y[r] Uncle Jos Shippen will come for you in our Phaeton [.] If the last s[d] be the case you will not be able to bring all you will want with our poor horses but you can leave the rest with M[rs] Radclift to come in the first waggon fisher sends—I have received all y[r] dear letters by John, who rejoiced my heart by telling me you were *very* well, thank God for it—Y[r] B[r] Edward [Livingston] has been in Philadelphia some days & with us great part of the time [.] He says he hears Col. L intends to come with you. Indeed it is absolutely necessary he s[d] & you must use y[r] influence, but let y[r] influence be left to the very last—

I wou'd have you pay the Old Lady every comp[t] "I believe you "when you say you have great confidence in the old L & wou'd stay "with her as she desires you s[d] if your Papa & myself wou'd consent. "But my dear how can you feel easy if you disoblige us so much as "to refuse to come when we insist upon it." Read the above paragrafs to her—Y[r] dear B[r] begs you will excuse his writing now as he is obliged to be with Edward L [Livingston] but he will send his letter by the stage— M[rs] Knox has been in this town a fortnight &

is now gone to Virginia & will spend some time with Mrs Washington, & you can't be afraid to come thus far when M^rs K in the same situation will go as far again. Mrs Knox speaks highly of you. You are a great favorite with her & she made me very happy by telling me so. She says Lady Stirling & Lady Kitty thinks of you as she does. O! how I love them for doing so. I will pray for a thousand blessings for them. I have sent [to] France for Baby Linnen but you must expect nothing from me unless you come here. Mrs Price sends her com^ts She stays with me a few days till she can get a Lodging. I s^d like her company if she had not so many visitors but I like best to be still & quiet & I shall be very much so when she is gone—

Adieu my darling, pray for & love

Your very aff^t Mother

A Shippen

The watchman is just crying make hast[e] eleven o'clock, or I would certainly write. You may expect to hear from me very soon, but am your loving and affectionate brother at all times and in all seasons

T. L. Shippen

I have received but one letter from you since I left you—

Addressed: Mrs Col. H. B. Livingston
at Rhinebeck
on the North River.
Hon^d by Mr E. Livingston.

In Nancy's reply to this letter from her mother her penmanship is tremulous and broken, as if she could scarcely hold the quill. Wretchedness of spirit and body are heavy upon her. Her husband in his brutal, jealous rage has become her gaoler, and Nancy helplessly pleads for papers, doubtless meaning legal documents of some sort. She is losing hope itself:

123

Rhinebeck Octr 4 1781

My dear Mamma,

I have just now received your dear affectionate letter of the 25 of Sep^r, & thank you for it; the Chancellor sets off To-morrow, & will take care of this—I am affraid it will be too late in the season when you receive it, to send for me. I hope my uncle will set out before, but alass! my dear Mamma what will avail his coming for me when Col. L. has told me positively I shall not come. If my uncle Joe comes for me my Papa must give them *Papers* to bring with him to try what they can do for me; Col. L. says they shall have no weight with him—O! my dear Mamma what cruelty to deprive me of being with the best of Parents at such a critical period. However I submit it to the disposer of all things to do with me & for me what he pleases.

If Col. L. shou'd prevail, & I shou'd not at last come to Phi^a can't you & Papa try & come to me? but I will try every thing in my power before I give it up. I am, & shall be very uneasy about it till I see you in Phi^a. I would write you a long letter but am troubled with the toothach.

Adieu my dear Mamma you know how much I am yours, as well from inclination as by the ties of nature.

A H S

Col. L. says if I will give him the *papers* he will let me come, & that if I do not I shall never come. I leave it to you & Papa to advise me for the best.

Some influence or persuasion, doubtless that of Madam Livingston, at length prevailed upon Henry Livingston to let his wife return to Philadelphia to have their baby in her parents' home. For Nancy was permitted to go back to Shippen House late in October of 1781. In her condition the several days' trip to Philadelphia must have been a severe ordeal, involving the crossing of the river, the long rough travel on execrable roads. But any danger or hardship that would help her to escape from Livingston she must have welcomed.

The triumphant end of the war of the revolution was near. When Nancy reached Philadelphia, the news that Cornwallis was taken had thrilled the city. She was at home on that first historic Sunday of November following the surrender of the British at Yorktown and must have seen the stirring events in St. Mary's Catholic Church next door. Representatives of the victorious armies of the young republic and of its ally, France, once again assembled in Philadelphia and marched down Fourth Street beneath the windows of Shippen House into the arched doors of the church, where they united in a solemn High Mass of Thanksgiving and laid the conquered flags of Great Britain upon the altar steps.

A few weeks later, on December 26, 1781, Nancy's child, a daughter, was born and named for Colonel Livingston's mother, Margaret Beekman Livingston. Nancy called the little one "Peggy," her "sweet Peggy," her "Darling Baby" and her "Angel Child," and from the moment of her birth wrapped her in ecstatic devotion. With the advent of the first grandchild to Shippen House, all world events passed into oblivion. Here at home the young mother was Nancy once again, and everyone worshipped her and waited on her and the baby. To have Nancy and her baby stay on at Shippen House doubtless was the desire of both her parents and herself. But her relatives and everyone she knew considered separation between husband and wife as a last resort; a terrible expedient which in the public mind made the wife responsible for all the vices to which the husband might become addicted thereafter. With strange inconsistency, they quite overlooked the circumstance that the husband might already be addicted to vices far from cured by the marriage bed and which entirely in themselves wrought the necessity for separation.

125

Another restraining factor too, no doubt, was the low state of her father's finances, the necessity of re-creating a practice shot to pieces by the war. Nancy remained as long as she could. So much was happening in Philadelphia and at Shippen House! Exciting news was always on the way from "dear Virginia." There was so much to hear and talk about. But Nancy must needs tear herself away and take her baby to its father's house. With her return to Clermont there is a break in the chronicle, a space of silence lasting a year and a half, in which there appears not a single letter or fragment of a letter. What must have happened is but a matter for surmise.

.   .   .   .

Once again Nancy was in the country of the Livingstons; that vast region of rolling majestic hills, blue-green and black, with deep caverns of cloud shadows and ravines, and ever the purple river flowing by. Under the venerable locusts of Clermont, how silently too the current of the world flowed on!

Besides her precious baby, Nancy had another treasure—the letters of Louis Otto. For her eyes alone, ever hidden from her parents and her husband, these letters were secretly carried by Nancy wherever she went. If they had not been in her cherishing care, they would not have survived. With the memory of Louis Otto's great love and tender friendship mingled all that was most gracious, lovely and inspiring of her girlhood— far away, now, it must have seemed. There were the books they read and loved together, the poems and philosophy, their dances and songs and music of harp and viol and harpsichord. Now they had come strangely to be mixed with the colors and shapes of the hills and the river and the clouds and with sunrise and sunset, moonlight and starshine. How completely she and Louis had met in heart and mind; how perfectly united they had been! Had any woman in all world's history ever a lover half so sweet as he?

All those delicate and hidden intricacies that nobody knew but they! She had still that little fragment of music he composed for her, his *Menuet of Strasburg* which he had dropped at her door and then run like a boy leaving his first valentine! There were the thousand and one funny, foolish little things they did and said and laughed about together; his mistakes in English; her mistakes in French . . . his use of "poison" of her eyes, as in "Eloisa to Abelard." . . . His prayer that she loan him her heart . . . that she heed the pleas of the tiny notes she wrote him which he called her children—for more little sisters to keep them company! . . . "I will take a ride on my Fancy it will carry me far!" he had said and straightway she too had leaped the same steed and laughing, in his dear arms had galloped over the heavens, footing the very stars!

"Fair as young light" . . . he had said she was in one of the poems he wrote to her . . . "Fair as young light." . . .

Time enough now to reflect upon all that she had lost. In him were power and wisdom united . . . and such adoration of her spirit and her body that the sweetness and force of his passion pierced every fibre of her being. Face to face she must have come with the truth; that he was the most blessed influence of her life; that marriage with him would have been a sacrament where with Livingston it was sacrilege.

So to dream by day of white love and then, by night to be forced to lie under black lust! What could she do? Where could she turn? Surely the desire came to her heart that her child might have been her lover's, not her husband's.

"I . . . Walkt forth to ease my payne." So she must have trodden Clermont's heights,

"And the bright euening star with golden creast
Appeare out of the East.
Fayre childe of beauty, glorious lampe of loue."

Walking thus alone in that solitude the memories of him
she loved so must have throbbed in her consciousness like sad
music, a poem too poignant, too beautiful ever to be imprisoned
in words.

III

Just when Nancy first learned of her husband's "amours,"
and of the existence of his several children by as many alliances, is not revealed in the letters or documents. That their
own little daughter was his only legitimate child was no secret
in the Livingston family. The Old Lady told Nancy that. His
other children were quite generally spoken of. Not once was
the evil done by Henry Livingston ever condoned or excused
by his family, least of all by his mother. But as one of their
own, he and all of his were under the ægis of their protection.
The law of their house forbade public scandal and, if he was
not honored or respected by them in private, at least he was in
public.

That out of a realm of beauty, of dignity and peace there
should develop the discord of a being like her husband must
have seemed to Nancy and others a strange and inexplicable
circumstance. Perhaps, she might have reflected, their ingrown
family life, their over-concentration upon their own, in itself
bred sometimes abnormal results. Secure within their own
closely knit households, devoted to their own and their children's pursuits, studies, works, joys and sorrows—had not
these become paramount, so that most of the Livingston women
in reality faced only the horizons of their own lives? Certainly

128

no one in her husband's family was concerned about the financial difficulties slowly creeping upon her father's household. Nor was anyone disturbed, except The Old Lady, about Nancy's problems and suffering as Henry's wife. She was not a blood relation and that made a difference. Henry, however, was their blood relation and his affairs were not to be criticized. But to Nancy Shippen, his conduct must have been appalling. To his gross licentiousness she makes but one reference in her *Journal Book*, when she speaks of "Lord B——'s squandering his money on miserable undeserving objects." She likewise emphasizes his jealousy of her and the dark suspicions that rode his mind about her; his talk that so frightened her, his fits of rage and brutality. The custom of her day decreed that a wife who had an unfaithful husband must not expostulate, but feign ignorance of his misconduct "and by superior agreeableness and attractions win him back." It is doubtful whether Nancy, being herself a woman of spirit and temper, would have stooped to this last cajolery, but to the first it seems she must have bowed until she learned through The Old Lady of Colonel Livingston's secret plan eventually to gather all of his children together under one roof—either in Rhinebeck or in far-off Georgia—and install Peggy, her own daughter, among them.

Little Margaret Beekman Livingston, namesake of Madam Livingston herself, the Little Princess of Clermont and daughter of Shippens and of Lees, cheek by jowl with his bastard breed!

Anne Home Livingston made her decision: to go back to her own home, back to the clean air and the warm hearth fires of Shippen House. On an early spring day in 1783 she packed her boxes, took her baby, and fled her husband's bed and board.

Soon after her return to her father's home she began the *Journal Book*.

Part Two

Journal Book and Letters

CHAPTER VI

1783-1784

THE KEY TO NANCY SHIPPEN'S JOURNAL BOOK

THE TIME—Last Quarter of the Eighteenth Century

THE PLACES—Shippen House and the French Legation in Philadelphia, Stratford Hall in Virginia, Manor Clermont, Rhinebeck in New York, and the President's House, New York City.

THE PERSONS IN THE BOOK

In the Order of Their Appearance

AMANDA, *the Heroine, the Author Herself*—Nancy Shippen (Anne Home Livingston).

LORD WORTHY, *her Father*—Doct͏ʳ William Shippen, the Younger, Director General of Military Hospitals of the Continental Army.

LORD B., *her Husband*—Leftenant Colonel Henry Beekman Livingston of the Continental Army, Scion of the Lords of the Manor Livingston.

LEANDER, *the Hero, her First and Last Love*—Louis Guillaume Otto, Comte de Mosloy: successively Attaché of French Legation in Philadelphia, Chargé d'Affaires of France in the United States; Secretary of Legation; Chief of the Political Division of Foreign Affairs in France; Minister to Munich; Minister to Vienna and Minister of State of France.

SWEET PEGGY, *her Darling Baby and Angel Child*—Margaret Beekman Livingston, aged seventeen months at beginning of "Journal." Only Child of Colonel Henry Beekman Livingston and Nancy Shippen his wife.

LADY WORTHY, *her Mother*—Alice Lee of Stratford Hall in Virginia, Mrs. Doct͏ʳ Shippen of Philadelphia.

MR. W. [ASHINGTON], *her Beau*—Bushrod Washington, of Bush-field in Virginia, nephew of President Washington, Justice of United States Supreme Court, heir of Mount Vernon.

YOUNG WORTHY, *her Brother*—Thomas Lee Shippen, Chronicler-Observer.

THE OLD LADY, *her Mother-in-Law*—Madam Livingston (Margaret Beekman), widow of Judge Robert R. Livingston, III, of Manor Clermont, Grand Dame of the Province of New York.

OLD WORTHY, *her Grandfather*—Doct^r William Shippen the Elder, eminent Physician of Colonial Philadelphia; Member of the Continental Congress.

R. H. L., *her Uncle*—Richard Henry Lee of Stratford and Chantilly in Virginia; Mover of Motion for Declaration of Independence and a Signer; President of the Congress.

A. L., *her Uncle*—Arthur Lee of Stratford and Landsdowne House in Virginia, and of London, Paris, Berlin, New York and Philadelphia: Patriot, Diplomatist: Signer with Benjamin Franklin of America's Treaty of Alliance with France.

THE COMPANY—President Washington and his Lady, Miss Eleanor Custis, the Chevalier de la Luzerne, French Minister, Thomas Jefferson, General Horatio Gates, General Henry Knox, Chancellor Livingston, Mrs. Richard Montgomery of Clermont, Mrs. Theodorick Bland of Cawsons in Virginia (Martha Dangerfield), Lady Kitty Duer, Colonel Henry Lee of the Legion, Mrs. Henry Lee (Matilda Lee) of Stratford Hall, Nancy Willing, Francisca de Miranda Lafayette, Vicomte de Noailles, Marquis de Chastellux, Joseph Wright, the Portrait Painter—Members of the Families Allen, Armstrong, Barrows, Bayard, Benden, Bingham, Blackwell, Blair, Blake, Bland, Bond, Boudenot, Bradford, Burd, Buston, Byrd, Chaumont, Clark, Coxe, Craik, Cutting, Dayton, Debuysson, Delaney, Duer, Duffield, DuPonceau, Edwards, Elesons, Elliot, Emlen, Filmore, Footman, Frazer, Gadsden, Hamilton, Harrison, Hazlet, Herd, Hodge, Hollingsworth, Horters, Ingraham, Jackson, James, Jervey, Jones, La Motte, Lee, Lenox, Livingston, Logan, Lyons, Magan, Magua,

Marbois, Marshall, McGaw, McQuerters, Mercer, Mifflin, Moore, Morris, Morton, Moyse, North, Peales, Peirce, Penn, Peters, Porter, Powell, Prager, Purviance, Redman, Ross, Russel, Rutherford, Rutledge, Sage, Samento, Secon, Sharp, Shippen, Smith, Spence, Sprout, Stead, Stewart, Terresson, Tilghman, Tillotson, Van Bercles, Vardon, Vaugh[a]n, Vendon, Voss, Walker, Webster, Wharton, White, Wikoff, Wilkinson, Williamson, Willing, Wilson, Winchester, Witherspoon, Woodbridge.

A Journal

Began

April 10th—1783
PHILADELPHIA
VOLUME THE FIRST

By

ANNA HUME LIVINGSTON

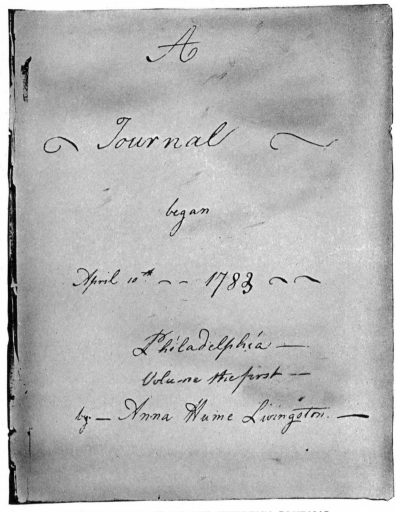

TITLE PAGE OF NANCY SHIPPEN'S JOURNAL

May 16.

Papa told me this morn'g at breakfast that I must send my dar'ing Child to its
Grandmama Livingston; that she had desir'd Mrs. Montgomery to request it of me, as
a particular favor — I told him I cou'd not
bear the Idea of it, that I had sooner part
with my life almost than my Child — he
told me it was for the future interest of
my baby, that its fortune depended on
the old Lady's pleasure in that particular — begg'd me to think of it, & to be reconciled to it — If I know my own heart
I never can — When will my misfortunes
End! I placed my happiness in her! she is
my all — & I must part with her! cruel
cruel fate ———

May 17.   10 oclock at night ———
I have been so unhappy all day, that I have not
stird out of my room except to dinner ——

A PAGE FROM NANCY SHIPPEN'S JOURNAL

Journal

April 10th—After Breakfast rode out with Lord Worthy. Had a conversation about Lord B. & dear Leander. His sentiments corresponding with mine made me extremely happy—wou'd to God it was a happiness that wou'd last—but the die is cast—& my life must be miserable! Lord Worthy sees the consequencies of my unhappy choice too late—it is well for me he sees it at all.

April 11th—Saw Leander—spoke to him—he praised my sweet Child—good man!

April 15—Dressed my darling baby, kissed her; & for some minutes was *happy*—recieved a message from Miss B——— & Miss M——— return'd an answer—wou'd be happy to see them—how insipid the company of formal acquaintances! Miss B. is handsome & well bred—but unentertaining. Miss M. agreeable. We chatted—sung—walk'd in the Garden—the afternoon more agreable than I expected.

April 16th—Work'd at my needle in the morning as usual, & read.—In the afternoon visited Mrs Bland—found a great deal of company—a great part of it insignificant & trifling.

April 17—This Morn^g went to St Pauls Church where I heard a lively discourse preach'd by Mr Magan.—In the afternoon had Company.

April 18—This day I spent entirely alone, enjoying my own meditations—they were not unpleasant—I feel calm & composed, & please myself with the reflection of having conform'd to the will of my parents in the most important action of my life—O! may I reap the benefit of it! I'm sure I shall! I have the sweetest Child that ever was born—in her I shall be most blest.

April 19—Mr Tillotson[1] visited me this Morning—he has lately seen Lord B—— but did not mention him; which made me uneasy—sure he can't have forgot me—not even send me his good wishes—I am unhappy—I shall in time get used to his neglect— But Oh! it will always make me wretched— Why did I believe him when he swore so often he loved me, & that he wou'd make me eternally happy.

April 20—This day I writ to Louisa—& read the remaining part of the forenoon. This afternoon was visited by the presidents Lady & Daughter—Sally & Molly Shippen—Miss Fanny Witherspoon—& several gentle men both young & old— Upon the whole it was an agreable after noon.

Apl. 21—Lady Worthy spent great part of the morning in my Chamber with me—directing & advising me about bringing up my sweet Child—I need it much—for sure I am a very young & inexperienced Mother—the afternoon we spent enfamile.

April 22^d—Sollitary & Unhappy—

April 23^d—This was a very fine day—I rode out in the Morning with Betsy & the Child—met Leander in third street—he look'd—smil'd & bow'd—he is all thats good, & my best friend. When I return'd found a letter from Harriett which gave me great pleasure. She congratulates me on the birth of my dear Child.—Ought I to repine, when blest with health, friends, indulgent parents & the sweetest Child that ever was born—but still I am unhappy.

[1] A brother-in-law of Lord B. (Colonel Livingston).

April 24th—Breakfasted this Mornᵍ with Cleander & Emelia.² Happy couple! surrounded by their beauteous Offspring & happy in their loves, they live a life of uninterrupted bliss. Spent the rest of the day at home with Lady Worthy.—I read Milton to her while she work'd.

April 25—Dress'd my Angel Child, kiss'd her a hundred times, thought her the most beautiful Child in the world & sent her to be admir'd by Miss Tilghman, who said a thousand things in her favor—in which I perfectly agreed.—

April 27—heard from Lord B.—obdurate man! he still continues to persecute me with his reproaches—God knows that I do not deserve them. How miserable shou'd I be if it was not for my dear Child.—Wou'd to Heaven he cou'd but see it perhaps it perhaps it wou'd soften him & make him relent.

April 28—Spent this day with Mʳˢ Bland working Tambour returned about 8 this Evenᵍ Found my baby asleep.—Innocent lamb! it knows not what its unhappy Mother suffers, from its unrelenting father.

April 29—Today my sweet infant was taken sick. She will now engross all my time & care.

April 30—She has Had a fever all day, something better this Evenᵍ—sleeps sweetly.

May 1.—Better still today—How thankful I am!—

May 2ᵈ—perfectly recover'd, spent great part of the day in returnᵍ thanks to God for her recovery—

May 3ᵈ—10 o'clock at night—Spent a most delightfull Evenᵍ at Mʳˢ Powells. I heard in the Morning there was to be a very

² Unidentified friends of Nancy's, not to be confused with Leander.

large Company.—I spent great part of the day in making preparation—I wish'd to look well. Sett off about six oclock—my glass told me I look'd well—was dressed in pink with a gause peticoat—an Elegant french Hat on, with five white plumes nodding different ways—a bouquet of natural flowers—& a white satin muff. Found a roomfull—& in the midst of them *Leander*—he told me what I believed—that I look'd like an Angel—shall I confess that I felt pleas'd to be approved of by him? Why? because he is my sincere friend—& was once (O! happy time!) my lover. I passed a most agreable even'ing—though a large company—which is seldom the case—a most admirable supper—excellent wine an elegant desert of preserv'd fruits & every body in spirits & good humor.—It is now late & I am sleepy.—Found my Child well.—

May 4.—felt dull & stupid all day.—Mr Washington drank tea with me in ye Afternoon. We sung, Laugh'd—& play^d at Chess.—Upon the whole spent the Even^g very merrily.—Lady Worthy & young Worthy of the party.

May 6—Spent this day at home, w^h Lord & Lady Worthy. We were all alone—my sweet Child amused us all.

May 7—It being a very fine day I rode out & took betsy & the Child with me—Called upon Mrs R. [obert] Livingston [3]—but found only Mrs Montgomery [4] at home, Mrs L. [ivingston] came soon after. They made me happy by praising my darling Child—& Caressing it very much. Spent the Afternoon at home with Lady Worthy my good Mother.

May 8—This morn^g paid a visit to Miss Tilghman & Mrs Hamilton. Found them both out—walk'd afterwards to Peals

[3] Nancy's mother-in-law, the Old Lady.
[4] Nancy's sister-in-law, widow of General Montgomery.

[Peale's] with S. & M. Shippen, M Cox, Mr Mif[f]lin, Major Moore, & My brother dined at Mr Jones & spent the Even^g there. Came home about 8 & found Mr Washington. We went together to Mrs Jerveys, & found her at piquet with Mr Jervey. We join'd them & made a party at Whist. Staid till ten oclock.

May 10. 10 at night—Miserable all day—in consequence of a letter from Lord B. He tells me—O what is it that bad he does not tell me! but what affect[s] me most is his accusing me of infedelity. Wretched Unhappy man—Nothing but your being jealous, & treating me ill in consequence of that jealousy, shou'd have tempted me to leave you—& now you say I left you because I loved another.—Had you not decieved me by so often swearing you loved me to distraction I shou'd not have been the wretch I am. O I'm wretched indeed! & the father too of my sweet baby—I'm almost distracted—

7 in the even^g May 11. felt more composed today—comforted by my dear Mamma—she begs me not to murmur but be re-sign'd the will of providence. My dear friend Maria drank Tea with me—

May 12—10 at night—At home all day—this afternoon was honor'd with a visit from Mr Marbois.[5] He staid about half an hour. I chatter'd a little french very imperfectly—but he said I spoke well. The french are too polite to be sincere.

May 13—This Morn^g I read Madame de Maintenons advice to the D—De B—g. I will transcribe so much of it as relates to the woman, because it corresponds so much with my Ideas on that subject. My Child calls for my assistance. Therefore I must defer writing what I intended till Evening. I come my darling—

[5] See *Supplementary Records* (2).

May 14—Detain'd all last Even^g by Company & to-day I am engaged to go out of Town with Lady Worthy & Mrs Bland, & Mr Washington spend the day at Chaillot. We shall spend a very rural day.—8 in the Even^g—Just come home—undrest & play'd with Peggy, & sit down now to write. It was one of the most agreeable jaunts I ever had in my life. The day fine, the Company agreable, & the best rural dinner I ever eat. We walk'd by the River deleware—we sung—we rambl'd about the woods; play'd at Chess—in short the variety of the scene, & the sociability that prevail'd throughout the company serv'd to make it a delightfull day. I am now sleepy—& my darling baby cries for her bedfellow.—

May 15—*10 in the morning*—I sit down to write now what I intended to write the day before yesterday. I hope I shall not be disturb'd. My baby lies assleep in the Cradle before me—I will write till she awakes—

Do not hope for perfect happiness; there is no such thing in this sublunary state. Your sex is the more exposed to suffer, because it is always in dependance: be neither angry nor asham'd of this dependance on a husband. . . .

Do not hope that your union will procure you perfect peace: the best Marriages are those where with softness & patience they bear by turns with each other . . .

Do not expect the same degree of friendship that you feel: men are in general less tender than women; and you will be unhappy if you are too delicate in your friendships.

Beg of God to guard your heart from jealousy: do not hope to bring back a husband by complaints, ill humor, or reproaches. The only means which promise success, are patience & softness: impatience sours & alienats hearts: softness leads them back to their duty. In sacrificing your own will, pretend to no right over that of a husband: men are more attach'd to theirs than Women, because educated with less constraint.

144

They are naturally tyrannical; they will have pleasures & liberty, yet insist that Women renounce both: do not examine whether their rights are well founded; let it suffice to you that they are established; They are masters, we have only to suffer & obey with a good grace.

Thus far Madame de Maintenon must be allow'd to have known the heart of man. I cannot agree with her that Women are only born to suffer & to obey—that men are generally tyrannical I will own, but such as know how to be happy, willingly give up the harsh title of master for the more tender & endearing one of Friend. Equality is the soul of friendship: marriage, to give delight, must join *two minds*, not devote a slave to the will of an imperious Lord.

9, at night—Spent this Even^g at Mrs Gadsdens; a Carolina Lady. She is an Elegant woman & very Chatty & agreable. Found a good deal of Company.

May 16—Papa told me this morn^g at breakfast that I must send my darling Child to its Grandmama Livingston; that she had desir'd Mrs Montgomery to request it of me, as a particular favor. I told him I cou'd not bear the Idea of it, that I had sooner part with my life almost than my Child. He told me it was for the future interest of my baby, that its fortune depended on the old Lady's pleasure in that particular—beg'd me to think of it, & to be reconciled to it. If I know my own heart I never can. When will my misfortunes end! I placed my happiness in her! She is my all—& I must part with her! cruel cruel fate—

May 17—10 oclock at night—I have been so unhappy all day that I have not stir'd out of my room except to dinner. Mamma then ask'd me if I had thought of Mrs L's proposal. I told her, I had thought of nothing else—she ask'd me my determination

—I told her I wou'd not part with my Child if I cou'd possibly help it. she then told me Mrs M.—y did not go to the Manor till the middle of June; that Papa had determin'd that the Child shou'd go at any rate—that he cou'd not be answerable for the Childs losing her fortune which she wou'd certainly do, if I kept her from her Grandmother. I cried all the time she was speaking & then retir'd to my room—which I have not left since. I feel pleased however that I have a month to determine in, & be with my angel Child.—I have kiss'd her a thousand times since.—& find I love her as well as myself. I must think of some thing in order to keep her with me, & yet secure her fortune.

May 18—Spent the day at home—Papa has not mentioned that dreadful subject to me since. I begin to flatter myself that with a little persuasion I may keep her with me—at least some time longer. My sweet Child! my whole soul is wrapp'd up in *you!* if I am oblig'd to part with you (O! dreadfull Thought!) I will look upon myself as the most miserable of woman kind. Why was my heart made so susceptible, since I am to experience nothing but misery?

May 19—I Visit'd Miss E Livingston this morn^g I like her extreamly. I had a long conversation with her. I think her very sensible—was much affected at a little annecdote I heard this morn^g of a young Lady who was sacrificed to the avarice & ambition of her parents to a man she hated—& her death was the natural consequence of her misery. She had a soul form'd for friendship—she found it not at home, her elegance of mind prevented her seeking it abroad; & she died a meloncholy victim to the Tyranny of her friends & the tenderness of her heart. It is a painful consideration, that the happiness or misery

146

of our lives are generally determin'd, before we are proper judges of either.

May 20.—To-day wrote to Eliza—told her my misfortune—told her it was the greatest but one I had ever experienced. But I have not yet experienced it. I know not yet how much I shall suffer when the time comes.—O! what a separation! how much I dread it! but I will if possible stay with her. Ah! It will be impossible I'm affraid, because it depends on the *disposition* of her father.—Alass! he will never change.

May 21—This morn^g I sent Betsy out with the Child to give it an airing—then set down to work at the Tambour. I was working a work-bag for my mamma. It is very pretty work—& I am fond of it—my Brother read to me while I work'd—he read Gill Blas. It diverted me & made me for a time forget my unhappiness. When the child return'd I allmost devour'd it with kisses.

May 22—I spend so much of my time in caressing & playing with Peggy that I allmost forget I have any thing else to do—I forget to read—to write—to work—in short I neglect the business of the day. At night I sit down to unfold my thoughts on paper—I love it much—me thinks it is allmost as pleasing as telling them to a friend. My child sleeps—I am sitting close by her—I feel happy at present because I put off the future prospect from my thoughts—I hope for the best—& enjoy the present moment.

May 24—Afternoon—I thought seriously this Morn^g about my sweet Childs education. I form'd many schemes which I believe it would be very difficult to put in execution. I wish in some particulars that it may differ from mine. In some respects I wish it may be as good. I have her wellfare at heart more than

147

any earthly object. God grant she may be in every respect what I wish her.—I have met with sentiments on that head that please me. I will insert them here that I may not forget them:

SOME DIRECTIONS CONCERNING A DAUGHTERS EDUCATION

1st. Study well her constitution & genious
2d. Follow nature & proceed patiently.
3d. Suffer not Servants to terrify her with stories of Ghosts & Goblins.
4th. Give her a fine pleasing idea of Good, & an ugly frightful one of Evil.
5th. Keep her to a good & natural regimen of diet.
6th. Observe strictly the little seeds of reason in her, & cultivate the first appearance of it diligently.
7th. Watch over her childish Passions & prejudices, & labour sweetly to cure her of them.
8th. Never use any little *dissembling* arts, either to pacify her or to persuade her to anything.
9th. Win her to be in love with openness, in all her acts, & words.
10th. Fail not to instill into her an abhorance of all "serpentine" wit.
11th. If she be a brisk witty child do not applaud her too much.
12th. If she be a dul heavy child, do not discourage her at all.
13th. Seem not to admire her wit, but rather study to rectify her judgment.
14th. Use her to put little questions, & give her ready & short answers.
15th. Insinuate into her the principles of politeness & true modesty, & christian humility.
16th. Inculcate upon her that most honorable duty & virtue SINCERITY.
17th. Be sure to possess her with the baseness of telling a Lye on any account.
18th. Shew her the deformity of Rage & anger.
19th. Never let her converse with servants.

148

20th. Acquaint her in the most pleasant & insinuating manner, with the sacred History, nor let it seem her lesson, but her recreation.

21st. Set before her the gospel in its simplicity & purity, & the great Examples of Antiquity unsophisticated.

22d. Explain to her the nature of the baptismal san[c]tion

23d. Prepare her in the best manner for confirmation.

24th. Animate, & instruct her for the holy communion.

25th. Particularly inform her in the duties of a single & married state.

26th. Let her be prepared for the duties & employment of a city life, if her lot should be among citizens.

27th. See she be inform'd in all that belongs to a country life.

28th. Discreetly check her desires after things pleasant, & use * her to frequent disappointments. * Ro[u]sseau

29th. Let her be instructed to do every thing seasonably & in order, & what ever she is set to do let her study to do it well, & peaceably;

30th. Teach her to improve everything that nothing may be lost or wasted, nor let her hurry herself about any thing.

31st. Let her always be employ'd about what is profitable or necessary.

32d. Let nothing of what is committed to her care be spoil'd by her neglect.

33d. Let her eat deliberately, chew well, & drink in moderate proportions.

34th. Let her use exercise in the morning.

35th. Use her to rise betimes in the morning, & set before her in the most winning manner an order for the whole day.

When wisdom enters into her heart, & knowledge is made pleasant to her soul, "discretion shall preserve her, & understanding shall keep her."

May 24—8 at night. There is such a sameness in my life at present that the particulars of it are hardly worth the pains of writing, tho' it is very agreable to look back upon ones life &

see whether our actions & thoughts alter for the better. My past life has been chequer'd with misfortunes. I will write every particular occurrence some future day when I have a great deal more time than I have at present—tho' I cou'd never make a better use of my time. I cannot have a more pleasing task than takeing care of my precious Child—It is an amusement to me preferable to all others. . . .

May 27—I received an invitation this Morn^g to spend the Even^g with Mrs Bland—but I was engaged—& I spent the Afternoon & Even^g with Maria. . . . I never was more happy —I kept my lovely Child with me all the time. The dear angel was the life of the company—Leander went past the window while we were at Tea—he look'd in—& his Eyes told me he wou'd be happy to join us—but I did not ask him—prudence forbid it—Why shou'd it? he is my friend—& I am his—but because he was once my lover I must not see him—Cruell custom—I have read or heard, I forget which, "that the best friendship is the child of love"—why am I not at liberty to indulge that friendship? Why? because it wou'd displease my husband.

May 28—I was wake'd this Morn^g at five oclock with the cries of my baby. It seem'd to be at a distance. I jump'd up— frighten'd half to death—run to mammas room where the child was, & found it almost in fitts with pain. I scream'd as loud as the Child—to see her in such agonies. Papa was obliged to take me out of the room or I shou'd have fainted. I never in all my life felt as I did then. She continued in that situation almost an hour,—& then slept two. In that time the maid told me that the child woke as usual at day break—that she being very sleepy she forgot to take care of her—& left the dear creature all alone —that she give *her* her snuff box to play with—& then went to sleep. In the meantime the child open'd the box & the snuff flew into her Eyes, nose, & mouth—& very near strangled her. I never will permit her to be taken up again when she wakes. Her dear Eyes are always open at daybreak—therefore she is generally taken up out of my bed softly & carried down stairs without waking me. For the future I will take her up myself. After her nap she seem'd pretty well—& eat hearty. About ten she went to sleep again—& woke with a high fever. I was very much alarm'd & call'd Papa—he thou't her ill—she continued to grow worse—he order'd balm Tea & lime juice & sugar—I gave it her—then he gave her a dose of nitre—In the afternoon a little better—I never left her all day except to eat a little dinner & then I staid but five minutes. This Even^g her fever grew worse—I was almost distracted—I believe I sent for Papa near a hundred times—He gave her a dose this Even^g that has done her good—she sleeps sweetly—her fever is abated—It is near Twelve oclock—every creature in the house sleeps but me —I have no inclination. I will watch my dear baby all night— I feel pleasure in doing her this service—I begin to be alarm'd —she has slept without stiring for four hours—I will call my father—The watchman calls one o'clock—I went to Papa & told him my fears—he relieved them by telling me the longer she sleeps the better—she may he thinks sleep off her disorder.

June 1—My baby thank God is much recover'd. These six days past she has been so ill her life has been despair'd off. I nurs'd her attentively—I never left her more than an hour altogether —O! what I have suffer'd! for several hours I thought she was dying—what I felt then it is impossible to describe—I have been ill too myself with fatigue & want of sleep—Mamma was much affected & fain wou'd have taken part of the trouble off my hands but I would not permit it she being in a very weak state of health.

June 7—8 oclock—My darling Child begins to be herself again. She has lost that beautiful color that used to adorn her lovely cheeks—but that makes no alteration in my love for her, she is dearer to me than ever—my time is so much taken up with her at present I cant find time to write all I wish—*June 8.* Today was the finest we have had a great while—Mamma insisted on my taking a little ride to refresh me—she said she would stay with the dear baby till my return—I went—called upon Emelia & took her with me—we had a very pleasant ride —I mention'd Peggys illness—she advised me to try the country Air for the reestablishment of the Childs health—M^{rs} M[argaret] L—n's [Livingston] proposal then popp'd into my head—I told her of it—She at first lamented with me—that there shou'd be a necessity for my parting with it—Ask'd me if I had resolv'd. I told her I had:—that Mrs Montgomery shou'd not take it—that it—if it did go, I wou'd carry it myself. Emelia agreed with me that it was best for me to go with it— said the Childs ill health—the length of the journey—every thing requir'd it—& further—she said may be after I got there Lord B. might relent—& we might live happy together *once more.* She thought the sooner I set off the better. I agreed with her. She proposed Cleanders accompanying me—How good! How friendly in her to part with her better half so long purely for my advantage. I've thought of it ever since. How happy shall I be if my plan succeeds & I stay with my darling, sweet Child.

June 9—Told Mamma yesterday my intention. At first she disapprov'd—but afterward was reconcil'd—because she saw my heart was set upon it.—then said, she shou'd be very unhappy to part with us both—it was very hard to part with her sweet grandchild—but to lose us both wou'd almost kill her. It cant be help'd said I my dear Mamma. You as well as Papa have agreed that it is absolutely necessary for the Child to go & I am determin'd she shall not go without me. The dear baby continues pale & thin—2 or 3 days before that dreadfull accident happen'd Betsy the Childs maid was taken ill with the measles. She was sent immediately to another house—the baby never having had that disorder I was affraid she might take it. She is ill yet—& I feel her loss sensibly. It was with Mammas maid the accident happen'd. *7 oclock* Nothing talk'd of but the journey. It is a very long one—two hundred miles—but if it was as far again I wou'd go to have the satisfaction of accompanying my darling Child.—O I'm wrapt up in her! & if at last I shou'd be so happy as to have it in my power to remain with her—to find that she makes an impression on the heart of her father—that he will love her—O it will be a happy jaunt for me indeed!—What a sweet little mediator!—can he but relent when he sees her—his picture in miniature—will he not be glad to see me—fold me in his arms—& repent that he has treated me ill—wonder at my forgiveness & condescension—& become a new man.—happy prospect—I will immediately write to him —tell him that I am going to take our dear Child to his Mothers—tell him I will expect to see him before I arrive—ask him to meet us & conduct us to his Mothers—

[July] *June 3*—Yesterday I wrote & this Morn⁸ sent the letter by post. I have been more composed since I have determined to go. My darling is so weak she cant be left by me hardly a minute—how she loves me—she wont rest aminute out of my arms except when asleep. Yesterday I hir'd a maid for her—Im affraid she wont be like Betsy—at least in Peggys eyes. She lov'd her almost as well as she does me. Before she was sick she prefer'd her Grand mamma to anybody.

[July] *June 4*—Today Mr Wright finish'd My Portrait. Is a very strong likeness. My dear girl is drawn sitting in my lap. Mr. W. began her before her illness—Her face is not quite finish'd. I desir'd him to wait till she looks better before he proceeds—as she was taken ill after she had set only twice.

[July] *June 5*—The day after tomorrow is fix'd for my departure—Mamma is much affected—& so am I—but shou'd be much more so if I had let Peggy go without me. It is very hard to be obliged to go 2 hundred miles from my parents or part with my Child. But alass! I am affraid I shall part with her at last. However it will be some comfort to "see" her fix'd with Mrs L. & to know at the same time that I have done my duty.

[July] *June 6*—Every thing is pack'd up—& to-morrow I go. Mr Wright finish'd my dear Peggys picture yesterday. It is like her but not half so handsome. She is dress'd in White & has a peach in her dear hand—sweet innocent! she looks like an Angel.—He has dress'd Me in Leylack satin edged with gold, with a blue girdle—My hair thrown back negligently—& tied with pearls—ringlets in my neck—long sleeves with white satin Cuffs & cape—but what adorns me most is my Angel Child sitting in my lap & one of my arms encircling her dear waist— Papa calls me—He called me to beg I would stay a few days longer. I told him the season was so far advanced that I was affraid it wou'd be too warm to travel—But he & Mamma insisted upon it & so it is put off—Untill the day after.

[July] *June 7*—My sweet Child grows better every day. I hope travelling will agree with her. I like my new maid much—& so does Peggy. I am to have a great deal of Company this Even^g.

I must dress. I shall see Leander perhaps for the last time—11 o'clock—They are just gone. The room was full—too many to Name—Maria came in just as the company was assembled— she thought to find me alone—she look'd disapointed—& went away soon. After Tea We walk'd in Mr Vendons garden. He had it Lighted up—it really look'd delightful. I walk'd with Miss E[liza] Livingston & Leander. We were obliged to stay but a short time. A gust came & frightend us home. I had a long conversation before Tea with Miss L [ivingston]. I love her very much. She is just what a Woman ought to be—Sensible—polite—tender—& sympathizes in the distresses of her friends. I believe Leander is in love with her—I hope he is— what a delightful Couple—How happy wou'd be their lives.— Mrs Morton—an Elegant Woman from Boston was here. She is thought a beauty. I wish to write more but it is late & I must rise betimes. I shan't have it in my power to write again untill I arrive at the End of My Journey.

In my Chamber at the Manor Livingston—

[July] *June* 7—I have so much to say I do not know where to begin. I will go back to the day I set off from Phil^a—Mama came early—found me in Tears—tried to console me—I hid my face in my Mothers bosom—she cried as much as me—Papa was obliged to part us—or I shou'd not have remember'd that I had yet to put on my riding habit. O! How I felt! the Idea that I was going to leave such kind indulgent Parents *perhaps forever* made me almost inconsolable. I am called to dinner. About 12 oclock we set off—Cleander & Kitty & Peggy—& poor me. Mamma & Maria rode a little way with us—& Pappa & my Brother on horseback. At last we parted—such a parting! I shall never forget it—I hung round the neck of my mother sobbing with her. Maria cried too sweet Girl—& Peggy was almost eat up between them. My dear Girl said Mamma, return to us if you dont find your husband alter'd for the better—dont let your love for our sweet baby tempt you to throw your self into Misery—No my dear Mamma cried I, I will return if I dont find *him* very much Changed for the better—But the sight of the Child must make him relent—& he will treat me well for her sake. My dear Papa too said—My dear Nancy I love you very much—your happiness I am concern'd for—be sure you return if you dont see a greater prospect of happiness than you ever saw before with him. I shou'd write a volume if I was to write all that pass'd on that occasion. I'll let it suffice to say that every thing that is tender & affection^t was said to me—& I was loaded with presents. I cried without ceasing all the way we went that day. I wrote to my dear Mamma from the three first stages. I afterwards had no opportunity. My dear Peggy Miss'd her Grand mamma—& wou'd stroke me on the face & say poor Ma Poor Ma altho' she is but 1 year & 7 months old. I lodged with good Mrs Smith at Princeton—at Wood-bridge lodged at Genl Herds—dined next day at M^r M^cquerters at Newark—At night arrived at Hackensack.—& stay'd at M^r [illegible] 2 day[s] after arrived at Mrs Ellson's near fish Kills where Col. & —— Stewart lodged. M^rs S— insisted on my staying there 2 or 3 days—I did & spent them very agreeably play'd at Chess great part of the time—The Morn^g I left M^rs S—t's I arrived at Head Quarters [Newburgh] & breakfasted with Mrs Washington—cross'd the North River in the Gen^ls Barge—& dined with Lady Kitty Duer [6]—that night reach'd PoughKepsie. I was then within 20 miles of Lord B— & 30 of Mrs L. I had not heard one word from Lord B. I began to be

[6] Lady Kitty was a daughter of Lord Stirling, married to Colonel William Duer in 1779. She and her sister Lady Mary Watts were among the belles of New York when it was called the Republican Court.

alarm'd. After Cleander had retir'd to his room—& the child gone to sleep & Kitty was eating her supper in the next room I sent for the landlady to stay with me till Kitty return'd: I ask^d her if she knew any of Lord B's family? She said yes—that she knew several of them—said there was *one* in particular that was much spoke of. My heart told me who that was. She said he was a very bad [man] & had very near kill'd one of his servants very lately, & that he had a *Wife* & *Child* in Phi^a ah! says I, you see his wife & Child before you. The woman look'd petrified, & Im sure I felt so.

The next day I proceeded to M^{rs} L—s [Livingston], determin'd to consult her before I saw Lord B—. I left a letter for him on the way to be given him, after I pass'd. Last night I arrived here—was received with a great deal of politeness, & affection. It is indeed an Amiable family. They are very fond of there little relation & she begins to be sociable with them. The Old Lady intends to write to her son Lord B— & interests herself much in my welfare. 5 oclock; he has answer'd his mothers letter but not mine. She read me part of it—he continues Obdurate—will not come & see me & his dear infant—continues to repeat his false suspicions & to be jealous of me—O! how miserable has he made me! I flatter'd myself when I brought him his dear Child his suspicions wou'd close—I will write to him again—& bid him adieu—his Mother thinks him unalterable in his resolutions—& that it will be impossible to live happily with him—but what wou'd I not bear to be able to keep my Child with me? I will write the Copy of what I send here. O! may it have the desir'd effect—

Sir   Manor Clermont

I did not expect after the information I left you when I passed thro' R. B—, that I shou'd have no other communication with you than by letter. A new state of things very different from what I expected when I left Phi[a] have taken place. It is supposed you will excuse your conduct on the footing of my having passed by without stopping at your house on my way to Clermont. From the view of things I then had, I really tho't that upon the whole it wou'd be most agreeable to yourself. It was reasonable for me to suppose from my not seeing you or hearing from you at any stage of the road that your disposition towards me was very unfavorable; & you know it wou'd be a Mortification I cou'd Ill brook, if when conscious of the best intentions, I shou'd either be indignantly recieved or rejected with scorn. From some reports also, part of which I have since found to be true, I supposed you wou'd wish to make some previous changes in your house. Upon the whole I am sorry to find in you a disposition so very unfavorable, & so repugnant to every Idea of future peace & comfort together. It is in the affliction of my soul I often repeat to myself the question— what am I to expect from returning into the immediate power & possession of a man, who can manifest at the present so ungracious a temper? But I am ready to believe that what has a principal influence on your conduct is the resentful reflection on my having so long delay'd my return from Phi[a] There is not Sir, a sentiment of my heart I wou'd wish to conceal; I have been faulty in many instances & mistaken in more, since I have been your unfortunate wife, but heaven is witness to the purity & uprightness of my intentions in this, & to the propriety of my sentiments respecting my past conduct. What is past cannot indeed be undone, I freely own I wish it had not been done.

But it is no small addition to my unhappiness, that you have put it out of my power to make these declarations with more agreeable prospects. However Sir, tho I return to my parents I return not *all;* All that is now dear to you, I leave with you; But what in this case will be your greatest happiness, will be to me, in the pangs of parting & continued separation, unspeakable Anguish. Yet I will not envy you—I will rejoice in this at least—that there will always be one dear Centre where our affections will meet—& that under the care of an affec^te & prudent Grandmother, this one precious fruit of our otherwise unhappy connection, will be train'd up to be an honor & a comfort to you. I shall not stay longer than today as a bar in your way to seeing it, & when you see it you will then perhaps drop at least one tear on the reflection—that, had you been generous & tender as *she* was well disposed ye mournfull Mother might yet have shar'd in the happiness of being near it. I shou'd have very little difficulty as to the punctilio of going to your house, had I not full & clear evidence of a governing disposition in you subversive to every agreeable hope. 'tis on this I ground my intentions of returning—& however awkward & unfortunate the condition of my future life shall be, I shall after this enjoy at least one happiness—ye happiness of a self-approveing mind, & thro' Gods Mercy shall hope to die in peace. In the meantime let mutual benevolence & mutual forgiveness, as we hope to be forgiven, supply as far as may be the place of mutual complacency, this shall be the endeavour of your unfortunate

Ann H L——

[August] *June 8*—I sent the letter yesterday Morn^g & in ye Even^g I recieved an answer—but such a one! I am asham'd to transcribe it—O! my heart! what I suffer! & must I part with you my angel Child? Yes I must—How shall I bear it? & Tomorrow is the day. O no! I cant go so soon. I will make one more effort to stay—I will ask the old Lady to write again—

[August] *June 9*—She did write again, & reciev'd an answer just like the former. To-morrow I go! I can spare no more time from my angel—this night is the last I shall have her in my arms for this year—this age to me—

[August] *June 21.*   Phil* My Chamber

   I have been in such a state of misery since I left my beloved Child I have not been able to continue my journal. Alass! how shall I paint my sufferings at & since that dreadfull moment that I parted with my beloved baby! I will not, I cannot attempt it—I will only say that I have never known a happy moment since—O! what a sacrifice! but it was for her—therefore let me try to be resign'd—

[August] *June 22*—Spent the day at Mount Peace, a delightful place—but every place is equal to me now. I am wretched every where; I do nothing but cry & repine at my fate.

[August] *June 23d*—My Journal will now be very insipid indeed. I spend my time mostly in my room. I read when I can, but it is seldom I can collect my thoughts sufficiently. I work at my needle, I have time enough now! Ah me! how sweetly did it used to be taken up with my dear Child—but now I can only think of her, & cry for her, & be the most miserable creature existing for her. Sweet Angel, she's happy—tho' her unhappy Mother is miserable—

[August] *June 25*—Spent the day at Challiot with Mamma M*ʳˢ* B. & M*ʳ* Washington—was more composed than I expected —I laugh'd a little—but I have felt more since I have been by myself this Even*ᵍ* than I have felt these 2 days before; every object around me reminds me of what I have lost—reminds me that once I was an happy mother—& that now I am wretched.

Cruel cruel man! You have now wreck'd all your vengence on me—you have deprived me of my only comfort.

Yet a letter from Otto, full of affectionate counsel, coming just at this time, must have been a source of comfort and strength:

My Dear Friend

Tho' your sudden return to Philadelphia was quite unexpected to me it does not strike me in the same manner in which it appears to affect your tender feelings. The whole of your conduct has been so extreemely proper that the last injury you received was only wanting to bring on your Side those few who had been prejudiced by misrepresentations. You know my tender Friendship for you and you must be sensible that your misfortunes have rendered you still dearer to a man who had so many reasons to prevent them and who sacrificed his own tranquillity to your apparent happiness. As I have constantly heard the opinion of the public I advised you to take a Step, rather below your dignity, but consistant with the duties of a Mother and of a Lady who prefers her reputation even to happiness. In this view the Step has not miscarried and you have satisfied both the Public and your heart.

As to your future conduct it ought to be such as to convince the World that you are sensible of your Situation, but let me entreat you not to indulge the melancholy thoughts which it may suggest you. The only means to bear misfortunes with fortitude is to be innocent, and if this is true who should feel them less than my Friend? To avoid the World would be a proof of guilt, to appear quite unconcerned would be a mark of insensibility, but there is a decent and reserved Behaviour of which you are perfectly mistress and which is the only ornament of innocence and Virtue.—If the esteem and admiration of your acquaintances can alleviate your grief I am happy to tell you that these Sentiments have never been more universal than in this moment.

Your most devoted Friend.

[August] *June 29*—I awoke this morning with the thought that I had my beloved child with me; sweet delusion! why will ye not last! Why so soon fleet away—I thought I had her in my arms, & that I was pressing her to my bosom—& for the moment was happy—But alass when I awoke I was miserable— . . .

[September] *July 10*—My time passes away without any thing material happening. I live retir'd, I am now fond of solitude. Every thing seems indifferent for me; except thinking of my dear lost Child, lost at least to me, for the most endearing part of her infancy; but I will not repine, I have done my duty; I have try'd to be reconciled to my unhappy husband; & I am now convinced that were I to live with him with all the discretion that ever fell to the lot of woman, my life wou'd be made miserable by him, for jealousy like ye jaundiced Eye wou'd discolor all my actions. But why these reflections, they will do me alass no good—I only write to ease my oppress'd heart.

[September] *July*—I spent yesterday with my dear Maria. She does all in her power to console me; she tells me I ought to be chearful, & happy, because I am rid of my tyrant husband—but ah me! I'm deprived of *all* my happiness. I am so melancholy I make her a very poor companion, but she is *good*, & sympathizes with me in all my distresses.

My dear Maria will shortly be married, & then I shall lose a friend for she goes to Carolina.

October 1—Yesterday my dear friend & companion left me, almost inconsolable for her loss. It is a loss indeed for we cannot replace a friend. The most powerful & lasting friendships are usually the produce of the early season of our lives when we are most susceptible of the warm, & affectionate impressions. The heart of Maria was formed for friendship—sweet, gentle amiable, with the most pleasing manners, & winning address— she has beauty; & accomplishments, both personal, & mental—

she makes one of the best of wives, as well as the most delightful of friends. She was a great comfort to me in my solitude. I was form'd for the world & educated to live in it. I had already been admitted into some share of its societies—so that the cheif comfort of my situation, is in the reflection that I have avoided a great evil. If my memory glances on any other circumstance of former pleasure, my heart can scarce sustain the mortification. I have however to thank heaven for having taken me from a situation where I must have been compleatly miserable, to place me in a state where I cannot be happy—

In the interval between the dates September—and October 1, the following letter, from Nancy to her mother-in-law Mrs. Livingston, must have been written:

Impressed with a sense of your politeness, & goodness to me, & with a heart full of the tenderest anxiety for my darling Child, I sit down to write to you Madam, & tho' I am perfectly satisfied that your care of her is the best possible, yet I have all the fears of a Mother; I fear she pines after me, I fear she is sick, & that your humanity prevents you from letting me know it, & perhaps this is the reason I have not heard by the two last posts; my distress is greater than I can express, I can never be happy without her, I feel that she is "close twisted" with the fibres of my heart,— do my dear Madam let me hear by the next post, if it be but one line, only to let me know how my sweet Child does, & you will lay me under an everlasting obligation—I send with this the reciept you mention'd, with some medicine; My Papa, Mamma, & Brother, beg me to present their respectful compliments with mine, to you Madam, & all your good family—
I have the honor to be with the greatest respect

Your dutiful Daughter
[Nancy Livingston]

P.S. Please to let me know my dear Madam if our dear Child is much loved by her father, & what effect seeing her had upon him; and if she can yet walk alone.

The reply from Mrs. Robert Livingston in September shows that Nancy wrote often, but that her in-laws were still inclined to look upon her as the offender and not the offended, in her relation to the family.

Cleremont 10 Sep^t 1783

Mad^m

I have the honor of 3 of your Letters received all within the last fortnight, and your papas very obliging Letter with the Medecines at the same time, for which I return him my best thanks. I will freely own, that when I did my self the honor to write to Dr Shippen I was most Mortifyed that you had not made one inquiry (as I then conceived) conserning our Lovely baby. But I am now fully convinced that you possess the feelings of a Mother, and ask your pardon for not doing you Justice till I had your Letters. You ask how she is. I can only repeat what I wrote before that she is in perfect health, pleased with every thing, and every Body. No person especially Gentlemen enters the Room, but she goes to them and says upe, and sits on their Lap and begins a conversation intirely her own. But her favorite one is her baby that ingroces all her time and all her care, next to the Harpsichord of which she is Extreamly fond. Her looks are much improved, having grown quite fat. To be short, for I dare not trust myself when speaking or writing of this dear Child, I will only ad that she is the sweetest and best tempered Child in the world, and as happy as an Angel, when the weather is fine to run about the Garden with her cousin betsey who is very fond of her, and her maid Gitty who is intirely devoted to her. Peggy Lewis came here some time agoe from Albany. You would have been highly delighted had you seen the Goodness of heart our Baby discovered at that time. She was so delighted y^t she knew no way to shew her affection but by taking betsey in one hand, and peggy Luis, as she calls her, in the other; then kissing one, then the other, repeating it five or six times to each. In short she is the darling of every body—her papa is very fond of her and she of him, altho she calls the Chancellor by no other name but papa and M^{rs} L mama.

Please to present my Compliments to all your family. Peggy stands at my knee. She has repeated the words give my Duty to

164

my Dear Mama, Grand Mama and G Papa, and twice kissed the Letter to send you a kiss. The negro who bears this to you has orders to deliver it to y^r hand.

I have the honor to be

Y^r Most ob^d S.

M. Livingston

November 13—Sunday—I passed this day at home. I do not think it prudent to go out as I hear Lord B. is in Town. I believe it—for the other Even^g somebody disguis'd came to the door & ask'd for me; he was told I was out—he ask'd where I slept—he was told; he ask'd in which room my picture, & the Childs was, he was told it was upstairs. He ask'd several more questions concerning me & then left the house. It must have been Lord B. & nobody else. Today I was told he had been seen & ask'd if he had seen me—he made answer, that he had been several times & cou'd find nobody at home but the servants. I am terefied at the Idea of seeing him. What shall I do if he comes & forces me away. I realy think my life will be in danger from his jealousy & unmanaged passions.

Monday—I am distressed past all discription at not hearing of my dear Child for so long a time. What can be the reason? is she sick or, what? unhappy creature that I am! a state of suspense is without exception the most disagreeable.

Wednesday—Drank Tea with Molly & Sally Shippen, a large company. Their merriment only served to make me the more sad—oh! My Child—I will write no more untill I hear from her—

December 2^d

Thursday—I have heard at last from my dear Baby, she is well & happy & Mrs L. [ivingston] is on her way to N. York with her; this piece of news has raised my spirits amazingly.

Monday—Spent the morn^g as usual read & work'd & drank Tea in the afternoon at Mrs Lenox's—heard the most delightful news, my Peggy is safely arrived at N York—Genl Washington told papa he saw her, & kiss'd her, happy Man! I saw Leander this even^g at Mrs Shippens he has been to N. Y. & saw Peggy, & kiss'd her he says a thousand times, & says she looks beautiful. I am delighted beyond measure; I am sure I shall not sleep a wink tonight.

Tuesday—It happen'd as I suspected, I did not sleep more than two hours, awoke at day break. I dream'd I saw her, & was pressing her to my fond bosom, when I awoke. I lay thinking of her 'till 9 o'clock & then fell into a sweet slumber & slept till 11—when Mamma came & call'd me up. She said she thou't I was sick; Ah! said I, I was never so far from it in my life, for I pass'd my night in the most delightful Manner. I have walk'd out this morn^g & am to drink Tea with Mrs Moore, this afternoon, & go from there to the concert. I am afraid I shall be foolish enough to tell every body I meet how happy I am.

Wednesday—Spent a delightful Even^g at the Concert, the music was fine, & the company agreable. I had a letter given me while I was there, by a gentleman lately from N. Y. my curiosity was so great I open'd it immediately, & to my great joy found it was from my mother in law giving me an account of my sweet baby. I was in great spirits the remainder of the even^g; the concert was concluded with a song to the praise of Genl Washington—he retired while it was sung—

Friday—8 o'clock—I have met with a great disappointment. This night there is a grand ball given by the Merchants in compliment to Genl W—n [Washington], I am invit'd & intended to go, but *alass!*—the hairdresser did not come till seven—

Saturday night at 11 oclock—I had a very large company at Tea this Evening. The company is but just now broke up, I dont know when I spent a more merry Even^g. We had music, Cards, &c &c—

Sunday Even^g—*9 oclock*—I heard an excellent sermon preach'd this morn^g by Mr Blackwell, the text was "Remember to keep holy the sabbath day." He spoke in a very sensible manner, & said every thing suitable upon that subject. This Afternoon we were honor'd with the Company of Genl Washington to Tea, M^rs & Major Moore, Mrs Stewart Mr Powel M^r B Washington, & two or 3 more—

Monday Evening—Mr Willing waited on me this morning to let me know he was going to N Y to-morrow morning early; I am very unhappy that I can't get ready to go with him, but he gave me too short notice. I must content myself with writing by him to Mrs Livingston & Mrs Rutherford, & sending my sweet Child a baby—

Tuesday 17—Col. Miranda [7] lent me a book call'd Voltaires Henriade, I read part of it this Morning & admire it much; The style is Elegant, & the descriptions lively. Leander drank Tea with us this Even^g— . . .

The following, dated only "Tuesday Even'g," shows that Leander received from Nancy more than a cup of tea that evening. With his longer experience of the world, it is amusing to note the admiration he expresses for her "Wisdom & experience."

I thank you a thousand times my dear friend for your advice so full of Wisdom & experience. I flatter myself *you will see the good effects* of it in my future conduct. With how much tender-

[7] See *Supplementary Records* (3).

ness do you deal with me! how sweetly do you encourage me to be *in*genuous with you! Indeed I'm quite ashamed of my *vanity;*

Good night, I will try to-morrow to write something more worthy your perusal.

Tuesday Even'g.

I have seen the the good effect! ! ! [Otto's hand]

Wednesday 24—Still confin'd by the pain in my face & sore throat—felt lonesome all day—how I miss my dear Maria—& Emily—the latter I expect soon to return from her Uncle's but ah! when shall I see Maria! have not [heard] from her these 3 weeks they appear to me like ages—

Thursday 25—Altho' this was Christmas day & some company to dine here that I have a regard for I cou'd not leave my Chamber but spent the day alone; My friend Washington dined here also. . . .

Fryday 26—This morn^g I set in Lady W's Chamber; & read to her. She has been sick for some time but is getting better; I dined down stairs—tho' much indispos'd; because it is my sweet Childs birth day. She is this day at 3 oclock 2 years old— God grant she may see many happy returns of this day. Spent the Even^g in my Chamber—

Saturday 27—Still in so much pain I am obliged to keep my face Muffled. I am out of all patience, I have been confin'd near a week—& yet not bad enough to keep my bed. I am tir'd of being alone, Lady W. unwell also. Lord W. out most part of the day—& only me poor Amanda left at home alone. I have heard of my husband, he was seen in N.Y. in disguise—Poor man! when will he behave well, & re[s]tore to his wife a husband, his Child a father & his mother a son—

Tuesday 30—Set in my chamber all the morning at work, & drank Tea in the even^g with the Miss Shippens. Was introduced to the Dutch Ambasadors two sons, & found them very agreable, the eldest especially—who has a great deal of humor. I staid till ten oclock & was very happy all the time; we sung, & play'd at cards.

Wednesday 31—At home all day—read some of Ganganelli's letters—they are ful of wisdom & instruction—

Thursday—January 1st—1784—Spent the day at home, reading, & hearing delightful music; the Day extreamly cold—

Friday 2d—had a slaying party this Morn^g went 3 miles & drank mull'd cyder, & eat buiscuit, & then return'd home, almost perish'd with the cold—spent the even^g at home Old Lord Worthy join'd us & we play'd at Whist till ten oclock—& then went to supper—which consisted of hominy & milk, & mince pies—the Even^g was realy delightful—the party—Old lord W. his son, & daughter Amanda—

Saturday 3^d—Lady Worthy & myself spent this morn^g together in ye parlor alone, we had a great deal of conversation the subjects various. She is a woman of strong sense, & has a Masculine understanding; a generous heart, & a great share of sensibility. Sweet Sensibility! source of a thousand heaven born sensations, for the wealth of the Indies I wou'd not be without thee!—

Sunday 4th—Spent the day with the family as usual, without any thing Material happening—read, meditated &c—

Monday 5th—Spent the Morn^g at work & busying myself a little about domestic concerns, which I am very fond of, as it takes up my attention from meloncholy thoughts; & at the same time takes the trouble off my dear Mama's hands. Mr Washington drank Tea with us & play'd at Chess with me the remainder of the Evening. I will here mention Mr Washington in a particular manner as I am very much his friend. He has a handsome face, with sparkling black Eyes, & good complexion—a small person—his Manners particularly agreable & engaging—Strong sense & an improved understanding for he spends most part of his time in study. His conversation is interesting & agreable, & he never fails to please, & make his friends all those who have the happiness of knowing him. He very often favors me with his company, of which I am extreamly fond. He is an intimate friend of my brothers, & declares himself much interested in favor of this family—

Tuesday 6—My hours today pass'd as usual, saw no company, but passed a sociable Even^g with my Papa & Mamma.

It is strange that with these daily entries during January, 1784, there is no mention whatever of her husband, nor of his letters, of which two have been found dated January, 1784, "in Philadelphia." The dates are unmistakable, and yet the serene tenor of Nancy's journal at this time makes it seem incredible that she received them. A few entries were omitted because unimportant.

Philadelphia 5:th Jan:^{y} 1784.

Madam

I am still a Letter in your Debt which would carelessly have remained unpaid had not the Trifle enclosed accidentally happened to be with me, of Consequence perhaps to you, I therefore enclose it. Your Fav^r would have been Answer'd immediately on its reception had you not been decided in your Resolutions which you know, Madam, I could have no Expectations of altering, having never been blessed with such Success since our Connection. In your

BUSHROD WASHINGTON
FROM THE ORIGINAL PORTRAIT BY JAMES SHARPLES
Courtesy of The Brook, New York, and Frick Art Reference Library

last you were pleased to Misconstrue some Words, rather meant as a Caution than an implication of guilt. I Should have given you this Satisfaction sooner, had I not conceived myself injured. But I will not lenghthen out this Scrall because I do not (for Reasons before assigned you) chuse to Animadvert upon the exceptionable Parts of your Conduct or Letters: also because I wish not my own Justification in preference to your "future peace of Mind" which I am happy to hear you have secured. Your Child was well when I left N.Y.

I have the Honour to be Madam your most
Humble Serv!

Henry B. Livingston

The second is written Jan. 24, 1784:

Madam
. . . But the last part of your letter Conveys something that appears to me very singular for tho I allow nothing can be more Natural than your Inclination to have your Child with you: yet as the same reasons probably exist which induced you to place her under the care and protection of my Mother it certainly is an addition to my Distress that I have no pretence to interfere in a concern in which you did not think proper to allow me a Voice. . . .

I have the Hon^r to be with a deep sense of my Misfortune,
Madam,

Your most ob^d & very Humble Servt
[H. B. Livingston]

Wednesday 7—Very busy all the Morning, & in the Evening alone reading Clarissa H. I like it very much, her character is fine & her letters are full of sentiment—I must adopt some of her excellent rules.

Thursday 8—This Morning was entirely Taken up in preparing to go to a Ball at the French Ministers;[8] I went with M^{rs}

---

[8] This Ball, given on the birthday of the Dauphin of France was one of the historic entertainments of Philadelphia's social history. A dancing room sixty feet wide was built next to the French legation, its roof supported by

Powel,[9] & passed a delightful Even^g—Mr Washington my partner—danced a Minuet, I believed I look'd well at least My Partner told me so—came home at one.

Friday 9—At home all day. In the After noon had a dispute with my dear Mamma. We got to very high words; indeed I was faulty, very faulty to say any thing disrespectful to a parent—but she found fault with me, & I thought unjustly, & therefore I resented it; & so displeased her that she commanded me to keep my room that Even^g—

Saturday 10—This Morn^g I set alone in the parlour at Work, reflecting on what pass'd yesterday, & determined within myself to ask pardon of my Mamma altho' I was not in fault at first yet as I had been passionate & disrespectfull to her afterwards. She came down to dinner & we neither of us spoke, during the time, I felt *sullen* altho' I had made such a good resolution, before; after dinner I spoke first, she answer'd me mildly; we then enter'd into indifferent conversation—& in the Even^g praised me for *my* mild behaviour towards her that afternoon. We have been good friends ever since—& I am to have a party here on *Monday*. I spent a *happy* Even^g with my parents. My Papa read while I work'd. Dear good Man! he has the sweetest disposition in the world, affable & polite to every body, & to his Wife & Children he is sweetly indulgent.

Sunday 11—This day so extreamly cold I cou'd not attend on public Worship. Mr Hollingsworth visited me this morning. He is a youth of good natural parts, but is rather too concieted & vain, & looks as if he thought himself handsome—where as he is I think him quite the contrary—he has a tolerable person

lofty pillars painted and festooned, the walls covered with banners and appropriate pictures.
   [9] See *Supplementary Records* (4).

—& can be agreable & facetious, when he pleases—he aims in general at being witty—sometimes he fails—& too often joins satire to make up for his deficiency. As my Mamma has desir'd me not to admit Company on the sabbath I have refused myself to some gentlemen that were polite enough to call, & spent the Even'g in reading to my Mamma—

*Monday 12.—11 oclock in the Even*ᵍ—The most delightful Company has just left me, I never spent a more lively Evenᵍ As it was a young party my Mamma chose to set in her Chamber, & my Papa was engaged out, so I had the company to myself—there was twelve ladies & Gentlemen, Miss Moore, Mʳˢ H. Moore, Miss Footman, the Miss Shippens, Mʳ Van bercles, Mʳ Washington, Mʳ Hollingsworth, Mʳ P. Wikoff, Mʳ Moore; We play'd at Cards, play'd at Pawns, Danced, & were as merry as it was possible for a Company to be. Miss Moore is vastly agreeable, & very sprightly, Mʳˢ H. Moore is an Elegant Woman, but rather haughty in her manners. Miss Footman is very engaging & sociable, Miss S. Shippen is pretty in the face but badly Made, & appears to have a fund of good humor. Miss Molly Shippen is very Ugly, & very formal in her manners, but very good natur'd—Mʳ P. Wikoff who some suppose is courting Miss M. S. is very like her in his person, & for a man of his years (he being forty) is very lively & chatty—

The Mʳ Van bercles are sons of the Minister plenepo, from holland—one of them is rather handsome, & the other is very humorous; they are both agreable—Mʳ B. Moore is a youth that is generally silent—but when he does speak it is to the purpose—he is not handsome, but makes it up by his attention to the ladies. It is now twelve oclock, & I am not in the least sleepy—& the room is so comfortable I cant prevail upon myself to leave it, my Papa not yet return'd; I expected Leander this Even*g* but was disappointed. What can be the reason? but here comes Papa, I must troop to bed.

Wednesday 13—All day yesterday was laid up with a violent toothach. [sic] Leander Called in the evening but I did not see him. drank Tea at Miss Moores, staid till ten. Leander was here again, while I was out, & saw Papa. He came to take leave of us, as he is going to Anapolis, he made an apology for not coming on Monday—

One of Uncle Arthur Lee's gossipy letters to Nancy a month later gives her news of the gay capital of Maryland, about the time that Leander was to return to Philadelphia:

. . . Miss Plater is pretty but not killing. Miss Rideout & Miss Sprigg are the belles here & have Congress at their feet. Messrs. Marbois & Otto are favorites as you may suppose. Mrs. Thomson is very gay. We have a great deal of dancing, feasting, ogling & all that. The Players are to exhibit next week & Annapolis will far outshine Philadelphia.

. . . When you go to N. York do not forget to give Peggy 13 kisses for me. Adieu. Kiss your Mamma for me & warm your noses together over the hickory fire in a friendly manner.

Friday 15—Today I feel quite well in body—wou'd I were so in *Mind*, I had a dream last night about my dear Child that makes me uneasy, how I long to hear from her. The weather is so bad that it is impossible for me to think of going to N. York—

Saturday 16—M*r* Willing is return'd from N. York & I have heard from my precious Child. She is well, & happy, & her grand mamma doats on her, I recieved a letter also from M*rs* Rutherford. M*r* Washington spent the afternoon with us, & play'd with me at Chess.

Monday 18—A stormy day, alone till the afternoon; & then was honor'd with the Company of Mr Jones (a gentleman lately from Europe) M^r Du Ponceau, & Mr Hollingsworth at Tea— We convers'd on a variety of subjects & play^d at whist, upon the whole spent an agreable Even^g Mr Jones is rather handsome, & very agreable in his Manners, & I think is rather sensible, than otherwise—I expected S. Shippen but the evening was so bad she cou'd not come—

Thursday 21—This Even^g there was to have been a grand display of Fire works. A frame was built at great expence for the purpose, the pictures of all the great men (with General Washington at the head) was hung up, & the frame illuminated, with more than a thousand lamps, & a great many elegant representations were to have been made, when an accident happen'd that put an end to all, for by the carelessness of the managers the gunpowder caught fire, & blew it up in the air. The Explosion was great, & what with the Turpentine, pictures, frame, &c &c it was the largest bonfire that was ever seen in Market street. One man was kill'd & a great many hurt—Mr Van bercle & Mr Duke, & Susan Blair (who had spent the day with me) Papa, & grand Papa went with me to see the remains of the fire works; we had the pleasure to see a few rockets, & a large mass, & then returned to Tea after making several wise observations—

Friday & Saturday 22. & 23—Felt dull and disagreeable, very low spirited & out of humor—wherefore are there days that, given up to meloncholy without knowing the cause, we are a burden to ourselves? first, it is because we are dependant upon a body which is not always in perfect equilibrium—secondly because God Almighty wou'd make us sensible that this life is

not our happiness, & that we shall allways be ill at ease till
we leave it.

There are fogs in the moral as well as the natural world; &
the soul like the sky hath its clouds: the best way to dispel such
glooms is to seek employment.

Sunday 24—Not very well today therefore cou'd not attend
divine worship; but contented myself with reading Blairs Sermons; they are delightful indeed—sound doctrine dressed in
the most elegant style.

Thursday 28—Spent a charming even^g at Mrs P. Danced a
great deal had three partners—Mr H.[ollingsworth] M^r
W.[ashington] & Major Moore. An elegant supper concluded
the even^g much to the general satisfaction. Spent this day at
home—

Saturday 30—Passed this day at Mount Peace very agreably.
Came home in the Sleigh by moonlight, caught a little cold—

Sunday 1st February—rather better today but still feel some
effects of my cold. At home all the morn^g. Heard Mr Sprout
preach in the afternoon. Miss S[ally] Shippen came in at 8
oclock, & set with me till ten. We discuss'd several serious subjects—& was join'd by Mr Lyons who came in about nine &
agree'd with us in all we said having nothing to say of his own.
He is however, or, appears to be, very good natur'd. He is not
handsome but rather genteel, & has a simplicity in his manners
not displeasing. He waited on Miss S. home.

Monday 2. At eleven was much alarm'd by my Mammas being
taken suddenly ill in consequence I believe of her sitting too
near a stove. The symptoms of extream illness was so alarming
yt I dispatch'd every body out of the house for Papa who hap-

pen'd to sup out yt even^g. He came. She continued ill all night but recover'd towards Morn^g.

Tuesday 3d—Mamma continues weak & long after her illness which she thinks was something of the apoplexy. I am not well myself owing to fatigue & sitting up all last night, for I was affraid to leave Mamma a minute. Indeed I am so sleepy now I can hardly hold my pen—yawning again, pen begone—I have induldg'd myself with a doze in the chair, & feel refresh'd. Spent the even^g in Lady Worthys chamber. She is much better.

Wednesday 4—Mamma is so much better that she came down into the parlor this afternoon. The Miss Shippens & Mr Hollingsworth drank Tea with us. They staid till eleven.

Saturday 7—At Mount Peace this Morn^g—made up a little party, went in ye sleigh. Mr Washington, Mr Hollingsworth Miss S. Shippen & Myself, we return'd to dinner. Had company in ye evening—M^r & Mrs Horter, Mr Secon. & Mr Poyter—Mrs H. entertain'd us all the even^g by playing on her guittar & singing with it. She is a very accomplish'd woman.

Sunday 8—I am very uneasy at not hearing from my sweet Child.—It seems an age. When will my prospects begin to brighten. Heard from my dear Maria. She is well but not contented with her situation. There is no perfect happiness in this world. . . .

Monday 9—Went a shopping with Louisa & Mr Washington & Mr Hollingsworth were our beauxs.

Tuesday 10—Very busy all the Morn^g employ'd in domestic affairs. Emelia & Louisa Mr W. M^r H & Mr Lyons drank Tea with me, & then play'd at Cards. They staid till eleven. My Papa was not pleased with me, for keeping such late hours. I am sure I dont have company so often Papa that you need speak to me about it. However since you dont like it I will be more retir'd still. Poor Amanda, when will the time come, that I can be free & uncontrould!

Wednesday 11—At home all day employ'd as usual. Read Clarissa Harlowe in the evening. It's a charming book fraught with instruction.

Thursday 12—Saw nobody but the family. Heard from my brother. Tommy wrote from Williamsburgh:

My dear Sister,

I thank you for the entertainment your charming chit chat letter afforded me. Nothing gives me more pleasure than to hear of your balls, concerts and tea parties, I enjoy them all with you, and am always very happy when I hear of your being so. I should have liked very much to see Papa attract the admiration of the Ballroom by his graceful minuet, and not less to observe you with your handsome partners setting an example worthy of imitation.

I thank you for your kind congratulations on my situation, and assure you that I am as happy as I can be when absent from you and my dear parents. . . .

Friday 13—Received an affectionate note this morning from Emelia. She ask me to spend the afternoon with her. I believe I will. Had a very large party at Emelias—staid till near Eleven. She proposed a sleighing party for tomorrow & I agreed to it.

Saturday 14—The weather was too bad to go in a sleigh, & we went in a Coach & four.—Drank tea at Mount Peace which is about five miles from Phil^a & return'd at 8 oclock. Brought the company home with me & we play'd at Cards till ten.

Monday 16—Not very well today. Heard last night that Leander who has been some time at Anapolis is return'd. I feel happy to think that I shall soon see so dear a friend—one that is as much my friend in adversity, as in prosperity. At home all day & mostly alone.

Tuesday 17—Not seen Leander yet. My dear Mammas ill health prevents me from seeing any body. Her spirits are ex-treamly low; her mind is very much affected.

Tuesday 24—The last week I have been confin'd with my dear Mamma who has been very low, so as to require constant at-tendance. She is better today but still indisposed. Dear good woman she has had severe tryals. I pray God they may be of use to her. I think there is visible alteration in her character, since this illness—more composed, more serene, more indifer-ent about worldly matters than ever I saw her. This is my birth day.—This day I am twenty years old. When I look back what a moment of time it appears to be, & what account can I give of myself for not having made a better use of it. Let me try to improve then, let me try to spend the next twenty years (if I am permitted to live so long) in a better manner. My dear Papa & Mamma drank my health in a glass of wine wish-in[g] me many happy returns of this day. At home all day.

Monday 1ˢᵗ of March—Had company this Eveⁿᵍ that staid till ten. Saw Leander for the first time since his return. He look'd as usual—only a little more meloncholy—he spoke but little; & left us early. I wish'd to enquire after his health & happiness & have a little friendly chat with him but there was so much company it was impossible. I hope to see him soon again for I realy have a sincere friendship for him. I heard this evenᵍ that my friend Mʳ Washington is much afflicted at the loss of a favorite brother, who was kill'd by a very sad accident, a school fellow of his was playing with a loaded gun, & by accident shot W: thro' the body.

Thursday 4—Mamma a little better today but still very low & week. Her spirits are much depress'd; she called me to her bedside & told me she was not long for this world, & gave me some particular directions about laying her out—I am in hopes that as her body gathers strength her mind will become more easy. I was much affected but did not let her see it. . . .

Friday 5—O! I am so happy. I have reciev'd a letter concerning my darling Child from my Mother in Law. My baby has been ill but is recover'd & bids her G. M. tell me she is a good girl—sweet baby when shall I see you. Had company this even^g—Received another letter; it is from Venoni to his friend Amanda.

Sunday 7—A very bad day so staid at home. Mamma din'd with us today. I express'd a desire after dinner to go in the even^g to hear a new preacher who some say is an arien. Mamma advis'd me not to go. I persisted & said I determin'd to hear him that I might judge for myself. My papa said the walking was too bad. I then ask'd for the Chariot. He said angrily I shou'd not have it. I was overcome, I burst into Tears. He left the room. My dear Mamma tried to comfort me—& when Papa came back, dear soul she said so much in my favor that he said as much *all he cou'd say* to make up with his spoilt daughter & we spent the even^g together happily.

Tuesday 9—I reciev'd an affectionate note from Emelia this morn^g begging me to spend the Even^g with her. I wish'd to go. Papa told me he wou'd stay with Mamma if I wou'd go. I ask'd Mama if I ought [to] leave her. She said yes she beg'd

I wou'd, for when she was dead I must stay. I did not go but sent an excuse.

Wednesday 10—A dull day—out of spirits—

Thursday 11—I was invited to a Ball at the French Ministers, but I refus'd to go at my Papas request, but my heart was there; It was certainly prudent not to go; how happy am I to have a wise parent to judge for me. He went & made an apology for the rest of the family. Mamma drank Tea with Mrs Blair—I read French w^h Pamela, & pass^d a tolerable even^g

Monday 15—This morn^g I read french. In the afternoon was honor'd with the company of Emelia, Mr Duer Mr Washington & Mr Second at Tea—M^r D & M^r S went away early & Mr W. Emelia & myself set till ten. We convers'd upon a variety of subjects & I think I never spent a more sociable Even^g—but I forgot to mention that Mr Duer told me that he had seen My Darling baby—very lately. He said she run about & chatter'd, & was the most beautiful Child he ever saw.

Tuesday 16—This Even^g I went with Emelia to Mrs Voss's to visit Mrs L. Mrs Rutledge who is going to Carolina. From there we went to the concert & came home about ten oclock.

Wednesday 17—This is my Dear Brothers Birthday. He is nineteen. May he see many happy returns of this day. At home all day with Lady Worthy who continues much indisposed.

Thursday 18—Not very well today, read Swifts works.

Saturday 20—busy this morning clear starching, & lost my emerald ring worth 5 guineas in the suds & was foolish enough to cry for it.

181

Wednesday 24—Sent an answer to Emelias note this morning letting her know that I wou'd wait on her to Miss Footmans this After noon with her. I went & pass'd an agreable evening in a large company. Leander was there. I came home at ten & he waited upon me. We convers'd but little.

Saturday 27—Louisa spent the day wth me helping me to make up some milinary. Mrs Moore sent to me to drink Tea with her but I sent an excuse. I was happier in the company of Louisa. In the afternoon Mr Washington came & drank Tea with us & spent the Even^g in a very agreable manner, us three alone—chatting, reading & singing till ten oclock when Lord Worthy came in, & Mr W. went home wth Louisa. Reciev'd a letter this Even^g from Venoni. [Louis Otto]

Sunday Evening—How have I spent this day? let me reflect a little! I have not spent it well. In the morn^g I rode out (instead of going to Church) with Emelia, & Mr W. [ashington] to the falls of Schyllkill to see the Ice that is thrown up on the land almost an hundred feet high. We return'd to dinner. I put Emelia down at her house & came home. My father ask'd Mr W. to dine with us with another gentleman. We sat at the dinner table about an hour & then Papa & D^r C—y went to Dr Bonds funeral. When Mr W. & myself were alone I propos'd (I am almost asham'd to write it) a game at Chess I did not reflect at the time I am sure that it was the Lords day & ought to [be] kept holy, or I shou'd not thus have transgress'd. We had not play'd five minutes when Mrs Clark a very worthy woman came in & reproved me: I blush^d from a consciousness of my having done wrong & determ'd within myself never to commit the like again. Spent the even^g alone.

Monday 29—Walk'd out this morn^g with Emelia & Miss Footman spent three or four hours in shopping. In the after noon went with Mr Washington to Louisa's & drank Tea & then we all walk'd, it being a very fine evening, to hear some excellent music but it was so full & the door so crowded we were oblig'd to return. Aunt & Uncle Blair, & Susan dined with us.

Wednesday 31—Work'd at my needle all this morn^g very busy preparing to go to N. Y. In the afternoon went with Emelia to pay a visit to Mrs Robinson.

Saturday 3^d—At home reading Gibbons on the decline & fall of the roman Empire.

Sunday 4th—At home all day had a very large company in the afternoon. Expected my friend Mr Washington but he did not come.

Monday 5—Alone all day in the Even^g Mr Washington Mr Lyon[s] & Miss Delany drank Tea with me, Mr W. said he had quite forgot to he was engag'd to tea the evening before. Spent a happy even^g.

Tuesday 6—As usual at home. Mr Washington & Mr Willing din'd here, the former told me he was going to Virginia in two or three day[s] & Mr Willing goes with me to N York next monday.

Wednesday 7—Washington called on me again this Morning to ask me to be of a party to Mount Peace, the day was rather cold & so Papa refused to let me go. I was fool enough to cry & refuse to eat my dinner, but Papa made up with me in the afternoon & said I shou'd go tomorrow.

Thursday 8—Spent a most charming day. W. dined with us & immediately after dinner Miss Grace Cox Mr W. & myself went in our close carriage to Mount Peace return'd at eight oclock paid Mrs P. a visit then went to Miss Shippens. They were out, from there I came home. W. went home with Grace Cox & promised to come back & take leave of me & the rest of the family (as they were then out) at nine oclock. As soon as they were gone I went to see Louisa, staid with her an hour & then return'd. In about 2 minutes after the bell rung & in came my valuable friend—but ah what did [he] come for? to take Leave. We sat alone about ten minutes & said very little, what we did say was upon friendship. My father then came in, & presently after he got up to go. O! how I felt to think of losing such a friend & yet not to lose him neither but to be separated from him, never to see him, never to spend with him any more happy chearful days in conversing, hearing him read while I work'd, singing wth him, & playing on the harpsichord for him. I did all I cou'd to hide my concern but I saw that he was sorry to go, sorry to leave his friends & yet happy in the thought that he was going to the fond arms of his expecting parents. He came to me first & took me by the hand, gave it a gentle pressure, & bade me farewell. I cou'd not then speak but after he had left the room I called after him & wished him happiness. Ah! why was I form'd with a heart so repleat with sensibility! The parting with a relation or friend almost kills me. I spent a very meloncholy even^g after his departure, & tho' I went to bed very late I slept very little.

Good Friday 9—Rose early this morning in order to write a line to my Cousin Ludwell by Mr Washington, but he was gone when I sent the letter. As soon as I saw the letter brought back I cried like a Child. What for, not because of the disappointment because that was trifling, but because I then thought of his situation, going so far from us, & that perhaps we shou'd never see him again. Spent the morning in puting my papers to rights, & reading some letters from my friends. At one oclock Emelia sent me a note telling me that if I was disengaged she wou'd spend the even^g with me, I was disengaged & about 7 oclock she came & brought G. Cox with her, & we three alone spent a most sociable even'g together. After Tea Miss Cox & myself play^d by turns on the harpsichord while Emelia work'd. Then Emelia read to us the Sorrows of Werter while we work'd. It is a very affecting little history, & made Grace & myself sob & cry like Children, but there is certainly a luxury in some kind of sorrows, as well as bitterness in others. We separated at about eleven oclock, but I forgot to write that we convers'd at intervals about our dear absent friend, & I dare say it was reflecting on his absence that affected us much as the novel. They both think of the amiable youth as I do.

Saturday 10—Busily employ'd all day packing up for my jaunt to N. Y. I expect to go on Monday. How happy I feel in the thought of clasping my beloved child once more in my fond arms, & pressing her to my bosom—but alass! I shall be obliged to part with her again in a few days after I have seen her as I can't leave my mamma longer & my father won't permit me to take her from her good Grandmother. Indeed prudence forbids it also, as upon her must my dear Child depend. O! may I be enabled to bear all my trials with patience & fortitude.

Sunday 11—Papa inform'd me last night that Mr Willing cant go tomorrow. Again disappointed! said I—when shall I go to see my Child? If he can said my dear father he will go on Thursday. This morning about one oclock I recieved a note from Mr Willing informing me that he cou'd not possibly go before Monday week. I bore it as well as I cou'd, & as I knew then of no other opportunity resolved to wait with patience. Went to meeting in the afternoon & brought Cleander & his

Emelia home with me to Tea & one of their lovely Children. After Tea we all went to Even^g Meeting except Cleander who staid to converse with Lady Worthy.

Monday 12—Writ this morn^g to Mrs Livingston to inform her that I was disappointed & to let her know that I should set of on Monday. About half an hour after I had sent & thou't it was gone Papa came in with it in his hand & told me it shou'd not go. I started—he put on a stern countenance & told me to get drest immediately, that Col. Duer wou'd wait on me in half an hour & take me to N. Y. tomorrow. I was so delighted that I jum^d about the room for joy. Col. Duer came & we settled the plan for setting out on Wednesday, & he had politely invited me to stay at his house while I am in N. Y. I shall be very busy till the day comes. Cleander & Emelia dined with us & partook of my happiness. . . .

Tuesday 14—Tomorrow & Tomorrow & one day more, & then I shall see my Lovely Child. The Thought alone makes me happier than I can express. My heart has been as light as a fly all day. & I have thought of nothing else hardly all day. Lady Worthy rid out to Mount Peace, & Lord W. [orthy] went to see his farm, so I have been all alone. At my return I shall begin the second book of my journals.

𝕬

Journal

Continued from

April 15, [1784-1791]

PHILADELPHIA

VOLUME THE SECOND

by

ANN HUME LIVINGSTON

CHAPTER VII

1784-1791

(April, 1784)

Wednesday 15—My dear friend Louisa staid with me last night; at nine o'clock this morning I took leave of her & my dear Parents, & set off in the Stage[1] with Mr Duer for New York, dined at Bristol, & arrived at Princeton at 7 this Evening; eat a very hearty supper of oysters & retired to my room.

Thursday 16—Arose at 6 this morn'g & went as far as Brunswick to breakfast, & arrived at Elizabeth Town to Dinner; we cou'd proceed no farther this afternoon the weather being very bad. A stage arrived here about 8 this Even'g with Company in it that I was acquainted with, So we proceeded together as far as Newark & arrived about 10 oClock.

F. 17.—Set off after breakfast with the same company & after crossing 3 ferrys arrived at Powles Hook where we dined, & after dinner tho' the wind was very high crossed over to New York. It was about 4 in the afternoon when we reach'd the City. I parted with my fellow travellers at the landing & proceeded with Mr Duer to his house in Broad Way. There I tarry'd for a few minutes, & adjusted my dress, & then walk'd to the Old Ladies, in queen street accompanied by Miss Susan

---

[1] The earliest "stage waggons" from Philadelphia to New York were "Jersey" wagons without springs and protected from the weather only by leather curtains at the sides and rear. There were four benches, three in the interior seating nine passengers and a tenth accommodated beside the driver. There were usually no backs to the benches and no space for luggage, save under one's feet. By 1784 very little more of comfort had been added.

Livingston & her B^r Brockhurst L[ivingston] children of the Governors. When first I enter'd the room I cou'd scarce see any body in it my Eyes so eagerly search'd every part of it for the dear object of my affections, but she was not there so I paid my respects to the family as well as I cou'd, & seated my-self; M^rs L[ivingston] arose immediately after & said she wou'd go & fetch the Child. My heart leap'd for joy; & I was in such an agitation that I cou'd hardly answer the questions of the family concern'g my health & that of my Parents, with any tolerable propriety. At length in came Mrs L. with the dear Baby in her arms, but so much alter'd I should not have known her, had I seen her any where else; so much grown, so much more beautiful; I got up instantly that the door open'd, & ran to meet her & clasp'd her in my arms, but she had quite forgot me & told me to "get long."

I beg'd her to come [to] me & call'd her my darling Child & try'd to take her, by force. All wou'd not do, she wou'd not take ye least notice of me, nor let me take her from her grand-mother; it was more than I cou'd bear, I was distress'd & mortified, & burst into a flood of tears. Mrs L. & the rest of the family did all in their power to prevail on her to come to me, but in vain; I walk'd to the window to hide my tears, & thought of some trinkets I had in my pocket which I had brought for her. I set down and display'd them upon my lap, & called her to me, the sight of them made her come instantly. I took the dear creature upon my lap, & she sat with me con-tentedly for near an hour; I spent the remainder of the Even'g there. Some part of it she was quite sociable with me & in high spirits. About ten I took my leave of the family & went home with Lady Kitty Duer: I took the Child with me & her maid Kitty who she is very fond of.

LADY KITTY DUER, LADY CATHERINE ALEXANDER, DAUGHTER
OF LORD STIRLING

PORTRAIT BY AN UNKNOWN ARTIST

Courtesy of Mrs. S. Naudain Duer

Saturday 18—She has been contented all this day, & some part of it appear'd more reconciled to me than I cou'd have expected.—Several Ladies of this City & 2 of my sisters in law waited upon me this morn'g;—& one of them Mrs Tillotson has politely offer'd me her house for my home while I stay here. I believe I will accept her invitation as it will look better for me to lodge with one of the family. Mrs L. made me a very good apology for not asking me to lodge with her. O! the racking thought that I must part with all my soul holds most dear. Eliza L.[ivingston] call'd on me the day before yesterday, Early in the morn'g before I was up, as she heard I was to set off that day, but as it was a mistake we walk'd out together to pay some visits. Now I am really going & she dont know it; she is the best female friend I have here. She is possess'd of very shining quallities and has a mind well turn'd & much improv'd, has a great deal of tenderness in her disposition, & sympathizes with the distresses of every one. She receiv'd a packet the other day while I was with her from my friend Leander. I did not before know they corresponded tho' I knew of their friendship. She shew'd me the letter in confidence, as illeberal custom prevents a correspondence between the sexes. It was writ in the most friendly manner. His style is elegant. At my return to P. Eliza L is to correspond with me.

Elizabeth Town

Friday 1. of May.—I parted this morn'g with my darling Child, and tho' it was dreadful beyond all description, yet it was not near so painful as it was the time before. It was indeed nothing in comparison. I went in company with Genl Knox, & Col. & Mrs Hull. Cross'd the Bay from N. Y. to Eliz. T. in the Gen^{ls} barge, dine'd there, & expected to have met a stage here to take us on; but were disappointed, so I went to Governor Livingstons with the Genl in a chair. about a mile out of the Town, spent as agreable an afternoon as I well cou'd have expected having just left my dear Child. Spent the Evening at Genl Daytons, & then return'd to the Inn with the rest of my fellow travelers; set out in the morn'g by Day break, breakfasted at Brunswick—din'd at Trenton & arrived in Phi^a at 9 oclock at night. I was so exceedingly fatigued that I beg'd the stage driver to go to our house, which he did. When the Coach stop'd I was surpriz'd to see the house shut up—& no lights in the Hall as was usual; at first I thought my Mother was much worse, but the Children of the neighbourhood soon inform'd us that my Father liv'd there no longer, & y^t the house was let to the Spanish Ambassador. For a moment I felt petrified with astonishment & mortified to the last degree, to think y^t he wou'd move without my being there. I was handed out of the stage by one of the Gen^n & met my dear Papa on the Pavement near our house. I embrace'd him with all my heart, then bid Adieu to my fellow travellers, & proceeded with my Papa to the house he had taken which is next door to our own. I was welcom'd by my dear Papa to our new habitation & he ask'd me how I liked it? I told him I was pleas'd with it as his choice, but I thought it was rather small—he told me we were not to keep it long, it was a temporary habitation, that he was to live there alone & I was to live with my sick Mamma in the Country—I spent the remainder of the Even'g with him in talk'g of my dear Child, and pleas'd him much by the little Anecdotes I related of her & ye agreable reception I met with. When I retir'd to my *small* apartment I indulged my grief, & gave way to the sorrow I felt at the great change that appear'd to have taken place in our affairs. I slept very little all night tho very much fatigued with my journey.

Sunday 2. I was so unwell this morning y[t] I kept my chamber & breakfasted in bed. After breakfast my Papa came into my room & enquired after my health, & beg'd I wou'd dine with him. Altho' very unable at his request I din'd below, & answer'd as well as was in my power the many questions he ask'd me relating to my journey. He appeared delighted with what I told him of my darling and frequently interrupted me by saying he wished to see her. After dinner my Papa went to Church, & I spent a solitary afternoon on the bed, reflecting on my unhapiness; Alas!, I have enough to reflect on. I am parted from a beloved Child, & have a Mother in a very distressed situation. May I by my assiduity & attention be of service to her! My Papa came in to supper, & prevail'd on me to join him at the table, I did so & as I had kept my room all day, was in a loose deshabille. My cousin S[usan] B[lair] came to spend the Even'g with me, & we were all at the Table when Gen[l] Knox came in. I wou'd have run away but he and Papa prevented me, the former paying me the compliment to say I look'd so well he wish'd I wou'd allways dress in that manner.

The gallant old soldier was very fond of Nancy and writes her in lively vein:

My dear Mrs L—

Are you engaged with all the world this evening—to the grand card party—if not and you feel disposed to sit snug by a comfortable fireside and enjoy the chat of friendship—pray bring your work to the old rendevouz in my Cabbin. If on the contrary you are sacrificing to the fashionable world by standing perishing with cold before your mirror adorning your charming person—I wish you success in all your endeavours, That your head may be dress'd in an unusual stile of Elegance—that every curl may encircle the heart of a swain, that your hat may be placed with as much grace as the one that shades the beautious brow of the lovely Allen— that your handkerchief may be Buff'd to the exact point of Beauty

—That your waist may be dress'd with uncommon neatness—that its size shape and appearance may exactly resemble Miss Peggy Allens, and that though so unusually small all the world may acknowledge it contains the Heart of Mrs Livingston—fraught with all the virtues which have ever been conspicuous to your friend

H Knox

Monday 3—Slept tolerably last night. Got up early; & after breakfast put to rights several things that had been deranged in the moving. After that set out in the carriage with my Cousin to Mount Peace, to see my dear Mamma who stays there till our Country house is made ready to receive her. I found her very low in health & spirits. Dined there & then went to see our new country habitation. It is about half a mile from Mount Peace pleasantly situated on a hill with a green Meadow before it. The House is pretty large,—at the back of it a garden and a nursery of trees—an orchard on one side, & a field of barley on the other—an excellent springhouse & a good well of water. With all these conveniencys sure I ought to be contented alltho' I shall not live in as grand a style as I have been used to—nor see so much company. I pass'd an hour here giving orders & arranging some affairs, & then return'd to M. P. & spent the afternoon ' even'g.

Thursday 6—Papa & myself sett off this Morn'g from Town to take possession of our Country house, or rather to fix Mamma & myself there. We spent about 2 hours at the place, walking & talking & then walk'd over to M. Peace leaving orders for the carriage to come for us after dinner. We din'd at M. P. then Mamma & myself rode to Challiot, walked in the garden there, presently Papa join'd us—& we made a happy Trio for a little time Mammas spirits being better, & spent an agreeable afternoon. We then return'd to Quid vis (the name of our new place); had a sociable supper, heard Papa read a little in Hervey, & then went to bed—

Friday 7. Papa left us early this morning his business requiring his attendance, & we spent but a dull day. Sometimes I work'd, sometimes I read to Mamma, or talk'd to her, but nothing I cou'd do wou'd raise her spirits. I think there must be some what upon her mind that distresses her. She retired earlier than usual to her chamber. I offer'd to attend her but she refused, & shut herself in, & spent the Even'g in earnest prayer.

Saturday 8—This day I pass'd well, for I was very busy, gave every one their proper work—& settled several family affairs. Mamma still the same.

Sunday 9—Mamma had a very bad night I was with her the greatest part of it. Towards morning being much fatigued I laid down at the foot of her bed, & fell fast asleep. She waked me in the morn'g by calling me, between sleeps & awake I ask'd her what she wanted—she beg'd me to hear her last request for she was not long for this world. I started up at that, & ask'd her what was the matter, & if she was worse. She told me she was, & that as it [was] probable she shou'd not live to see Papa, beg'd I wou'd let him know that it was her particular request that neither he nor any of his family wou'd go in mourning for her—& beg'd that he wou'd write to her friends in Virginia requesting the same;—I beg'd her to be compos'd & told her that she was not so bad as she apprehended, that Papa wou'd be to see her today, & do for her what was necessary. She still persisted that she was dying; I got up & order'd some nourishment for her, & wou'd have sent to M. P. for my grand-papa but saw plainly that her health was no worse, only her spirits much affected, & her immagination disorder'd.

About 12 oClock Papa came with my Aunt B. & found Mamma still in bed & me very much dejected upon her account. Indeed I went so far as to complain to him of my situations being very disagreable, & that it was hard for me to be alone with Mamma when she was in such a distressed way—& cried heartily for my nerves are weak. I said too much for I made him angry tho' I saw he was sorry for me, he ask'd me who was so proper to take care of Mamma as her own Child? & if I shou'd not bear with patience any trouble I shou'd meet with? I still cried—& then went into another room, where I staid alone a few minutes to compose myself & then went down to my aunt. She comforted me as well as she cou'd, & said I was too young & inexperienc'd, (Alass! not in trouble) to have the care & trouble of Mamma alone, & that my Papa wou'd look for some careful good old Woman to stay with her, & take some of the trouble off my hands. Papa prevail'd on Mamma to get up, & dine below with Grand Papa, Aunt B, two of my little cousins, Papa & myself. She continued better the remainder of the day. After Tea my Aunt & G. P. went home, & Papa spent the Even'g with us. He read & I sung hymns.

Monday 10—After breakfast we all went to Mount Peace, & then Papa & myself went to Town & left Mamma there. . . . I went to Louisa's, staid with her an hour, & ask'd her to stay with me tonight in Town, as I shou'd be alone. She promised she wou'd. From their I went a shopping, & then home; after dinner I prepared myself to go & see some fire works, that were to be display'd in Market street.

Ten o clock at night—I have been to see the Show; it was very brilliant,—& vast crouds of people fill'd the streets. I went with Papa & was in a house where I had a good view of the whole. Afterwards I walk'd up to it with Papa & examined it minutely; I wish I had a descriptive talent to do it justice. It look'd like a large elegant house—painted & illuminated; on the top of it were placed at proper distances four statues, representing the four cardinal virtues, the pictures of Genl Washington the King of france &c. &c. were properly disposed, with four elegant pieces of painting—emblematic of our liberty & independance—the 3 hundred lamps with which it was illuminated were still burning w^n I left it. Eleven oclock & no Louisa. Papa came home with me but is gone out to sup, so here I am all alone—

Tuesday 11. Louisa came last night after I was in bed & apologized for not coming sooner, we lay & chatted till near morning. She arose early & went home before breakfast—I did not rise so early, for about ten oclock Papa & Genl Knox came in & found me at breakfast . . . came home with Mamma who I think is rather worse.

Wednesday—12. Pass'd this day solitary & alone—for Mamma keeps herself shut up all day.

Thursday 13. As usual.

Friday 14. Rode out with Mamma to Chaillot & for the first time since she has been ill made her smile. We walk'd in the Garden, & brought home a great many flowers.

Saturday 15—Mamma & myself rode to Town this afternoon for the purpose of going to Church tomorrow. In the Evening Genl Knox came in, & after he had set some time proposed my walking to see Mrs Hull who is so ill. I went with him & on our way met Papa, so we all went together & found her [the] poor woman, very ill. Papa prescribed for her, I wished it was

in my power to help her because she is a stranger. Afterwards
we went to Louisas, who was out & then went home with Papa.

Sunday 16—Papa took Gen[l] Knox to Mount Peace to Break-
fast this Morn'g & Mamma & myself went to Church. M[r]
Sproat preach'd an excellent sermon & Mamma seem'd more
compos'd after hearing it. After dinner Papa & I went together,
Mamma being not well enough to join us, to hear a sermon.
Spent the Even[g] in reading.

Monday 17. Went out very early this morning, & called upon
Louisa, to take her with me in the country, but she cou'd not
go; she said till Thursday upon the account of her being engaged,—so about ten oclock, Mamma & myself set out for our
seat in the Country where we spent a very dull day together.

Tuesday 18—This day was still duller for it rain'd all day, &
Mamma worse.

Wednesday 19. The same—

Thursday 20. Louisa came here this Morning to my great delight; received 2 letters from my friends in Virginia one from
M[r] Washington [2] & the other from my cousin M[atilda] Lee.
Spent a charming day. Mamma went to Town this afternoon, &
intends staying there this week, as the synod meets.

Fryday 21—Tho' this was a very rainy day we pass'd our time
delightfully. I read while Louisa work'd. In the afternoon I
answer'd the letters I reciev'd yesterday from Virginia.

Sunday 23—This afternoon Grandpapa came to see me & not
finding me in the parlour came up stairs, where Louisa & myself were seting on the bed in deshabille. I was reading & she

[2] See *Supplementary Records* (5).

hearing; he kiss'd us, & call'd us lazy girls—we got up immediately, dress'd ourselves & went down & drank a sociable dish of Tea with G Papa; in the Even'g Papa & Mamma came & join'd us.

Tuesday 25—Today was a very fine day indeed, & after breakfast we drest ourselves alike, & went to visit one or two of our poor neighbours. The first we went to see was an old man & his wife, very old indeed. They live in a very small house, & keep a good garden for a living. Their whole family consists of, besides themselves, a dog, a cow, & a few fowls; they gave us a very welcome reception, spread a clean white cloth upon a little clean table, & put on it some milk, some bread, dutch cheese, & redishes, the old woman put on a clean cap & apron, & the old man his new hat, & then placed himself to wait upon us. After we had finish'd our repast (& we ate very heartily) they shew'd us their garden, their spring, & pick'd us a bunch of flowers, & thank'd us for visiting them. They appear'd as happy & contented as if they inhabited a palace. We told them we were sisters, & they said they thought they saw a likeness; they ask'd us to come & drink Tea under their large Chesnut Tree, & said we should be very welcome. The next house we went to, my dear friend Maria once lived in for 2 summers. The large house is now empty & a poor family live in the kitchen.

We walk'd all thro' the house & every place reminded me of the happy hours I had once spent there with my dear Maria for I staid with her part of a summer; we then walk'd in the garden & went to the summer house & the fish pond. The sight of them brought Tears into our eyes; the remembrance of a thousand little sports & Teapartys we had together, & the tete-a-tetes & even'g walks all rush'd in upon my mind; the good people at our return gave us a nosegay, & we had a pleasant walk back, talking all the way of our dear dear friend. We spent the afternoon in ranging about the feilds, sometimes Mamma wou'd join us but not often, Grand Papa drank Tea with us, & after Tea we had a fine Syllabub, in the Even^g Louisa for a little sport mounted G Papa's horse, & rode towards Mount Peace. G. P. & I follow'd on foot, she rode about half a mile & then gave up the horse to its owner, we bid him good night & return'd home;—

Wednesday 26—This Morn^g the Chariot came for Louisa. I did all I cou'd to keep her but she must obey her mamma's orders, & away she went & left her friend Amanda, quite disconsolate at losing her companion. Felt very dull & dismal the remainder of the day, till towards even^g my spirits return'd & I enjoy'd the sweetness of the country air. Mamma still the same very low & dejected in mind.

Friday 28—After an early breakfast we all went to Mount Peace—staid about an hour, & then Papa & myself went to Town & Mamma & Uncle staid at Mount Peace.

Saturday 29—Zeleida [3] walked out with me yesterday morning. In the Even^g yesterday Louisa & Miss Stockton, came to see me. Leander also came, & after Tea they proposed a walk. We all agreed to it. Papa accompanied us, & we walk'd & talk'd till ten. I had not seen Leander for so long a time that I had a great deal to say to him; he told me, that he sett off for Europe in a fortnight & then I lose in a manner a friend, not I hope lose his friendship, but his company for ever. . . .

This Afternoon I dress'd myself & went with Zeleida & her sister & six more ladies & as many Gentlemen to visit M^rs

[3] An unidentified friend of Nancy's.

Moore who lives a mile from Town. We walk'd there, spent an agreable afternoon, were well entertained, walk'd in the most delightful gardens after Tea till Ten oclock & then return'd home. I went to Louisas where I have made my home since I have been in Town.

Tuesday 1 of June—This day we were to have spent at our Country retirement—Miss Stockton, Louisa, Major North, Major Jackson & myself. Mamma was to have staid in Town & I expected to have had one happy day—When Lo! (as usual) I was disappointed—for Louisas Mamma was so ill this Morn'g that she cou'd not leave her & so I broke up the party. I set off for the country by myself as Mamma setts off from P. tomorrow morn'g for Princeton. This was by far the hottest day I felt this year so that I enjoy'd the cool country air tho' I was alone.

Saturday 5—This morning Papa came to breakfast with me & brought with him a Mr Winthrop from Boston. I had had a very bad night & had taken tobacco to ease me, which acted upon me like an opiate so that I was asleep when Papa came into my chamber & awoke me. I told him how bad I was & try'd to excuse my coming down before a stranger when I was in so much pain, but he press'd me so much that at last I yeilded, got up & dress'd me & went down assuming as chearful an air as was in my power. We then breakfasted together, & I was charm'd with Mr Winthrop; he is a particular friend of my brothers. After breakfast we all went together to M. Peace where I took leave of Papa & Mr W. who sett off for Phi^a—I spent the remaining part of the day there, very much troubled at times with my face, tho being in so large a family serv'd to divert my attention. I came home very early in the even'g & very much indispos'd.

Sunday 6—I kept my bed all this day my face was so bad; in the afternoon two french Gentlemen came to see me, but were not admitted, nor wou'd they have been had I been ever so well, had my Papa & Mamma been absent as they were now.

Wednesday 9—Not so well today as yesterday. Papa came out this afternoon & told me that my Mamma was return'd & enliven'd me so much that I grew well presently.

Sunday 13—Felt very meloncholy all this morning, & kept my room, in the afternoon went with Mamma & Papa to hear Mr Duffield. After meeting I put Mamma down at our house & went to see Louisa. . . .

Spent the Evening at home with Mamma & a good old Lady nam'd Mrs Clarck.

Tuesday 15—This Morning after breakfast we drest ourselves, & order'd the carriage to pay Mrs Stewart a visit at Clifton. We found her & the rest of the family at home, & were treated with great politeness. We walk'd in their garden which is very beautiful, & found, when we return'd, a table cover'd with wine & fruit. They press'd us much to stay to dinner but as we were engaged to drink Tea with Mrs Peters in the afternoon we excus'd ourselves. We had an early dinner at home & set out immediately after to go to Bellville. But we were disappointed in our intended excursion for when we reach'd the ferry we found that the rope was broke & that the boat of consequence cou'd not go. So being nearer Town than Quid vis, we went there. I drank Tea and spent the Evening with Louisa and staid all night with her. In the morning about ten oclock I set off with Mamma for Quid vis.

Wednesday 16—This day I pass'd chiefly in reading to Mamma, & conversing with her. Expected Leander to Tea but he did not come.

Sunday 20—This day I think I spent chiefly as it ought to be spent with my dear mother: Grand Papa & my Uncle drank Tea with us.

Tuesday 22—I intended visiting Papa today as his business keeps him closely engaged in the City, but was prevented. I get used to disappointments. Spent the day at home employ'd as usual.

Thursday 24—Rode to Germantown today with Mamma who has been in very low spirits all day. I hear Leander sails next week & I shall not have it in my power to bid him farewell.

Friday 25—Reciev'd a letter from Leander, as a last testimony of his friendship. It was very affecting. He is gone! I am glad I did not take leave of him, it wou'd have affected me too much.

Undoubtedly a number of farewell notes passed between Nancy and Otto just before his departure for France. This fragment appears to be a part of the last one:

"Elmira has exceeded all my wishes; if it is possible to be happy in departing from the most amiable, the most generous Friend, I am rendered so by your note. The Idea that I shall hear from you or at least communicate my ideas and all my wishes to Elmira is not sufficient, *but condusive,* to my tranquillity. Elmira has seen me in various situations, every one of my Steps must deserve her approbation, and in leaving a Country in which I have been the *happiest* and the most *miserable* of men, I have at least the consolation to recollect that I have constantly acted according to the strictest rules of propriety. Permit me to think, Elmira, that this conduct gives me an unquestionable right upon your Friendship and that I ought to occupy a principal place in your esteem and perhaps—in your affection. Without these I should be miserable, whatever may be in other respects the agreable prospects that are bef[ore] me. Elmira will render me infinitely happy by informing me as often as possible of her situation, the means are easy and have been explained.

Adieu my amiable, my unfortunate Friend; May you remember that affection knows of no distance. May your past misfortunes be only preparation for the most delicious enjoyments which must be soon or late the reward of virtue.

[Unsigned]

Saturday 26—Mamma spent this day at Challiot & I spent the day at home very busy making sweet-meets for the winter.

Sunday 27—I spent this day entirely alone, except having the company of Books. I read, & meditated upon what I read. I transcribed some passages out of Blairs excellent sermons, & upon the whole spent the day much to my mind. Mamma return'd from Town this Even'g & my dear Brother whom I have not seen for this long long while accompanied her. I spent a delightful even'g with him.

Thursday July 1st—I went to Town this morning with my Brother—& had the happiness to see my dear Papa who[m] I had been absent from so long, & to bid my Uncle Shippen farewell before he went home; he has been upon a visit to Papa for this last three weeks. . . .

Friday 2ᵈ Louisa & myself spent the morning in rambling about the meadows & shady groves, & eating fruit which we have in abundance. After dinner we went to Belmont to see the beautiful Mʳˢ Peters. We spent a very agreable afternoon at that delightful place. We sett off for Town about 7 oclock,

& had a charming ride by moonlight untill we reach'd the suburbs of the city, where we were stop'd by a couple of highwaymen; as there was no gentlemen with us, not even the footman behind the carriage, we determin'd not to resist but give all the money we had about us. The Coachman attempted to defend us with his whip, but we call'd to him, & order'd him to be quick. Louisa gave all the change she had about her, & it satisfied the Robbers, after which we drove very rapidly into the Town.

Monday 5—Set off about nine oclock this morning for our retreat accompanied by Zeleida & Evelina in the charriot, & my Brother & Doct' James on Horse Back. We spent a charming day. Mamma at Mount Peace. We laugh'd, sung, play'd, walk'd talk'd & in short were as merry as possible; they left me in the Evening to enjoy my own reflections. Dear me! I'm quite tir'd of the country.

Monday 12—I feel happy to see my dear Mother so much better. This morn'g she appear'd quite composed & this afternoon rode to Town. I amused myself with book till just now, I am going to rest, & expect a more comfortable night than I have had this long time.

Tuesday 13—Mamma return'd from Town about 2 oclock & brought me a letter from Papa, who tells me that he has heard from the Manor, by a gentleman who is just come from there, & who brought me a message from my dear Child. She said "tell my dear Mamma that I am very well & love her dearly["]. Sweet soul! what wou'd I not give to see her—to embrace her. . . .

Friday 16—Still more alarm'd last night, so much so that I set up great part of it. The dog howl'd dreadfully. We thought

every door creak'd. We search'd all the house but found nobody. Mamma much worse all this day. Uncle A Lee paid us a
visit this Even'g, he enliven'd us a good deal.

Saturday 17—The country grows more & more disagreable to
me every day, but my fate has fix'd me here & I must try to
submit to it with a good grace. I spend all my time either alone
or with my distress'd Mother. Alass cou'd I console, or relieve
her misery it wou'd be some consolation to me, but it [is] out
[of] the power of mortals to do either so I hope & pray God
almighty will take pity on her. My Brother paid us a visit this
Evening, & gave us a pleasing account of a balloon that has been
exhibited 32 feet diameter which wou'd have answer'd the expectations of those who contrived it had it not taken fire.[4]

Sunday 18—This morning Mamma and my Brother went to
Town. I enjoy'd myself in reading, & meditating without being
disturb'd—& 2 or 3 hours pass'd away charmingly; a delightful
silence prevail'd all around me, till at length I was roused by a
number of country people who pass by & who were going into
a neighbouring wood to gather huckle berries. The simplicity,
& mirth w^h seem'd to reign among them, but above all I immagine a love of society tempted me from my solitary employments to join them. They were delighted and I no less happy,
in perceiving the emotions I excited in these innocent people.
We soon arrived in the wood, & having tir'd myself with pick-
ing and eating wild fruit I amused myself with the little children that were with us. I took one, a pretty little girl of about
4 years old with me to see one of my neighbours who lives in
the wood, a plain country family, but they were all gone to

---

[4] A contemporary reference to this balloon ascension is contained in the
Diary of Jacob Hiltzheimer, of Philadelphia, 1765-1798.

meeting, the House lock'd, & a faithful dog appear'd, who by his loud barking told us he kept good centry.

When I return'd I found the good people had left the place, & were on yᵉ way home. I follow'd with my little companion, who seem'd very fond of me & never once ask'd for her mammy. Just as I had left the woods, I perciev'd in the lane at some distance a Gentleman dress'd in black making hasty strides towards me. I cou'd not immagine who it cou'd be in that dress. I know none of my acquaintance that I cou'd suppose wou'd find me out in my retirement. At last he came near enough for me to discover that it was my old friend & acquaintance Dʳ Cutting. I was very glad to see him. We talk'd over old times on our way to the house, and ask'd so many questions on either side that it was with difficulty they were all answer'd. I ordered some cool punch & invited him to eat some fruit & milk which he refus'd being engaged to dine with Mʳˢ Craik ⁵—so I dined alone, & then took my book & went to stroll in the orchard. In the Evening my Uncle A Lee came to see me, & supp'd with me tete-a-tete.

Thursday 29—This retirement begins to be very tiresome. My poor Mammas state of health is not the greatest of my troubles. Alass my heart is ill at ease with regard to my lovely Child who I have not heard from this long long time. what can be the reason? Is she ill? Is she, alass— I know not what to think. Sure nobody has so many troubles as I have.

Friday 30—Mamma seem'd so much better today it revived in a manner my drooping spirits. She held a long conversation with me today equally instructing & entertaining.

⁵ The wife of Dr. Craik, Washington's personal physician.

Monday 2^d—Today I experienced a very great change from the still life in the country to the noisy bustle of the Town. The day too was remarkably warm, & I so fatigu'd with moving, I wish'd again for the retirement that yesterday I was wearied of. Tomorrow I shall have my wish.

Tuesday 3^d—I arrived here about 11 o'clock & found my Mamma as well as I left her.

Wednesday 4th—As usual, preventing reflection, by being employ'd.

Thursday 5—Very busy making my brother up a piece of linen.

Saturday 7—I work'd very industriously all this morn'g, & after dinner rode on horseback to pay a visit to Mrs Lenox an agreable neighbour I have where I found a large party.

Wednesday 11.—Nothing can be a more distressing sight than to see a beloved Parent dying before ones Eyes; alass I fear my poor Mother will not last long. She takes little nourishment & pines to death: when will my afflictions end. O may they prove of service to me & teach me not to set my heart on things below.

Thursday 12—My dear Mother more distress'd today than usual—wou'd I cou'd comfort her.

Friday 13—Good Mr Sproat visited my poor Mamma this after noon, & she I thou't derived some comfort from his conversation & prayers. My cousin S. B. paid me a short visit in the Evening.

Saturday 14—Mamma seem'd so much better today & so conversible that it made me quite happy.

Sunday 15—Pass'd this day entirely alone except an hour or two my poor distress'd mother permitted me to set with her.

Some time after the middle of August—allowing for the long passage from Europe in that day—Nancy heard from Louis Otto:

L'Orient, July 24th 1784

I was very sorry, my dear Friend, before my departure from Philadelphia to have it not in my power to see you. However there is something so distressing in taking leave of a person we esteem that it was perhaps better for me not to be gratified in my wishes.

Tho' our navigation has been pretty short and fortunate it has tired me almost to death. There is no situation in Life, no Company whatsoever that could render the Sea agreable to me. Particular circumstances of which you are well informed rendered it still more disgusting and the first happy moment I enjoy since my departure from Chester is our Landing at l'Orient. The remembrance of all my former connections seems to revive at once and I think myself already blessed by the embraces of some of my old bossom Friends and by the tender meeting with my Mother and Sisters whom I have not seen since six years.

Whatever may be the prospect of my future employments I shall always cherish the Memory of some of my particular Friends in America and to hear from them will be for me a great source of hapiness. You will remember, my amiable Friend, that you promised to write as often as possible and you know how interesting it must be for me to be acquainted with the particulars of your Situation and of your Family. Dr Shippen I believe is not the most copious Correspondent in the World and I have reason to put more confidence in your attention than in the little time he could spare me from so many avocations.

I shall not repeat the contents of my last note. I flatter myself you will not easily forget them.

If Mrs Shippen will accept of the tender wishes of a man she has once honoured with her esteem I hope you will remember me to her. I have received so many civilities in your Family that

I shall for ever remember them. In a few days we set off to Paris from whence I shall write to you more circumstancially.

Adieu, my amiable Friend; may you find in the Consciousness of your own worth those Blessings of which Fate has vainly attempted to deprive you. If in your philosophical retreat you remember your absent Friend think that you can not more effectually return his tender regard than by writing him very often.

O.

Monday 16—Being tired with setting so constantly at my work, In the forenoon I order'd my horse & took a pleasant little ride to Challiot & Mount Peace, & so home again. I felt great benefit from my ride.

Wednesday 18—Spent a most delightful day in Town. Papa had a very large company & he was pleased to say I graced the head of his Table. Pass'd a charming Even^g with Papa & Brother. set up till eleven oclock.

Thursday 19—I arose at 5. oclock this morn'g & set off to my dear Mamma in the country, found her as usual & spent as usual a solitary day.

Friday 20—This afternoon my grand Papa came to see us. Dear good old man, a happy serenity dwells allways in his countenance. His conversation is replete with good humor, & good sense.

Thursday 26—Dined in Town with a very large company. The dinner was made for my good friend Mr Duer; who is just come from N. Y. who I asked a hundred questions about my darling child.

Friday 27—I came from Town about 10 oclock & found my poor mamma as usual.

Saturday 28—This afternoon Mrs Mif[f]lin & her sister drank Tea with me & Mr Harrison Mrs Lee Mr Walker & my Brother. Mrs Blair & Mrs Hodge drank Tea in Mammas chamber with her. I spent a very lively afternoon.

Sunday 29—This day I spent as I do the Lord's day in general; & I read the divine Herveys meditations in the morn^{g} I enjoy'd the calm serenity of this morning in a particular manner. My Uncle Lee came to see me this Ev^{g}

Monday 30—I arose at about 5 oclock this Morning, & went to Town on Horseback accompanied by my Uncle.

Tuesday 31—I set out this Morn^{g} at six oclock for the country on horseback, alone, excepting a servant behind. I found my dear Mamma much indisposed. I was so indeed myself, but a little nap entirely recover'd me. In the afternoon I rode with a young lady that lives in the neighbourhood, thro' a most delightful wood, & call'd upon a country neighbour & spent part of the afternoon there. We then went round & stop'd at my Grandpapa's & drank Tea; poor dear old man, he is ill; I found my father there. The family seems a little alarm'd for him. We had a pleasant ride home on horseback my Papa accompanied us.

Wednesday 1 of September—My Uncle Arthur Lee came to spend the day with me, & we spent it very merrily & happily. In the Evening we went accompanied by my fair neighbour to take a pleasant walk in the fields. We had not walked far when we perceived a small house at the foot of hill with a little green lawn before the door & a very little garden on the right hand full of vegetables & a few flowers. The neatness of the place tempted us to walk in, where we found a venerable old man &

his wife, & dog which made the whole of this poor family. The old man was too old to work, & so the wife, who is not much younger, gathers wild herbs & carries them on her head to the market which is five mile[s] from where she lives—in order to get a living. I asked her what she lived on. She said a little bread when she cou'd get it, or any thing else. In a very hospitable manner she offer'd us some of a very brown loaf she had just made, we accepted it because it wou'd give her pleasure. My Uncle laid a piece of silver on their clean wooden table, which the old woman did not perceive till we were just going away when she honestly offer'd it to us, thinking it was left by mistake. It was return'd to her with assurances of our good opinion of her. It was late before we got home, & we talk'd much of our little adventure.

Tuesday 7—Received a letter from Papa desiring me to come & live in Town with him, as Mamma is so fond of solitude & I am not. I think to comply with his desires, leave her in the Country with some clever elderly person. Busy all day moving & packing up.

Wednesday 8—Finished packing & moving this morning & went to Town in the afternoon.

Thursday 9—Return'd this morn'g to the country, to bring some necessaries to Town. Found my poor dear Mamma walking in a solitary manner in the fresh mow'd meadow. I dined in the country & return'd to Town in the Evening.

Monday 13—This day employ'd as usual in domestic affairs, preserving peaches &c. Mr Duponceau & Mrs Jones drank Tea with me.

Tuesday 14—This afternoon Miss Shippens visited me & in the Even'g I visited Mrs Montgomery who is just arrived from France.

Thursday 16—Very busy all day. How happy it is for me I can be so, as it serves to take off my attention from those things that so distress me by the reflection. Col. Armstrong & Mr Prager, & Zeleida drank Tea with me, & we pass'd a very agreable Even^g

Sunday 19—Had company to Dinner w^h prevented my attending public worship. Oh how wrong! to be prevented by any thing, much less having company.

Monday 20—Passed the day at home attending to domestic duties. I was engaged out but excused myself, General Gates called on me after breakfast & brought me a letter from one of my sister in laws Mrs Tillotson. She mentions my darling child in a manner that gave me great delight. She is expected here soon.

Tuesday 21—I accompanied Mrs Stead this Morning to Bartrams Garden, 5 miles from Town, we had a charming party & Gentlemen attendants on Mrs S. & myself.

Wednesday 22—Zeleida called on me this Morning. About 12 oclock I went with Mrs Stead & a large party of Gentlemen to see some new paintings exquisitely finished. In the afternoon Miss Shippen, Mr Edwards, Mr Purviance & Mr Wikoff spent the afternoon with me.

Sunday 26—So much indisposed today, I cou'd not go to church. Ah! how seldom do I go when I am well, but I intended going today, had I been well enough.

Wednesday 29—I had a very bad night, my face was so bad I groan'd with pain. It is easier thank God today. This morning I received a letter from my Uncle A. Lee who has lately seen my dear Peggy. He speaks in her praise as does every body that has seen her; she has indeed in my opinion an angels mind. O! how I long to see her. Cruel separation! how hard my fate!

Arthur Lee's letter is dated Albany Sepr 22^d 1784:

Dear Nancy—

I call'd at Clermont as I promised. I was delighted with the old Lady, with Mrs Montgomery Miss Clida or Eliza Miss Kitty, & not the least with your dear little Peggy. I always tho't Eliza pretty & think so still—but Kitty is Peggy's friend & favorite. The family appear to love one another & to be very harmonious which always gives me great pleasure, as the contrary appearance is a constant cause of uneasiness to me. The Chancellor & Mrs Livingston supp'd with us & were very friendly with me. I do assure you that I think the old Lady a most respectable & agreeable Lady, & regret exceedingly that your fortune has removed you so far from her. She talked of Peggy's going to Philadelphia in the winter, but seem'd to think it would be a terrible journey for her, & upon the whole I think it will not be prudent to urge it.

I beat Mrs Montgomery at Chess. But it was by laying a trap for her. I made way for her pawn to go to Queen. Allur'd by the brilliancy of the attcheivement, she neglected her poor King, who the very move before she was to make a Queen, was taken prisoner without resource. Tell Tommy that this is the way to win all or any of your Sex. That to captivate them he must apply, not to their reason or their interest, but to their fancy. He must keep before them constantly an object attractive of that, & he may beguile them of any thing—This my sweet Nancy, you must allow, will win every daughter of our Mother Eve.

I have sent Peggy a compleat tea-apparatus for her Baby. Her Doll may now invite her Cousins Doll to tea, & parade her tea-table in form. This must be no small gratification to her. It would be fortunate if happiness were always attainable with equal ease.

My love to my Sister—Papa & Tommy.

Adieu my dear Nancy—take care of yourself & of the Family.
A. L.

Friday the 1ˢᵗ of October—I went this morning with my dear Papa to Quid vis to see my dear afflicted Mother. We found her low, & her spirits very much dejected. She won't hear of coming to Town but prefers the Country because she can be entirely alone. Mʳ Mercer a delegate of Congress play'd chess & drank Tea with me & was so obliging to offer me a Ticket for the Concert this Evening but I was so much undress'd I cou'd not go, so he went after Tea without me.

Saturday 2—Genˡ Gates called on me this morn'g. I play'd with him at Chess, he beat me 2 games to my great mortification. Spent the Even'g at Mʳˢ Steads. Mʳ Stead & Zeleida called on me this Morning; I play'd Cards at Steads this Even'g till ten oclock.

Monday 4ᵗʰ—While I [was] setting very busy trimming a new hat today I received an affecᵗ note from Mʳˢ Stead requesting me & the rest of the family to spend the Even'g there at Tea & Cards. Papa desired I wou'd go so I sent word that I'd wait upon her; but indeed I think it wrong for me to touch a card for I no sooner set down to them but I feel so great a propensity for gaming that I intend to make a resolution not to play at all. Grand Papa dined with us, Miss M. Shippen paid me a short visit in the afternoon return'd from Cards at Eleven. Play'd with Gen. Gates & lost 3 dollars.

Tuesday 5—Rode out with Emelia today to Mount Peace, found the family just recovering from the fall fever which they have had severely; gave my Aunt & Uncle B. a ride, then left Emelia at Mount Peace while I went to see my Mother. Found her very low & much dejected; the day was fine & I shou'd have had a very pleasant ride back if it had not been that my poor Mothers situation left a very impression on my mind & made me low spirited. How very unhappy is my situation at present separated perhaps for life from an only & beloved Child, & living with a Mother whose situation is by far more distressing than any one can conceive. I live retired & confined, but not so much so as I shou'd have thought my unhappy circumstances required. How much shou'd I have suffer'd in my present situation if those prejudices which are customary to people of my birth had holden their empire over me; if, for example, I had annexed much value to luxury & showy dress, I shou'd now cast a doleful look on my plain suit; whereas their happy form join'd to neatness, abundantly suffice my vanity.

Wednesday 6—Walk'd a great deal this morn'g doing some business in the shopping way; writ to Maria by Mrs Stead; in the afternoon was dress'd by the hairdresser to pay a brides visit to Mrs Bradford. Found a room full of company; but took my leave early not being pleased with the reception I met with from the Bride; perhaps she is one of those who think my Conduct with regard to my poor unhappy husband wrong—or perhaps it was accident—I was however mortified—especially as some of the company was ask'd to stay & dance, & as I was one of those who was not ask'd. I went to Mrs Vaughns where I drank Tea again & was treated with the greatest attention & politeness; the family have lately been to the Manor where they saw my sweet little girl. They told me they left her well & happy.

By some mistake a week was left out of this journal. [Note in Nancy's handwriting.]

Friday, the fifteenth—Ordered the Carriage early this morning & went to Quid vis to bring home my dear Mamma. I went alone & as I rid along thro' the most delightful country, I cou'd not help admiring how faithfully nature fulfills the eternal laws which are prescribed it to be useful & to subserve the welfare of the creatures at all times, & in all seasons. The winter approaches, the flowers disappear & even with the rays of the great lamp of day the earth hath lost its splendid appearance; but these despoiled plains still awoke in a sensible mind an emotion of pleasure. Here it is doth it say, that the copious harvest was collected and it raises to heaven an Eye of Gratitude. Dropped are the leaves of all the fruit trees, faded is the herbage of the fields. Here I stopped, then bringing my Ideas home to my own bosom I said to myself, the smiling aspect which my destiny offered is now equally obscured, & my exterior splendor is fallen like the foliage that crown'd this youthful shrub. Perhaps the lot of man hath also its seasons; if it be so, I will during the mournful days of my winter, nourish and support my soul with the fruits that education and experience have amassed for me. . . .

Saturday 16—This morning while I was taking my mornings walk my poor Mamma ordered the carriage to take a ride. I came home just as she was setting off, & offer'd to accompany her; as she was too weak to ride by herself, but she refused & said I wou'd oppose what she was going to do, therefore begged her maid might be call'd to go with her; she not being in the way I call'd mine, & ordered her to dress herself & wait upon my Mother. She did so & to my great surprize found after she was in the Carriage that she gave orders to be drove out of Town. I spent the remainder of the day in the greatest anxiety for her, indeed all the family were anxious upon her account. In the even'g the coachman return'd & said his Mistress was in the country & said she chose to be there alone; what a dreadful situation to be in! given up to the extreamest meloncholy; who knows alas! how soon that the happiness they now enjoy, may be torn from them. O may I be enabled to glean from my present unhappy Situation patience & resignation to the divine will.

Monday 18—I went to see my dear Mamma in the carriage this morn'g, before I had got a mile I met my sister Tillotson & her family coming to Town. It gave me great joy to meet them so opportunely & I begged they wou'd make our house their home while they stay'd but they excused themselves saying they had a great many servants & much baggage & only intended staying a day in Town. They were on their way to Baltimore. I turn'd back as soon as they left me & hurried home to dress & then went to visit them. They have a sweet little baby who I almost devour'd it is so like its sweet little Cousin my darling Peggy. I spent an hour with them in agreable Chit-Chat, invited them to dinner tomorrow, but they set out early in the morn'g. I then came home sent a servant off to Mamma with some necessarys for her & my respects & apologies for not waiting upon her. In the afternoon Mr Tillotson his Lady, Miss Livingston & Dr Armstrong favor'd me with their company to Tea & we spent a very agreable evening. Mrs T. delighted me with many anecdotes concerning my darling Child, & says she is the idol of all who know her.

Tuesday 19—I went to see my relations this morning; found them busy preparing for their journey. I embrace the dear Margaretta, my lovely little neice, & bid them adieu wishing them every happiness. I came home & filled a handsome basket with oranges & Cakes & sent to them for their journey; they are charming people & the family altogether, (except my unfortunate husband) delightful. How unhappy it is for me I am prevented by my unfortunate situation from being with them. They are all sensible, amiable, & pleasing to the greatest degree. I went to the Concert in the Evening with my papa & Mr Bendon. The company was very small, but the music was charming.

Wednesday 20—I pass'd almost all this morn'g in shopping, & made several pretty purchases. After dinner I gave some necessary orders in the family, & then began to dress for a Brides visit. It is a tedious employment this same dressing. It took me 3 hours at least, what a deal of time to be wasted! but custom, & fashion must be attended to. I was ready when Miss Morris call'd upon me & we went together to Mrs Whartons. The room was full of company, & the Bride look'd beautiful, & I judg'd from the looks at the Company towards me that I look'd tolerable; I was dres'd entirely in white except a suit of pink Beaus & had on a new Balloon Hat. I came home about 8 oclock & play'd piquet with Papa till ten.

Wednesday 21—I went this Morning to the Country with Louisa, to see my dear Mamma. She was worse in my opinion tho she thought she was much the same. I prevail'd on her to return with us to Town, & I think the ride did her some service. I visited another Bride this afternoon, found a great deal of company. After Tea, I paid a short visit to Mrs Stewart. I was taken at the Brides with a bad tooth ach which was so violent when I came home that I went to bed almost distracted with pain, which continued all night.

Wednesday 27—Last night I was worse than ever, I was obliged to have my Papa called. He gave me something to ease me, & I fell asleep & did not wake till late when to my great joy I found the gum bile broke & my face entirely easy, tho' very much swell'd. I spent the day in comfort as I cou'd read, & work alternately without pain.

Saturday 30—How very dull my time passes away! No company, & my eyes so painful that I can't read. I think, I meditate on my past life & my future prospects, but neither please me. Sweet hope now & then comes in to my relief that a change for the better may take place in my hitherto variagated life. I went down this morning to breakfast for the first time since my illness. My Father seemed much pleased to see me, & introduced my Uncle R H L [Richard Henry Lee] to me who is here upon a visit.

"How very dull my time passes away! No company . . . !" Nancy scarcely had use now for the two pages in the back of her journal with its careful apportionment of every precious minute of the day and headed: *A Proper distribution of the 24 hours.* A budgeteer before the days of budgeting, she had allotted:

For rest six hours only—in general—
The first three morning hours ought to be passed in study—& closet duties & occasionally in any epistolary amusements—
Two hours to be allotted to domestic management, at different times of the day as occasions require—
Five hours to your needle, music, drawings, geography, &c &c in these to be included the assistance & inspection, given to servants in the needle works requir'd for the family.

Two hours to be alloted to your first two meals but if conversation, or the desire of friends, require it to be otherwise never scruple to oblige and as it may be hard not to exceed in this appropriation I will put down

One hour more to dinner time conversation to be added or subtracted as occasions offer'd, or the desire of friends may require—

The remaining Five hours—

to be occasionally allotted to conversation, visiting or recieving the visits of friends, or to reading either to yourself alone or to the family—& this allotment of time may be called your fund, upon which you may draw to satisfy your other debts—

The seventh day to be kept as it ought to be kept & some part of it to be employ^d in works of mercy, & sometimes an hour allotted in it to visiting the neighbouring poor—

A journal ordinary ought to be kept by every young Lady—& once a week you should rekon with yourself—& if within the 144 hours contain'd in the six days you have made your account even, note it accordingly If otherwise carry the debit to the other weeks account; as thus: "Debtor to the artical of working so many hours" —and so the rest—

A Proper distribution of time indeed! But the next entry proves that it was scarcely possible to live by any set routine:

Tuesday 2^d—Let me see, how have I employ'd my time today? The same way that I employ'd it yesterday, & the day before, & the day before that—indeed there is such a sameness in my life that the particulars of it are hardly worth seting down. However it may be of service to me some future day to see how my life passes away now & compare it with the manner in which it passes away then. This morn'g I gave orders to the servants as usual for the business of the day, then took a little work in my hand, & set down before the fire, to think, how I shou'd dispose of myself in the Evening. The morn'g I generally devote to working or reading, and I concluded to go to the concert. Then I consider'd what I wou'd dress in, & having determined that important point, I felt light & easy, & set down to the table & eat a very hearty dinner; I then set down to my work for half an hour, paid a visit to my Mamma's Chamber, & seated myself to my toilet—I was ready at six, & called upon Emelia who was going & found her ready. Dr James accompanied us, we found a full room & spent a Charming Evening.

Here occurs a blank page and a long break in the journal. The orderly course of events is hopelessly broken. January, 1785, seems to have been a period of emotional strain for Nancy, although her correspondence with Otto was on the calm basis of affectionate friendship. The three letters here given must have reached her in late December and early January.

In the other world, December 4, [1784]
10,001,781.

Madam!

Since my death, that is, since the time on which circumstances prevented me from having the happiness of conversing with you, I did not receive the least intelligence from Your World. Permit me to take hold of this opportunity to send you a few lines from these gloomy abodes, Mr Ingersol who has resolved to return into life for a very important transaction, is so kind as to carry this letter and I hope you will give him a kind reception.

Travelling having allways been my greatest passion, his Plutonic Majesty condemned me on my arrival here to make a Journey into the moon. A Butterfly was immediately sadled to carry my baggage and my own person to that renowned planet. There I was happy enough to find a bottle with the inscription: *Good Sense of Mr Waittoolong.* I was a little ashamed of that discovery but had presence of mind enough to lay claim on the bottle and carry it with me in my *portemanteau.* My Butterfly, who had been once a very great *Beau,* proposed a little excursion into the planet *Venus,* but having recovered my bottle I could not possibly comply with his extravagant insinuations, and returned in this Kingdom, where I have got allready a number of acquaintances. These are of a very particular kind and you will perhaps be pleased with their description. One of them, a Lady of 20. Years, is extravagant enough to think before she speaks and to laugh only at her own follies. Another, an Attorney, pretends never to receive money but when he has gained his cause. An other, an old husband, is allways of the opinion of his wife, and his wife does never talk of books though she has read a great deal. A Republican, who thinks that virtue ought to be the principal foundation of a good Government; a Baron who talks of the equality of mankind; a Physician who is candid enough to say that he is ignorant; a Merchant, that offers his money at one per cent; a Lady who confesses that she is pass'd fifty, &c. &c. all these curious Caracters surround me, and I hope that you will pity my distressing situation and order me to return in Your world.—A thousand compliments to my Sweet Friend and believe me to be with the greatest respect and the most tender attachment

Madam

Your most obedient
humble servant

John Waittoolong

Patience Island in Elysium
the 13th December. [1784]

Madam

Nothing could be more agreeable to me in my gloomy retirement as a letter from you, the black Sylph who carried it to me disappeared as fast as happiness and I could not give him any answer. You will probably receive this letter by a traveller who intends to make a tour through the world upon the tail of a Comet. —This will appear extraordinary to you, but I am now so used to strange Scenes that nothing can surprise me; as to *Boston* he has not yet made his appearance here; besides his reception would be very indifferent, as it is a general prejudice in this world that Dogs are not worthy to be in company with human beings.

Since I recovered my bottle, Madam, the pretended instruction you received in my Company, must be looked at as a mere compliment, but even a compliment is agreeable when it is said with so much delicacy, and though I read your letter only ten times I am ashamed of the barbarous Style of my epistles if compared with yours. You will be surprised that we speak so bad English in Paradise, but you know that the better sort of people seldom come this way.—

Though I am very anxious to see you, Madam, I hope you will never pay me a visit on those terms you mention in your letter.

I respect very much your Councillors, but the task imposed upon me is too hard. An Astronomer just arrived from your World informs us that his Colleagues have discovered a new *planet;* when your *Resolve* will be known some ill natured *Rittenhouse* will discover still more planets and I should never have done travelling till I turn myself a Planet. Besides all our Buterflies have been ordered back to your World to attend your Churches, your Balls, Concerts and Weddings and it would be very difficult for me to get any accommodation for my Journey. It is true that *Rosinante* is still here but the poor animal is so lame that it would be cruel to propose her so long a Journey . . . my respectful Compliments, and contribute as much to her happiness as your own heart desires you to do—that is, more than any other human being can possibly conceive.—When nature had done all what was in her power to make a perfect Woman, when she had graced her Work with all the beauty of Youth, with all the Charms of domestic virtue, there was still something left—and that something was at last [mutilated] . . . She gave her the tender heart of [illegible] . . .

Your most devoted
J. *Wait patiently.*

CHAPTER VIII

1785-1787

I

SOMETIME during January, 1785, Colonel Livingston went to Philadelphia. In his desire for a reconciliation with Nancy he suggests formally and humbly an arrangement for an interview with her at his lodgings:

I know my Dearest Girl of no Objection to what you propose But a Necessity for some Arrangements which cannot be made previous to Your Determination at least Six Months before, perhaps future Considerations may make it longer, and if we were perfectly agreed in every thing else that Term could not be Shortened, however I press not for anything which may be disagreeable to you.

The Lodgings I am at are Retired & you will be sure of seeing no one but myself should you think it Advisable, add to this it will be in your Power to Shorten the Conference if displeasing. I give you my Honour no restraint shall be laid upon your Inclinations of which I hope you cannot doubt? My Reason for Pressing this matter more than I had any Idea I should ever have done is from a persuasion, which indeed amounts to Certainty, that if we ever again United, that Union will and can only be founded upon explanations that must from *Necessity* if ever take place before I leave Phila^da Therefore for the last time I entreat you seriously to Consider this Matter with the attention it deserves. Your Brother I hope will attend you.

But if you are Determined on the Contrary, I cannot miss the proper Conclusion, & in Consequence cannot ever again admit a Conference upon this Subject.

Do not Construe this last sentence into an attempt to force you into any Measures that you may think improper. I abhor & detest

225

the thought. I speak the Truth—& should despise you, if you could on any occasion swerve from the dignity of your Station, which I think can not receive the least Tarnish from a Conference with your Husband, after a three years *Cruel* absence.

I can no more farewell . . .

Yours sincerely & Affectionately

H. B. L.

Mrs. Ann Hume Livingston

Nancy, feeling encouraged and happy over the idea of a reconciliation with her husband, for the sake of being permanently with her child, takes up her journal again:

February 24ᵗʰ 1785—This is my Birth day. I intend from this time to continue my journal, which I have neglected doing for these (near) four Months past. I heartily pray that I may so spend my time as to make me here after happy in the reflection. But O! may I have a better motive for trying to act well. O that my principal aim may be to please God, & appear good in his sight. May I from this time never offend "Him" in act, word, or deed! May I be duly mindful of every duty so as to be acceptable to God & approved of by virtuous people. Within these last three months my time has passed in a continual round of insipid amusements, & trivial occupations. I have however in the meantime, not long since, seen my husband, after an absence of three years; he came to this City upon business. I contrived however to see him, and thank God am reconciled to him. I have now a prospect of living happily with him & my darling Child.

. . . .

Meanwhile, welcome news of Peggy comes from Nancy's uncle, Richard Henry Lee, who is President of the Congress now meeting in New York, and preparing to move into his new house:

226

New York, Jan—17, 1785

. . . I have twice seen my sweet little cousin Peggy Livinston [sic] since my arrival here— She is a very pretty & very chatty & loves her Uncle mightily. She promises to come & see me often when I get in the President's House which will be this week having hired Mrs. Franklin's house in the Street where little Peggy lives— It is a very elegant House, and provided with every accommodation— I think that little Peggy is very much like her picture in your father's House.

Mr de Barthold has by this time rigged me out in such a manner as to convert the old president into a young Beau Very well, if for the good of my country I must be a Beau why I will be a Beau. . . .

Meanwhile Nancy attends a series of lectures on physical geography and astronomy given by the itinerant blind philosopher Dr. Moyse; she reads French; takes lessons on the guitar; serves as hostess for her father's dinner guests, and goes to an occasional ball. On Tuesday, March 1st, she writes in her journal:

"Very busy preparing for a very large company who dined here today. I left them soon after dinner & drest for a Ball at Mrs Morris. I danced till 2 & came home much fatigued had 3 partners but not one that pleased me among them . . .

She is evidently in a happy frame of mind over the prospect of reconciliation. Suddenly, without a word of warning, Nancy gets a letter from her eccentric husband which abruptly ends all hope or chance for any adjustment.

Eight o'Clock

Tomorrow Morning at Nine I leave this Fatal Place, dreadfully so to me as tis from here I must Continually date my Misfortunes. I take my Passage by Water in hopes some happy Accident may Rid you of a painfull Restraint and me of My Woes.

I have this Day endeavoured to Flatter myself, that you would have deigned to see me at the Only Place where we could meet with Propriety. But I Confess more with a View to keep up my almost exhausted Spirits than from real expectation.

And I write now more for the purpose of Venting an almost Bursting Heart, than from Design of Obtaining any other Advantage. And as—in such Situations of it I have in the Anguish that wrung my Soul more than once offended without intention, or premeditation, which I hope you will do me the justice to acquit me of. I therefore Beseech you to pardon any expressions of the above Description which may in our Intercourse may have Escaped me & be assured that tho I feel myself Cruelly Injured, my Heart will never allow me to Complain. With every wish for your felicity, I Remain

Henry B. Livingston

Nancy's reaction to this letter is revealed in her journal:

"I shew'd it to Papa & received his advice concerning it. This letter has destroy'd all my hopes." Some days later she writes:

Saturday 5— . . . Supp'd tete a tete with Papa, who says he sees it will never do for me to return to my inflexible husband . . .

Tuesday 8—Spent part of this day in read[ing] to my poor Mamma who is much better than she has been but is still afflicted with the most strange affection of the mind. Spent a most charming Evening at a Ball given by Mr D^e Marbois.

Wednesday 9—Heard Dr Moyse again this Even^g upon trade winds & he gave us an account of the formation of the earth.

Thursday 10—Worked a little at my needle, read, sang, play'd upon the guittar &c &c in the morn'g gave the necessary orders to the servants of the family. After dinner prepar'd for the Assembly where I spent a most agreable Even'g; had five agreable partners. . . . When I came home about one oclock I was much alarm^d with [news] I had given me of the coachmans falling off of the box & nearly killing himself. After he put me down at the assembly he came home, took up the maids & carried them to a Tavern, treated them with wine & cakes & got so drunk himself that off he tumbled. There was every thing done for him that was necessary, but the poor creatures groans still vibrate in my ears.

Friday 11—Spent the morn'g as usual sometimes doing something, sometimes nothing. About 4 in the Afternoon Dr Cutting came in, & we spent the afternoon in the most agreable chit-chat manner, drank a very good dish of Tea together & then separated. . . . I read a little & then retired early to rest.

Saturday 12—Have not been well today; afflicted with a very bad cold but saw a large company at home, the Craig family, Mrs Vardon & several Gent^n—the Even'g pass'd off in the most agreable manner. When the company was gone Mamma join'd us & appeared better than usual which gave us all the greatest pleasure.

[Here a leaf has been torn out]

Very little is told in the journals for the rest of the year of 1785, but a great deal in the letters from Tommy, Mrs. Theodorick Bland, Uncle Arthur Lee and Uncle Richard Henry Lee.

An engaging letter from Tommy describes the stately elegance of the President's house in New York City now occupied by Uncle Richard Henry as President of the Congress and also gives an intriguing picture of little Peggy:

I find my uncle here in a Palace, and think indeed that he does the honors of it, with as much ease and dignity as if he had been always crowned with a real diadem. My chamber is a spacious and elegant one and prettily furnished. I now write in it, and which way soever I turn my eyes I find a triumphal Car, a Liberty Cap, a Temple of Fame or the Hero of Heroes, all these and many more objects of a piece with them, being finely represented on the hangings—Never were more honors I believe paid to any man, and very seldom with more cordiality than are daily heaped upon the head of the master of this Castle. I rejoice at it because I believe no man ever better deserved them. Billets of invitation without number, visiting cards and letters of friendly congratulations fill every mantle piece and corner of every chamber. Centinels guard his door, crowds of obedient domestics run to his call and fly at his command, and a profusion of the delicacies & luxuries of good living crowns his hospitable board. This you will say is not among the most unpleasant circumstances of the business in your son's estimation. I acknowledge it my good father, I acknowledge that from a strict observance of you and a constant endeavor from my youth to do as my father did, I have imbibed an Epicurean taste, and really I think with Monsr De St Evremond whose expression I have just used, that even Cato's virtues without it would not make us completely estimable or happy. But he speaks as I mean to do of all the pleasures we are suseptible of when he uses the word Epicurean—

Last night I paid my first visit to the Old Lady, my uncle introduced me to her; She received me with very great politeness and made many affectionate enquiries after my Sister my dear Mamma and yourself, & expressed great concern for Mamma's situation; She then sent for the little darling; Miss Margaret had heard in the course of the afternoon that her Uncle Tommy Shippen was come to town, and had made the name re-echo through every part of the Entry Staircase and parlour—Yet when she was brought in, she put on the most old maidenist coyness you can conceive, and said that I was not her uncle, for I was a *Gentleman*, by which I suppose she meant a Stranger. However with the assistance of a Cake (for she is Mother's own daughter in that respect) and a good deal of coaxing she owned that she conceived me to be her own Uncle, but not her uncle Tom, for he was in Baltim? but her Uncle Shippen. The old Lady tells me that when my Uncle Arthur came to take leave of her he had been asking her what he must say to her Mamma, her Grand-Papa Shippen, her Grand Mamma Shippen, and her uncle Tommy Shippen, she accordingly sent them her love, and when he had been gone a few minutes, she very gravely broke forth in this Soliloquy: Grand-Papa Shippen! Grand Mamma Shippen! Uncle Shippen! What then am I Shippen!

The old Lady supposes her a prodigy of good sense. But I should have told you that after I had bribed her with Cake and Tea, and with a sight of my red pocketbook which she insisted on being allowed to call hers, she seated herself very much at her ease on my lap & held up her little ruby lips, as often as I wished to kiss them, which was every minute, and practised so many little endearing ways upon me that the old Lady could not keep her hands off of her, but almost smothered her with kisses. She is excessively fond of her Uncle the Pres*—he sends her Good things as she calls them, and she searches his pockets with the greatest freedom imaginable for something which she thinks he must have at the bottom of them for her. She takes the round two or three times in the Evening to dispense her Curtesys and her kisses to all her uncles and aunts, whom she mentions by name before she makes her curtesy, and then offers up the little mouth which really appears to me in great danger of being kissed to pieces.

Nancy's devoted friend, Martha Bland, writes her from Virginia during May and June, referring pleasantly to old times together in Philadelphia:

Cawsons May 12th 1785 Virginia
. . . I have had a thousand times a Mind to begin a Correspondence with you, but I fear'd to venture upon your time knowing how well you Can, and do, fill it up. But for the future you shall have no Cause to complain of me for few people take so much delight as I do in dweling on scenes which have given me such *Pleasure* as I've experienced under your dear Papa and Mam-

mas Happy, Hospitable, & Cheerfull roof. Tell your Mamma I yet flatter myself we shall see the whole groop from forth Street, in Virginia, and then we will Laugh at all the little foolerys we have past together & by no means leave our friend Arthur out. Sweet little Peggy too, Bob sends her twenty kisses. . . .

As to my situ[ation] it is as pleasing as my Country will admit of. I want nothing to make me Happy in this life but a little more agreable society; such as a charming Evening in Philadelphia affords, what tho it gives My Lady Scandal an opportunity, to thro' her shafts—yet innocence & true virtue hold her at arms length especially when Supported by the best of Husbands. Good [God] Bless you my dear Nancy! and if you *cou'd be* as happy as I wish you to be your Lot wou'd be perfect felicity. . . .

M Bland

Tommy is making preparations for a voyage to England and a several years' stay abroad, for his father plans for him to study law at the Inner Temple in London and then to make the grand tour. In one of his letters to his sister in the summer, Tommy refers to Uncle Arthur Lee's appointment to the Treasury Board and adds his opinion—uncommon in that day—that women should be interested in public affairs:

I know that in all governments Republican as well as Monarchical who direct and manage the purse must have a great share in the government of the Nation and because I know of no person better qualified or more to be relied on than our good Uncle A Lee.

You see I cant help wanting you to be a little of a politician and indeed I do most exceedingly and always have reprobated that fashionable notion of entirely excluding from political study or action, all your sex, on the pretence forsooth that they are too weak to be useful, too unsteady to be learned and because they I mean the men undertake to assert that God has intended you for an inferior sphere. . . .

The important event of Louis Otto's return from France in a new official capacity for his government stirs Nancy to write again in her journal, Sept. 6, 1785—Sunday:

I have lived as usual with my dear indulgent Father trying to be happy, & to make him so, since I wrote the journal of last June. This Morn'g I was disturbed again in my mind, by hearing that my Friend Leander is arrived from France in the honorable character of Secretary to the Embassy & chargé des affairs of France. Now must I be wretched in the reflection of what I have lost. O! had I waited till the obstacles were remov'd that stood in my Fathers way, then had I been compleatly happy. Now they are removed, but what is my unfortunate situation! —A wretched slave—doom'd to be the wife of a Tyrant I hate but from whom, thank God, I am separated. My amiable & still sincere friend writ me an account of his arrival & appointment. I answer'd his letter by an opportunity I heard of today. I wish'd him happiness! I sincer^ely wish it him tho' I am deprived of it. What have I not suffer'd in my mind since his arrival; all my woes revived afresh. . . .

Sep^tr 15—The strangest alteration has taken place in my feelings that can be conceived; my tranquility is fled, I am absent, thoughtfull & unhappy; I make a thousand mistakes in a day. This last week what miseries have I not suffer'd in my mind; my dear Father too observes it. Alass! my behavior does not please him. I appear discontented. I neglect my duties—I seek in the charms of disipation for happiness. I find none—I return home more unhappy than before, displeased with every thing I have said or heard—I will for the future stay more at home, see less company; for two reasons, my Father wishes it, & I feel more than ever that retirement *suits me best*.

Ah! me where shall I seek for consolation? My darling

Child! If I had but her; I shou'd not be quite unhappy, she wou'd serve to console me, but she is taken from me, for I know not how long. O! my God teach me resignation to thy divine will, & let me not suffer *in vain!* I staid at home all this day till the Even'g, I then went with my Mamma to harrowgate springs. I return'd early & drank Tea alone with Papa. He is now gone out & I am alone. My Mother is gone to bed—what shall I do—it is two hours before my bed time—I wont go out. I can't fix my attention to read. Had I but my Child with what care I'd watch *over her.*

October 15ᵗʰ—Another Month is pass'd & no alteration has taken place in my situation; I am however more reconciled to it than ever I was. I find an infinite pleasure in trying to improve myself & my mind is much more composed since I have determin'd to employ every hour of my time usefully, except those destin'd by every body to amusement & relaxation. Music & reading & writing fill up half the day; work, family duties & dressing, the other; the evening I devote to seeing my friends either at home or abroad. Thus I enjoy at present a negative happiness—disturb'd it is occasionally, by some few cross accident[s] & disagreable reflections. Now & then I hear of my Child—& some times form plans of having her with me, & as often am disappointed. My Husband (what misery, alass to me, that I have one) lives in his old way trying to deprive his wife & lawful heir of their property by throwing it away on miserable undeserving objects. I have another new scource of woe, for the authoriz'd separation that I have been so long expecting to take place, is given over entirely. Thus am I situated differently from all the human race, for I am deprived of all hope of ever being more happy in this world—the next I leave to HEAVEN.

During this period Nancy finds in The Old Lady a sympathizing friend. Madam Livingston writes her:

. . . I often think of you my poor girl, your Mother so situated as she is—your unhappy Marriage arising from events disagreeable on both sides, your brother absent, y^r child at a distance & y^r father's profession by which you must lead a solitary life. God I hope will make all things work together for good to your soul & that all these trials may lead your heart to himself & that you may find afflictions sanctified to you & receive a bowed will in conforming to that of God's. Peggy sends her love & thanks for the fine presents. You cant think how happy she is with your letters.

In order to be in closer touch with Peggy, Nancy begins to make plans to spend the winter in New York. Her mother's health is improving and the prospects are so promising, she writes Martha Bland, who replies:

Virginia, Cawsons, October 23^d 1785.

To tell you, my dear Mrs Livingston, that your letter gave me infinite pleasure wou'd be tautology. Be assured, that every remembrance of yours will ever be inexpressibly agreable to me. I will not take it as mearly a Compliment, when you say I added to your felicity during the time I resided in Philadelphia. It wou'd have been unpardonable, had I not thrown in my poor pittance of abilities, to the social Circle. Ah! my dear Nancy! what pleasurable moments have we pass'd together! How sweetly glided the evening off. It seems like a pleasing dream, yet it was a dream of long continuance, of three Charming years. Oh! I cou'd dream my whole life away just so; but fate has sunder'd us; we are thrown to every point of the Compass, and perhaps, nay, 'tis too probable, may never *all* meet again. Cruel reflection! it alwais imbitters my gayest moments when I suffer myself to think upon the Subject.

I rejoice to hear of your Mammas recovery. May it be permanent! Beg of your Pappa to Continue to me that partiality, which has so often distinguish'd me as his favorite. To hear of your brothers Happy & successful progress in that line of life which he has mark'd out for himself—will ever be pleasing to Mr Bland and myself, as his sincere friends. . . .

I think Mr Marbois has Excellent luck to be chosen Intandant of an Island which will render him both honor and profit. I have an exalted opinion of Mr Ottos heart, it is an honest and an upright one, therefore I rejoice at any event which can reward his merit; but I long to hear of some Duke or Marquess, being sent by *our friend Lewes,* to *take Charge of his affairs.* Me thinks Merchants from Spain, and Secretarys from france, make our Sovereignty but a poor Compliment. But this entre nous, my dear Nancy! as I both esteem, and admire Otto.

You will spend a delightful winter in New York. Wou'd to heaven! I cou'd join you there, but I dont know how it is. The Virginian ladies are almost in a State of vegitation. Our familys are so situated, that we must attend to the innumerable wants of them, or make one great effort and cast off all Care, as to ourselves it is only the cost of a dollar, which directs us either way. A few weeks past, we were at Norfolk (a Seaport town in Virginia) and hearing of a packet boat about to sail for N. York Mr B. immediately proposed a jaunt, to me. However, we recollected some little domestick matters, which were rather against such a sudden trip, such as clothing our Negroes for the winter, before we left them. At length it was determin'd that Heads or pillars shou'd carry it. However, it was not a favorable throw, for our trip, and we determin'd to return to Cawson. But as far advanced as the winter is, if I was to propose, spending it in N. Y. my Excellent Husband wou'd immediately second me.

We are here in all the Luxury of domestick ease, & Happiness. I want nothing but a bustle to make my time pass off delightfully. There is so much calm and passive Happiness in my Situation it some time fills me [with] ennui, and at the same time my reason reproves me for it, for do not the poets paint the very life I am leading, as the summit of all earthly joys? If I lived in the vicinity of a large city, I shou'd be in paradise but so remote from the *noise* of the *bon mond,* such a sameness, nothing to agitate the

Spirits. However we have not ceased to think of, and promote our European trip. It gains ground every day in our hearts. Pray my dear, be so good as to tell Sally Dill that it is only in case I shou'd go to Europe, that I shall send for her. Here I have so many attendants that I can have no want of others. I shall wish as ardently for a letter from you & my friend *Tom* as a lover wishes for a sight of his Mistress. No matter how trifling the subject so that the letter is long. Indeed every little thing interests me. Mr Bland sends you a kiss. I send one to y^r Pappa. My best love and sincere affections to y^r Mamma, yourself, the whole family & to all inquiring friends. Adieu my dear Nancy. Nobody loves you better than I do. Montesquieu sends his comp^{ts} to you

Yours for ever

M. B.

As Mrs. Bland's letter indicates, Alice Lee's extreme mental depression at this period of her life was more or less temporary in its nature. Apart from physical causes, her spiritual trials had been exceptionally severe: a shadowed girlhood, too frequent childbearing, the death of six children in infancy, distress over the war with England, and separation from her family during the first years of the Revolution. After they were all reunited, she had encouraged and approved the attachment between Nancy and Louis Otto. But in obedience to her husband's dictates, and the unwritten law that made a wife subordinate in all things, she had taken part in the conspiracy to force Nancy to break her troth to Otto and marry Colonel Livingston. And she had stood by, helpless before the train of evils and disasters for her daughter that followed that marriage.

The coming of her first grandchild, for whom she had sent to France for "Baby linnen," was for her the greatest event in the history of Shippen House. Yet she agreed to have that child banished by her own husband, her "lov'd and honor'd husband," for the sake of securing for little Peggy a future fortune. She was a mute and helpless witness to her daughter's anguish—a prolonged torture which was eventually to bring its one inevitable result. She realized, too, her part in spoiling her son, in making him vain and irresponsible, and she repented that too late. Besides all this, Alice Lee, inheriting her mother's pitying mind, had come to know the poverty and misery with which a physician's wife was ever in contact and could neither remedy nor alleviate.

Her decision to leave Dr. Shippen and Nancy for "the still and quiet" of the country she loved, was made so that in the solitude she might pray forgiveness for her sins, regain by meditation and prayer her mental and spiritual strength—her lost self, as it were. She read the Bible continuously. It was woman's only refuge in a world aligned against her. She became almost a religious fanatic. While she never did recover completely, it is significant that several years later, after Tommy's marriage and the coming of grandsons who became dependent upon her, she became normal, active, intelligent and kind. When her husband died in 1808 she carried the full responsibility of the rearing and education of Tommy's two boys. For Thomas Lee Shippen died prematurely in 1798, and his widow remarried soon after.

With the approach of winter, Nancy's uncle Richard Henry Lee, back in Virginia once more, refers to little Peggy in one of his letters from Chantilly:

". . . Our felicity would be complete indeed if our Philadelphia friends made part of our Circle—I am not without hopes that it may one day or other be the case. . . . You have numerous friends here who will all rejoice to see you and the fine sparkling black eyes of little Frank will glisten wonderfully at the beautiful blue eyes of his fair cousin Peggy Livingston."

Though the journals record nothing about Peggy at this time, news of her came in a letter from Otto:

New York Nov^{ber} 5th 1785

My dear Friend

I have till now defered writing to you because I constantly expected to go to Philadelphia but this agreeable Journey does not yet appear to be very near and your Brother being on his return I take the liberty to trouble him with a few lines. Some people here, (and amongst them I am myself) believe that you will spend a part of next Winter in New York. This would be the more agreable for you as your little daughter is expected in town. Mrs Montgommery and Miss Livingston are already arrived and would be as well as the Misses at Hanover Square very happy to see you. The Winter it is supposed will be very gay. Balls, assemblies, plays and concerts are already projected and the New York beauties are preparing offensive and defensive Weapons for the approaching season. In your Philosophical retreat, my dear Friend, these little things will perhaps not interest you, but the Friends you have here will certainly be a great inducement.—I am very happy to hear that you are still very sociable with Mrs Craig; there are not two persons in the World worthier to live in a perfect union with each other and I flatter myself to be a Wittness of your happiness on my arrival in Philadelphia.

The departure of the President is generally regretted here and I am on my own account very sorry to loose him; but the restoration of his health is equally dear to me and I hope that the air of his native Country will be of great use to him.

Please to present my best Compl. [compliments] to M^r and Mrs Shippen and to be persuaded that I constantly am

Your sincere Friend
and humble servant

L. G. O.

When Nancy was obliged to abandon her plans for a winter in New York—where she could see and be with the two she loved most,—it was a crushing blow. She took up her journal on the last day of the year 1785:

December the last day—With what speed has the last year passed away! It seems but as yesterday, since the last new years day! but alass it is a whole year taken from my life—And a whole year of experience added to it; I cannot accuse myself of vanity, when I say I think myself more wise, more patient, more resign'd to my situation than I was the last year. Yes! I think I am upon the whole much happier! altho' there is no difference in my manner of living—no prospect yet of there being a change for the better; but I begin to think that happiness consists more in our minds being at ease, than in all the variety of accidental circumstances. If that is really the case, why may I not be happy! Yes I may be compleatly so if I persevere in the path of my duty, & always remember that a virtuous life insures happiness, & eternal felicity.

1786

January 1ˢᵗ—Dined at home alone with Papa.

Saturday 3ᵈ—went with Mʳˢ Vardon & Mʳˢ Samento to Mʳ Peales exhibition.

Sunday 4—company at dinner—spent the afternoon & evening alone reading Young's Night Thoughts. Received a letter from my Uncle Arthur & heard from sweet Peggy.

The letters were reassuring: "Late news from the Manor says that Peggy was perfectly well at school," writes Uncle Arthur: "learns with great quickness and is very charming . . . Peggy's father came to see her & was fond of her. . . ."

Later he refers to Louis Otto,—doubtless in reply to a query from Nancy,—but not by name:

I very seldom have an opportunity of conversing with the charming person you mention. He looks always gentle—[illegible]

& pleasing. When the season renders my country residence pleasant, I shall often invite him to breakfast, for I have a real esteem for him and his conversation is always pleasing. But as he supposes his swaining proceedings are profoundly secret from me, I never venture to touch upon them. The overture must come from him . . . My brother is well & desires his love. I saw your friend the other day. He looked exceedingly handsome. . . .

Arthur Lee does not appear to have the slightest realization of the depth of feeling between his niece and the French Diplomat. When he refers to the current gossip then linking Eliza Livingston's name with Otto's, he says "Susan and Eliza are certainly to be married to Kean & Otto—wormwood for somebody & rue for you. . . ."

For a long time Nancy had known of the possibility of a marriage between Louis Otto and Eliza Livingston, a kinswoman of her husband and Nancy's best friend in New York. She had even expressed a hope that Otto would in time love Eliza, "who is just what a woman ought to be, sensible, polite, tender" . . . to repeat her own words of some years before.

Their wedding took place shortly after Nancy received her Uncle Arthur's teasing letter. The register of the chapel of the French Legation in New York contains the record that on March 13, 1787, Sieur Louis Guillaume Otto, chargé d'affaires for France in the United States, married Miss Eliza Livingston, daughter of Peter Van Brugh Livingston, Esq.

Nancy commended Otto's course as the only path of wisdom or happiness for him, as in truth it was. With her inborn pride and courtesy, she would pray God's blessing on the man she so loved, and upon his wife and his children in the sweet relationships that she could never hold.

There are comparatively few entries in the journal during

the next weeks. Several items refer to Nancy's attendance at a series of lectures on physical geography, astronomy, etc., being given in Philadelphia that season by the blind philosopher Dr. Moyse. Interest in pseudo-science was then the fad of the hour not only in Philadelphia and New York but also in London and Paris. Nancy mentions "a lecture on Grammar & Pronunci-ation, by Mr Webster author of a Grammatical Institute. He was eloquent & just in his criticisms. . . ."

Tuesday 6th—Spent my day at home as usual, & the even'g went to a very large & brilliant Party at Mrs Vaughans, above fifty people, & every body in high spirits.

Thursday 8th—The Philosopher Dr Moyse drank a sociable dish of Tea with Papa & Myself, after which I went with him to Miss Craigs, where I spent the remainder of the evening agreably. The good D^r entertained us on the Piano Forti, on which he play'd delightfully. He insisted on my performing, I did, & accompanied it with my voice.

Saturday 10—Had a small party at home this even'g. The blind Philosopher made one of the company. The even'g the most disagreable I ever spent—owing altogether to Mr S.'s ill-timed raillery. His extreme ill natur'd criticisms made every one unhappy. Dr Moyse far from being entertaining.

Sunday 11—Pass'd this day in writing by Dr Moyse to some of my friends in Charleston. I recommend him in the strongest terms to their civility & protection. Major Jackson drank Tea & spent the even'g with us in a sociable way.

Monday 12—A Company of learned men dined here today— The little time I stay'd at table I was very highly entertained.

Wednesday 14—Saw nobody & went nowhere.

Thursday 15—This Evening I shall always remember as one of the happiest I ever spent. Mrs Allen & the Miss Chews drank Tea with me & spent the even'g. There was half a dozen agreable & sensible men that was of the party. The conversation was carried on in the most sprightly, agreable manner, the Ladies bearing by far the greatest part—till nine when cards was proposed, & about ten, refreshments were introduced which concluded the Evening.

Friday 16—I was awak'd this morn'g with a present from my dear Papa of a nosegay, composed of hyacinths & myrtle. As I proposed spending the day out of Town I thought I cou'd not dispose of my bouquet better than by presenting it to the charming Mrs Craig who I knew was to have a Party this Even'g to which I was invited but had pleaded an excuse. I enclos'd it in this little note:

Dear Madam,
    I think I have heard you say you are fond of flowers, give me leave to present you with the first hyacinth I have seen this Spring. The charming little stranger certainly deserves some recompense for paying us a visit so early in the season at the risk of its tender & delicate constitution. The greatest reward I think it can meet with is your permitting it to live & die in your bosom.

She received it & sent me a most gallant answer.

Saturday 17—Louisa & myself staid all night with our friend Mrs Burrows who insisted on our staying & dining with her today also. We agreed & after dinner had a pleasant ride to Town accompanied by Mr Bond. We stop'd by the way to see the beautiful greenhouse & garden of Mr Francis.

243

Wednesday 21—Drank Tea at Mrs Vardons with Miss Craig, Zeleida & Louisa—a so so even'g which must be the case when cards are the sole amusement.

Thursday 22—Must I acknowledge that the greatest part of this day was spent in preparing for the assembly. I went with M^rs & Miss Coxe & danced with Mr Coxe.

The monotony of Nancy's days is occasionally broken by the diverting letters written her and her father by Brother Tommy, now studying law at the Inner Temple in London:

Thirteen vessels from Philadelphia and New York and not one line from Mrs L. to T. L. S. How unaccountable,! how unfriendly! how unsisterly! If you have any regard left for the gentleman above named, I beg that you will oblige him to alter his tone in his very next letter, and change his upbraidings into thanks which he assures me, he shall be always ready to do and with the utmost chearfulness, whenever you give him occasion by writing him a very long, very circumstantial, and very particular letter, informing him of all the news (except what belongs to ye region of Scandal) which is now in circulation among the great and fair, at Council-chambers, at Coffee houses, at tea tables and at toilets.

And all this, being a very curious gentleman indeed, he most assuredly expects from you; so that if you do not wish to grieve and disappoint him, you know your course. And this is being open with you. He presents to you on this occasion his sincere affection and brotherly love, and to your little feet and legs a half dozen of white cotton hose, which he hopes will not be unacceptable or uncomfortable. Remembering that *you* never wear silk, he has chosen these for you to wear when other ladies do, and hopes that by their fineness and softness, they will confirm you still more in your preference to cotton which he thinks from experience to be by much the best wear. He has worn socks and under stockings of cotton gauze ever since his arrival in England with great advantage. He would send you a hat also by this occasion, but as it is not yet determined what will be the fashionable one this winter, and as he wishes to let you know the fashions by what he sends, he waits with patience until their high Mightinesses the Dutchesses, the Marchionesses and the wives of Earls (commonly called Countesses) come to town, hold their Council and decide the knotty point. There are almost no fashionable people in town at present, nor does any other topic present itself upon which to write to a fine lady if we except Theatrical ones, and they are so much ye same yesterday today and forever in a mediocrity of actorial excellence, (which is all that I have yet seen) that when you have once touched them, you cannot write upon them again without a dull and tedious repetition.

Yet I expect that when The Siddons shall make her appearance, a new field will be opened, and I will ramble in it I promise you, whenever I think it to your satisfaction. In the meantime, will you do me the favor to bear my best compliments to Mrs Craig, Mrs Vardon and the whole circle of our pretty acquaintances. In it a Miss Sally Shippen holds a distinguished, I might have said super-eminent rank, I beg that I may be remembered to her with particular emphasis, and assurance of strong consanguineal attachment as well as that which results from her beauty and accomplishments. Tell Mrs Craig that England boasts no such woman, as far as I can see or learn.

October 4. I have indeed beheld, I have heard, I have felt, through my whole system felt her, the matchless queen of tears, the incomparable Siddons. And Oh! for power equal to my inclination to do justice to her merits, to give you an idea however inadequate, how sublime she is, how exquisite my feelings were. But to describe her perfections or to convey a just idea of their effects, would be almost as difficult as to equal the one without supernatural assistance, or without being a spectator to conceive of the other. She shone in the character of Belvidera in the Tragedy of Venice preserved and you are too well versed in Dramatic lore, in particular too zealous a votary of Melpomene not to know that the character is admirably suited to the exertion of great abilities. In the mad scene she was particularly great, and in the cry of murder, piercing to the most phlegmatic breast.

But as I despair of giving you any idea of this prodigy at present, I must wait until I have seen her again, which I hope to do and again before I proceed farther in my description. At present suffice it to say, and do not I pray you think me profane for the sentiment limited as it is in its nature, that she surpassed every idea I had found of powers oratorical in the Heaven above, in the Earth beneath, or in the Waters under the Earth.

I am indeed your affectionate brother and sincere friend

Thomas Lee Shippen

At length Nancy receives the welcome news that Madam Livingston is sending Peggy to her:

Your Daughter shall [be home] on Sat under the care of her Uncle Tillotson & my Dinah who is very careful & tender of her . . . You will remember I deposite to your maternal arms a sweet and tender plant, watch over her I entreat you, spoil her not by winking at disobedience nor on the other hand be not severe as she has so much sensibility that it would make her unhappy without complaining of it . . . Ask her to show you her pocket hdf which she has hemmed [be] Surpris[ed] how well it is done. Her book do not suffer her to neglect . . .

Peggy was to be placed in the loving care of Uncle Arthur who wrote to Nancy:

Our dear little Peggy is expected hourly with her Aunt Montgomery & Mrs. Lee [Matilda] will speedily bring her next week. My Brother will be with you I expect on Monday next & by him I hope to inform you that your darling is here.

P.S. Sat. Morning. I have this moment kissed your little Dear who arrived the day before yesterday with her Aunt Montgomery. She is in high health & is a charming girl. Next week Mrs. Lee will set out with her for Philadelphia & you will press her to your

246

heart. Quelle joie! My love to Shippen. Adieu. My brother brings you a letter from the good old Lady. Matilda's love.

Matilda Lee was Nancy's dear Stratford cousin, with whom she had corresponded years before, from Mistress Rogers' School in Trenton. Shortly after Peggy was born—a few months following the surrender of Cornwallis—news had come from Virginia of the marriage of Matilda Lee to their cousin Light Horse Harry Lee. During 1785-86 Colonel Harry had been elected to the Congress in New York. On their way North he and Matilda, "his Mrs. Lee," as he called her, had visited Shippen House and Nancy. They were to be frequent guests henceforth and, best of all, from Nancy's viewpoint, they were to provide ways and means for little Peggy's coming oftener to Philadelphia to see her mother.

With Peggy back, a happy winter must have followed. Madam Livingston writes frequently of Peggy and, through the child, is often in touch with Uncle Arthur Lee whose gentleness and goodness lead her to question in amazement why he should have so many "Enemyes!"

My Dear Mad . . .

I am very much obliged by the favorable oppinion you form of my Judgment in training her in sentiments of Virtue and honor. You may rest assured that the Same line of conduct that I have persued in the Education of my Daughters (and I flatter myself I have succeeded to my wish with them) shall be observed with respect to so beloved a Child invariably. . . .

M⟨r⟩ Lee is so obliging as to take Charge of this for you. He will be able to answere all your inquiries about her little improvements much better then I can at this time. Give me leave to observe to you our Mutual obligation to him for his tender attention to the dear Child in which we have often admired the goodness of his Heart, which joined to his Mental and acquired Abilities have

procured to him the Esteem of all my family—whence has that
Gentleman so many Enemyes (this in confidence to you alone)
. . . Believe me to be with Great respect

Yours Sincerely

N. York 3 April 1786 Marg^t Livingston

With the change for her following Otto's marriage, how
fortunate it was for Nancy to have Peggy with her! She had no
time for her journal now. In spite of her excellent theories
and counsel, Madam Livingston had, in her overweening fondness for the child, quite spoiled her. Nancy evidently had her
hands full. Dr. Shippen casts some light on this situation when
he writes to Tommy describing Peggy's first tea party:

Who do you imagine had a Tea Party & Ball last night? Miss
Livingston invited by card 3 days before, 20 young misses, treated
them with all good things, & a violin,—Miss Morris, Bingham,
Chew, Willing, &c. &c., 5 coaches at ye door at 10 when they departed. I was much amused 2 hours. Peg behaved with great politeness & danced a cottillion well. She is a very sensible & improved
child. Nancy has great credit from the difference y^t appears in her
conduct from what it was when she came here.

Little more than a week later Tommy is sent an account of
his birthday celebration at his home in Philadelphia:

17th: This day my son is 22 years of age. God grant he may live to
more [years] very honorably & happily to himself & profitably to
his country! Remember what Mr. Pitt was at 25!

Miss Bingham & Miss Livingston your niece have been dancing
minuets & Cottilions in *their* way in honor of your Birthday all this
evening before Mrs. Bingham, Miss Willing, your sister, Major
Jackson, Mr. Pollard, Mr. McPrager & your father. Prager &
Mr. Moses Franks played for ye children. They all joined in
wishing you many, very many, happy Patricks Days.

Another letter, filled with praise for the little girl, goes forward on April 20:

Your Sister has gained great credit in the management of Peggy who is amazingly improved, & much admired by ye whole Town. She says 5 of your old speeches, sings 6 songs & behaves with the most engaging propriety. She loves & fears her Mamma much. Not one in the house from Tom. L. Ryan up, but will be sorry when she goes to New York. Your Mamma is in Town, is better, & much delighted with Peg. She joined this evening in a hymn with her & your Sister & Piano Forte. . . . W. S.

Another letter of Dr. Shippen refers to his wife:

My d^r Son—

Your dear Mamma has paid us a visit of 10 days & has been sitting with Peggy & me 3 hours in my room—seems much more composed than she was; tho now she begins to think it is too great an indulgence for her to live w^h us any longer—she wishes you would not harbour any illwill against Tories or Britons—you ought to think America was to blame as well as england &c &c.

After Peggy's departure the summer is a busy one for Nancy, so busy that she continues to neglect her journal. Accounts of these months come only from Dr. Shippen's letters to Tommy:

My d^r Son—
         Philadelphia 1st June 1787.
. . . Your Sister had an elegant Teaparty last night—7 carriages at ye door—Miss Allen look'd remarkably well & sung her best; as I handed Mrs A. to her coach I mentioned the conquest I had discovered Miss had made of my Son—She put more of her hand into mine & said, Well D^r, Raney is a good Girl & he is a very clever Fellow, it will do very well. Mrs Morris, Mrs Ridley, formerly Miss K. Livingston, Mrs Bingham, Mrs King, Mrs Pinckney (Miss Stead) Mrs Moore & their husbands—P Bond & his 3 Sisters Messrs G. Harrison, Rutledge, F. Corbin, ye 2 Franks John Livingston & Mr Reinagle were the party. Genl Washington, the Penns, the Chews & the Coxes were invited but engaged. Nancy made a great exertion at the nobility & acquitted herself to a charm as you know she can when every thing is to her mind—

. . . Your Grandfather came to town last evening, & seem'd pleased with the show his Grand-daughter made. . . .

June 4. 1787.

We live very frugally & are very well satisfied with each other —when a Tea party is on foot Miss makes a little racket, however as nobody contradicts her she is generally well pleased & good humor'd, looks much ye better for it. Little Becky is married to a cober womans shoe maker & lives in my wooden house next ye Chappel. her sister Kitty attends your Sister—& a big Becky cooks & scrubs. Bill & Tom are waiters and Stephen is hired when we have company, the horses are at pasture ye summer Season therefore no Coachman necessary—Whenever I go into ye country to see a patient or to take a ride my old Friend T. Smith is ready to accompany me in his chair.

Novr 7. 1787.

Col. Harry [1] & Mrs Lee have spent this evening with us in a very friendly sociable manner, Oysters & Eggs our Repast—M^r & Mrs Bingham called in the evening & sat with us about an hour, Mrs Lee had never seen her, was much delighted with her indeed & Mrs B. thought Mrs Lee very like what your Mamma was— your Letters pleased them much, The Col speaks highly of your abilities & enviable prospects—They set off tomorrow for Virginia —Nancy behaved like a Virginian like her Mother. . . .

Good night my d^r Boy

A diverting incident was the protracted journey of a fashionable hat sent by Tommy to his sister, and consigned to the care of their Uncle Arthur Lee. It so inspired that gentleman's sense of humor that he devoted almost an entire letter to its wonders:

[June 3, 1787]

I cannot gratify the dear Mother about her dear daughter farther than that she arrived safe at Clermont with her Grand

---

[1] Light Horse Harry Lee.

mamma & her Aunt Montgomery. I forwarded your letter, my
dear Nancy, by post; but have not heard from the old Lady. At
length the dear delightful, long expected hat is arrived. It came
in a square box, somewhat smaller than a common [?] Imperial.
I was obliged to open it in order to pay the duty on the value of
the contents & those contents were—a hat. This vast machine contained—a hat. The mountain labored & brought forth—a mouse.
The rim of this hat is somewhat less than a yard diameter & the
crown not above two feet & a half high. The Crown is of blue
tiffiny, or some such stuff with a large bunch of white ribband
appended & hanging down about two feet; the rim is white silk
edged with a kind of white velvet, or silk plush, as the mens hats
used to be. I apprehend, upon the whole, that it is a winter hat &
will be useless to you now; except to shew how much your Brother
wished to gratify you. Mr Harrison, to whose care your B^r committed it, & I, have had a consultation about the mode of forward-
ing it. We are of opinion that if sent by the stage it will be rubbed
to pieces, & therefore I have determined to send it by the first
opportunity by sea. By what vessel I shall advise you. There were
a dozen pair of kid gloves also in the box, which I shall forward by
Mr Harrison. This Gentleman is much in the interest of the hat—
very tender of it, & duly impressed with the very great importance
to the fair head in Philadelphia that it shou'd reach its destination
uninjured. It is in my opinion—an absolute fright—but what is
my opinion to the—fashon—a dear, fascinating word, that renders
every thing charming. Your Father will be my debtor for the
charges upon it, & he likes that situation so well, that I dare answer
for it, he will give himself no trouble to get out of my debt. M^r
Harrison brought also some parcels for your Mother, which he will
deliver himself in a few days. Write me all that passes in the
Convention.   Adieu

[A. L.]

Between New York and Philadelphia the hat seems to have
been in transit three months. It was the subject of anxious inquiries from Nancy, to which her Uncle Arthur replies at last:

. . . O the hat! it is gone by the Philadelphia packet that comes to Mease's wharf. I delivered it with my own hands to the Captain praying & beseeching his tender care of it as being more pretious than all the things his vessel had ever carried before.

Again something happened to delay matters and Uncle Arthur writes again:

What a sinner that skipper was for not sailing away quietly with his precious charge—your hat. When it arrives & arrive it will unless (Thetis?) should bribe the skipper to betray his trust & deliver it to her; I hope it will be announced by a general ringing of bells & discharge of artillery & be carried in procession through the streets . . . & Dr. Rush deliver a lecture on this wondrous work of the millener.

But Nancy, perturbed by the continued delay, must have written her uncle another letter which evoked an essay on "The Hat":

That hat—that charming hat—my dear Nancy, where shall we find it. I have searched Ancient & Modern history for it, in vain. Certainly, said I, we shall find it among the Ornaments which Venus furnished to Juno, when they plotted to enchant poor Jupiter—a desperate undertaking, since you will own it would be easier to blind a dozen lovers than one husband. But Homer, among all the charming things he mentions on that occasion, has not one so charming as this hat. Whether Helen wore such a hat, when she enamoured Paris, & involved not only all Greece & Asia, but all the Gods & Goddesses in war; is what I cannot discover in any book Ancient or Modern. I next examined, whether it was among the ornaments that rendered Lucretia so fatally fair in the eyes of young Turquin, & made him hazard his life & crown upon a kiss. But I find in that critical moment, the Lady was undressed. Nor could I trace one glimpse of it among those enchanting things that enabled Cleopatra to seduce Anthony from the empire of the world. After having read 12 volumes of Ancient history, with 24 of German commentaries and illustrations in folio,

I have not been able to determine whether such a hat was among the imperial ornaments of Semiramis or of Queen Zenobia, or whether that renowned Princess Thalestris wore it, when she marched six thousand miles to try whether Alexander was as invincible in the fields of Venus as of Mars. History says that in fifteen days this illustrious Amazon overthrew the renowned warrior, tho in modern times men are supposed to hold out for a month. The books of Chronicles and of Kings with the assistance of Josephus, would not inform me whether the amorous Queen of Sheba, wore this hat, when she came envelopped in spices, to hold dalliance with the sapient king. When will our country produce such heroines in love?

You see, my dear Nancy, with what arduous assiduity I have labored to trace this hat, because you are anxious about it. After all, perhaps Mr Herschell's forty foot telescope will discover it to have become one of the brightest satellites of the Georgium Sidus. Oh that we had another Pope to consecrate its transmutation to everlasting fame. Then might Nancy's hat outshine Belinda's hair; and reign among the most brilliant & beautiful constellations that adorn our Poetic sky.

Do not forget to lay me at Mrs Bingham's feet. Ask her by what means she escaped from France after robbing the ladies there of all their graces & attractions. It was no petty Larceny; & had she been arraigned, she must have been convicted, as the stolen goods would have been found upon her.

Tommy's letters from London bring news of Alice Lee's old friend, Anne Home, for whom Nancy was named. Though she had been married to Sir John Hunter for many years she could still charm, so the impressionable Tommy declares:

. . . From her appearance you would suppose her 23 or 30 years of age, & she is graceful, genteel & elegant beyond anything I have seen in England. I do not think my mother's friendship & attachment for her have made me blind to her real character tho I feel that there was a strong preprofessian in her favor from the time of my being apprized of the circumstance. If I had not known

253

it however I am convinced that I should have admired her extremely. I am sure I do no injustice to Mr Hunter in giving Mrs Hunter the sole credit of the elegant arrangement of everything that I saw at the house and I might also say that I had seen nothing so elegant as the entertainment of this day since I have been here. Lord Lansdown forms the only exception Mad^n was very attentive and flattering in her manner of speaking of my dear Mamma. She said she made particular enquiry when Mrs Arnold came here whether she was ye daughter of her friend as she certainly should have waited on her as such.

Lady Hunter was apparently delighted to be reminded once more of her girlhood friend and set about dressing a doll for Alice Lee's grandchild, Peggy Livingston. Tommy writes of having dinner with them:

. . . Before I take leave of them entirely I must speak of *the doll*, because Mrs. Hunter has become a party concerned. This doll then which has been matter of so great expectation, which has so often been promised and so long neglected, which is to be ever memorable when finished and to unite all the taste and graces of a fashionable lady, having been purchased in embryo by your brother, is now at the house of Mrs. Hunter, and from all I can learn engages great part of the attention of the whole family. The hair dresser is making for it a wig or chevelure, the whalebone man a pair of stays, the milliner a full dress, and the—shifts—petticoat and handkerchief divide the cares of the ladies. In short no pains are sparing to send the lady in question complete and perfect into the world, where very few can boast as much at going out of it. But every picture that is justly drawn has its black as well as its fair side, and so must also the picture of the doll. By some ill-fated misadventure the toy woman in Bond Street, perceiving perhaps that I looked at the beauty of her face more eagerly than at that of the toy I was purchasing, gave me O! wicked mischief! a face with a crooked mouth. I saw clearly that hers was as it should be and not suspecting so fair a face of a deed so foul I paid her at hazard for what I had trusted to her generosity. I will not believe that she knew of this defect herself. Rather let it be ascribed to chance which so often over throws the best designs of mortals, than to the wicked machinations of so fair a one. But after all what will the doll be the worse because its mouth is on one side. The uglier the face the more attention will be paid say I to Mrs. Hunter's taste in dressing it; but Mrs. Home is afraid that *our ladies* will think it a part of the fashion and will attempt to imitate it, I reply to her that if they did, they would fail, their mouths being too beautiful to admit of distortion and if they should succeed they would make defect perfection. So much and no more of the present for my dear little niece except a fear that so fine a lady will demand an extraordinary *portion* . . .

This extraordinary doll reached Peggy before she went back to her grandmother in New York, but she liked best her dear little dog.

II

Not until fall does Nancy write again in her journal. This time she is moved by the death of a beautiful young acquaintance.

Here is September the 7th 1787—My poor journal has been neglected for one year & more.—This evening I have been led to reflection, by hearing of the untimely death of Miss P. Ross, a young & blooming girl of 17 years of age. I sat alone, ruminating on my past life, & lamenting the uncertainty of all human hopes, when I recollected that I used to pass some evenings agreably, in setting down the occurrences of the day; this reminded me of my journal, I took it out of my escrutoire, & how much was I astonished to find that almost two years has pass'd almost imperceptibly away, since I last wrote in it!

Before the year closes the melancholy event of Eliza Livingston's unexpected death takes place. It is not directly referred to in a letter, but from Otto's mention at a later date of a little daughter, Eliza, it appears that his young wife died in childbirth. Deeply touched over Otto's grief and loss, which are also her own, Nancy must have written him a letter of condolence. His reply expresses a sense of gratitude and a deep affection that has never been dimmed. Nancy is to him a source of comfort and of joy given him by no one else. Yet even in his need for her help he realizes that a happy reconciliation with her husband would be the best solution for Nancy and for her child.

If anything can surpass the satisfaction I have had in writing to you it is the happiness of receiving your answer. I felt the emotions of meeting a Friend after a long and tedious absence—a Friend always indulging, always disposed to comfort and to oblige. I must confess that when I first took the pen, different reasons seemed to detain me from renewing a correspondence without having received your approbation. This your goodness has now afforded me and I have every motive to rejoice at the step I have taken. Your flattering Letter convinces me, not that I possess the many good qualities, which you are so indulging as to suppose in me, but that your partial Friendship has not yet removed the coloured glass, which embellishes every object. Your esteem I always wished and succeeded to deserve, but the great interest you are pleased to take in my fate is more than I expected and must be entirely attributed to the Excellence of your heart.—of a heart so full of its own sorrow, that there seemed to be no room left for those of a Stranger. I always reflect with self approbation on the Steps I have taken to contribute to your happiness, tho' they were entirely contrary to my own interest and tho' they have not been successful. Your tranquillity, your duty . . . let me not enquire into the motives of my conduct, but I have every reason to believe that they were just. Even now, if every means is not yet exhausted I should recommend new endeavours to effectuate a reconciliation. But doubtless you have done more than could be expected from the most enduring temper and I am afraid every remedy has been tried in vain. Nothing is left but—patience, a long, a [illegible] remedy, the last ressource of disappointment.

As to me, my amiable Friend, I am destracted with a thousand thoughts, equally incoherent, equally distressing. Every former prospect of happiness being at once vanished, I am wandering thro' this World, without knowing where to stop or whether to go. I was born for the peaceable enjoyments of domestic Life. The most flattering views of fortune can give me no satisfaction, for who will partake of them with me?

Shortly afterwards he writes again:

. . . I must confess that I rely more upon you than upon myself. I was resolved to set out for Philadelphia & surprise you at your fireside . . .

The good judgment of both prevails and prevents a reunion that might have had disastrous consequences. Nancy considers taking steps for a divorce from Livingston. Otto tells her:

. . . My old acquaintance with you seems to give me the privilege of being candid. I have known you at a time when you hardly entered the world; since that I have seen you but a few days. The improvements, which experience, perhaps misfortune, must have afforded to a mind like yours have not escaped my observation . . . but in reading your letters I still discover greater perfections. Perhaps a riper age and a long acquaintance with a Lady whose mind had the principal claim to admiration have rendered me more attentive to those accomplishments which, contrary to eternal beauty, are improved by time . . .

December 19, 1788

It is really uncertain how long I shall remain in America, perhaps many years, perhaps a few months. . . .

To see you again, and in the same room where I have passed so many agreeable hours, is a satisfaction of which I can form no proper idea; I know only that I shall feel very embarrassed particularly if witnesses are admitted at the first interview . . .

A continuation of the present tranquillity of your mind and heart is the most desirable of all blessings, and I sincerely hope will not be interrupted.

. . . by cherishing & cultivating that Friendship which you have permitted me to indulge & which can only cease with my life.

Adieu

As the days pass she becomes more and more dear to him and his yearning for her more than he can put into words:

August 26th

My dearest Friend. . . .

Yes, my inestimable Friend, you are now dearer to me than ever: Your indulgence has placed you in such an amiable light that I am some times on the point of running to Philadelphia and thanking you verbally.—My Eyes, the ton[e] of my voice would probably better express my feelings than the cold paper you are now perusing. Would to God I was near you in this instant, without that disgusting wittness whom you mention and whose faded charms are now floating on the ocean. To spend one Evening with you and to become thoroughly acquainted with our present Ideas, would be the most enchanting of all moments. But whilst I am thinking of all this the remembrance of my late disappointment at once overclouds this pleasing prospect—if instead of my correspondent Julia I was to find that Julia who has lately received me with so much indifference I should be miserable indeed. But no more of this.

Once again Louis begins a regular correspondence with Nancy. While his letters are sent secretly, as always, there is nothing clandestine about them. They are entirely on the basis of devoted friendship.

Your obliging Letter of the 17th instant is a convincing proof, my amiable Friend, that my conjectures on that of the 2^d, which I have not yet answered, were groundless. In the latter I had found the following expression: "I beg too as you must write with as

much ease as propriety *not to wait for returns* to all your Letters."
This I considered as a very polite intimation not to write too often
and resolved, tho' with great reluctance, to indulge myself only
once in a Month in this pleasing occupation. I now discover to my
great satisfaction that I have put a false construction on the meaning of my charming Correspondent and instead of complaining I
find myself obliged to implore her forgiveness and to offer her my
warmest acknowledgements. Can you then really set any value on
my Letters?—Can Julia, who is so good a Judge of English Lit-
terature, be pleased with my rude and imperfect performances?—
To indulge the feelings of my Heart; to follow that impetuosity
of Fancy and imagination, which I have unfortunately received
from nature, would be disapproved even by Your Friendship, tho'
it might amuse an impartial reader. I am constantly checked by the
apprehension of saying too much or too little—too much for you
to read; too little for my feelings. This naturally introduces in my
Letters an ambiguity or perhaps a stiffness, of which I am sensible
without being able to remedy it. I can never forget, and would to
God you had never forgotten, that you have still in your possession some former Letters, written under different circumstances.
You once promised to return them; they are still yours; they are
still wittnesses of those sentiments which you have inspired. By
keeping them you seemed to approve of, even to cherish their
contents. Whenever I take the Pen to write to you, some expression, which so long an acquaintance seems to justify, but which
other considerations must render improper, immediately offers and
notwithstanding my care to remove every sentiment that might
displease you I have every reason to believe that in my last Letter
I have not been equally successful. The answer you gave me
seemed to confirm my apprehensions; particularly as you finished
it by the unusual expression of *having the honor to be most re-
spectfully* &c. Therefore to write to you, my amiable Friend, is
not so easy a task as you suppose, tho' it is a very charming one. I
at once pass over the interesting Scenes of former times, when I
was the affectionate and, I may say so, the worthy confident of
your Heart, when the longest Winter Evenings appeared to be
minutes. Those times are no more, but they have left a deep, an

everlasting impression, which even the most cruel disappointments could not since efface.

You say nothing of your charming Daughter for whom I really feel a tender affection. Do not forget to kiss her in my name. . . .

To comment on your goodness, my charming Friend, would be to repeat, what I have already expressed a thousand times. I acknowledge myself under the highest obligations not only for having received a supernumerary Letter, but for having received any Letter at all; this being fully granted and my gratitude for ever pledged, permit me to acquaint you with a new kind of apprehensions, which your kind encouragement has not yet removed. If I once admit the propriety of writing to you without being answered, it is difficult to determine where a concession of this sort will stop; you may be pretty well pleased to receive, without thinking to return any Letters; probably because you can not conceive how important they are to me.

To avoid any difficulty of this nature I have had till now strength enough never to write without being answered; I may even communicate you a Secret, which Julia must not hear for the World. I have burnt several Letters, which were directed to her, merely because I thought it impolitic not to insist upon a regular exchange. To banish all etiquette is in my opinion most essential in Friendship; even in a more tender connection it may be useful to live upon a perfect equality. Any pretention to superiority must offend the feelings of one and lessen the tenderness of the other. This at least has been always my opinion on this subject; and *when the heart offers the pen,* there can be very little difficulty about etiquette. I confess, my most indulging Friend, the error I committed in reading the Letter which your goodness calls an *unhappy* one but which I can not remember without the greatest satisfaction. It gave birth to an explanation which has greatly contributed to the calmness of my present situation. If it was in my power to see you for a few hours, several remaining doubts would be perfectly removed. This supreme degree of happiness I anticipate with inexpressible Fondness. To see you again, to read in your Eyes that tender concern which you so lively express, to forget for a moment that seven years have wrought an inavoidable separation, to talk over a thousand innocent Scenes, which could only interest *us*—Oh! and let Julia be present, let her know how much I love, esteem and respect her, that I never ceased to take the warmest interest in her Fate and that, if it had depended upon me, she would have been perfectly happy. All this I shall tell her with the sincerity of a heart, which has been always devoted to her. But will it not be imprudent to indulge sensations which seem to be no more calculated for her than for me? Advise me, my dearest Friend; your opinion shall be a Law for me. If you think it better not to see her—not to see her!—forgive, I believe I should not follow your advise.

The information you give of your charming little Daughter is extreemly interesting. Never you [mutilated] can say too much of her. May she be blessed with the temper of her Mother; talents are pleasing, Wit is entertaining, but in the heart she must find the source of her happiness. Will you be so kind as to kiss her in my name, tho' I might probably not have that privilege myself. Your delegated powers in this particular will exceed my own. Adieu, my amiable Philosopher, I feel better every time I receive your soft remonstrances. Would you refuse to devote a few moments to the instruction and improvement of

Your most affectionate Friend   M.

Meanwhile Madam Livingston again enlists Arthur Lee's aid in escorting Peggy to her mother in order to prevent the child's father from taking her by force.

My Dear Madam

By Mr Lee's obliging attention you will I hope be made happy in receiving our Dear Child to your maternal arms. May she answer all your expectations and prove your comfort and Joy. I fear she will be rather a trouble to her uncle on her Journey as she is not fond of long rides but she has promised me that he will tell you she has been a good Girl. I am sure she ought to love him. May she never hereafter when she thinks she does not need his attentions receive any intimation from him with contempt, or return his affection with disrespect in no one instance. Let me intreat that you will upon every occasion attend to her Mind, to inculcate the fear and Love of God as the first Step to insure her principals —to shew her the necessity and Beauty of practising Virtue truth benevolence and delicacy so as these may be the Governing principals of all her actions and never my dear Madam suffer her to violate the truth by prevarication or deception of any kind, except in only one Instance. You will easily Guess—I mean when it comes in competition with delicacy & there it must not be taken in too great a latitude.

These are the steps in which I have led my Girls and I thank God I have succeeded. I remember the education of my three youngest best altho I think I may say it of 3 sons also that I have never known them to deviate from the truth in any one instance or ever had occasion to give them a Blow. I do not think that whipping upon every occasion can be of service unless you have to deal with children of vicious dispositions. There indeed it becomes necessary. You will pardon what I have written and Impute it to my anxiety for my childs Temporal and Eternal happyness.

I received your pamphlet upon Education (which Mr Lee franked and directed for which I am obliged to him) at dinner, surrounded by 17 or 18 people. It was handed about and at last the Chancellor took it. . . .

With respect to your confidential Questions in your Last. Would to Heaven that I could give you such an answer as would give you pleasure or me comfort, but both are impossible. I am a Mother and every misconduct every Sin and Immorality recoils upon my heart and makes it Vibrate with ten fold force. I cannot tell you all I hear for I have seen him only three times in about a year. He never comes here nor I at his house in which I have not been near three years. He has seen his Daughter only once and that by accident at Mr Tillotsons. His behaviour was so cool to her that I felt the utmost pain. It has convinced me that she must not be often with [illegible] her Father and she shall not. I have not let him know of her going as I had thought to do, as I have been advised if she had come to her aunt (for at his house she shall go) that he would have taken her home. . . .

Believe me to be sincerely yours,

M Livingston

It does not appear precisely at what time an agreement was made between Nancy and her mother-in-law, Mrs. Livingston, to have Peggy spend a part of her time with her mother in Philadelphia, but that it was made is clearly stated by Arthur Lee, and this fragment of a letter from him was written in the early spring of 1788:

There can hardly be a doubt as to the propriety of your plan, but how the old Lady will receive it I cannot say. I am rather afraid not favorably. Poor little Peggy—it should be flattering to her to know what a contention there is for her company.

It is evident that Peggy was in Philadelphia a few weeks later for Arthur Lee asks:

May 1788

How fares it with our little Peggy? Does she continue to be a good girl & improve in her reading, music, friends & dancing? If she does, kiss her & thank her for me. . . .

But shortly afterwards, Arthur Lee is urging upon Nancy the justice of Mrs. Livingston's urgent request that the child should come back to her:

I enclose you, my dear Nancy, a letter from Mrs Livingston, which came to me yesterday in one from her, in which she most earnestly entreats me to second her sollicitation for little Peggy, being sent to her by Col. Lewis. It is a delicate matter for me to interfere in, & I am sensible it must be a great affliction to you to part with such a little darling. But all things considered it seems to me to be your duty to send her back. I presume it was a condition of her grand Mama's sending her to you, that she shou'd return, & in detaining her you wou'd commit a breach of honor in that engagem^t Considering how much the dear Girl depends on her Grand Mama, how much her heart is set upon the Child & how grievous it wou'd be for her to be deprived of her entirely for the time she has yet to live, it seems to be an ill-judged fondness that wou'd sever them entirely. Her grandmama's good sense, the proofs she has given, in the young Ladies her daughters may satisfy you that you risque nothing essential to good morals & good behaviour, the most substantial parts of Education, by the Child's being with her. I own that Philadelphia furnishes, with your attentions, more means of rendering her accomplished in female graces. But I wou'd submit to your reason, whether it is not sacrificing too much to the Graces, to deprive her of the patronage of such a Grandmother.

I understood it was the plan agreed on that Peggy shou'd be with you & her Grandmama by turns. This appears to be the only modification that can satisfy the fondness of each. In the substantial parts of Education you will co-operate & the finer & more ornamental ones you will easily graft upon them. Let me hope then that you will shew yourself superior to the gratification of your own feelings which wou'd be attended with so much danger to the essential interests of your Child.

Adieu

A. Lee

Nancy consents to Peggy's return to her grandmother for the summer months. Madam Livingston is so pleased with the child's improvement that she makes a more definite proposal that Nancy have the little girl every winter under her guidance and instruction.

. . . Your sweet child's improvement has kept pace with her groth.—She has given great credit to her fair instructor and returned to me as accomplished as one of her age is capable of being. Indeed we are all delighted with the dawnings of reason and reflection which she constantly discovers.—The other evening sitting in my arms & looking at the River in pensive thought she asked— Had God a beginning, Who was his father, "Grandma, if I fall in the river will I be drowned, What will become of my body if my soul goes to heaven?" . . . Your town is now I suppose the gayest of all the States as all the wise men of the west are now met together. May God give them wisdom and direction for the good of the whole. . . .

Later in the summer The Old Lady again wrote of Peggy:

. . . She continues a sweet Child & often speaks of you—Poor N. Y. is quite deserted & all the gay world are in your Town. Your uncle I hear is also with you. That I am sure will be an addition to your happiness. Time will shew wether the report of his courting a young and Beautiful Lady at N. York is true. The Chancellor assured me when he was in town it was the prevailing report and as a proof he said her family by some thing which dropped believed that there was truth in the report and by another Gent^n I heard the Ladys sentiments upon the occasion I shall not anticipate he may over come difficulty and I may congratulate you upon the occasion. Miss Maria is certainly very pretty. I suppose you dont know her. My son John who is fond of rising Beauty was much in her praise last winter but would much rather see her M^r L[ee]s wife than his sister, to which he is amazingly averse from no other motive than the desparity of ages, but this is only between us. . . . The Chancellor lives just at my door but alass these my expectations are in part defeated. Mr Hindman was in treaty for a fine farm also near me, but he writes from Santa Cruz that the Doctors have ordered him to the South of france and I have no hope he will ever recover. Just now I hear a neighbour who lives but 2 miles off upon the most elegant Situation the Hudson affords offer to sell his farm which is an Excellent one for £600 at easy payments. How happy should I esteem myself to have another settled there. But why do I trouble you with these things. But the account I had heard laid in my head about this place.

I have not mentioned our Childs going to you next winter [illegible] to her father, you know his temper and I must say nothing about it till the time comes. God who has all hearts in his hand will I hope change his. I shall conclude this with the words of my dear [illegible] Last Letter Oh that Heaven may bless us with contented minds & Submissive hearts to its divine will—May we indeed. Present my Compliments to Mr Lee and tell him I have Received a Letter with one Inclosed from Mrs Washington & that I thank him for his care. Y^r Sweet girl says she loves her Ma and sends her duty.

I am My Dear Madam   Yours Sincerely   M. L.

265

Upon reviving [reviewing] I find I ought not to have mentioned what the C[hancellor] told me as it may be the cause of displeasure or pain should my Friend hear it, neither of which heaven knows I would be the cause of in him without bearing my full share of pain. From the knowledge I have of his Sentiments I think him incapable of any thing but strict honor and truth—but it has been his ill fate that whenever his prospects were brightning to have Reports of the like nature in addition to other disagreeable tales, cast in his way which has given a handle to those who were opposed to his views to call him faithfulness in Question thereby weakning her confidence and raining fears for futurity. Tell him my best Blessings if he will accept of it shall attend him in their fullest extent. I need not tell you my dear Madam that this is a confidential Letter.

CHAPTER IX

1787-1800

I

Having exhausted all other means of adjusting the profound differences between herself and her husband, Nancy at last decided to sue for divorce. In the early summer she appealed for advice to her Uncle Arthur Lee, himself a lawyer. In reply he wrote:

July 11ᵗʰ 1789

My dear Nancy, your *undated* letter reach'd me yesterday. It is, in more respects than this, precisely the letter of a fine Lady. It talks of a Divorce with as much nonchalance as of a discarded Lover. At the advice of all your friends—good—both here & at Philadᵃ—your humble Servant being out of the question—better still—now for execution. Do enquire which of the Lawyers in N. Y. is most learned & successful—in obtaining divorces I suppose you mean & I cannot find one who has had any success that way. There is one—who married an old woman being himself very young & he I think must be the most learned—Another married a Lady with fifty thousand pounds, & he I conceive must be deemed the most successful. To these therefore I would recommend you. Their names are Burr & King, than whom I imagine you will find none here, more fit to do justice to a fair Lady's desires. But if you are serious—which is rather too much to expect—my opinion is—that yʳ Father should come here & instruct those Gentlemen in every thing necessary to conduct the business. If it be necessary to apply to the Legislature here; it is now sitting, & no time is to be lost. It must be obvious to your reflection, that no one, but your Father —while he is living—can with propriety, or even decency, interpose in an affair which so immediately concerns the honor & interests of his daughter. . . .

[Arthur Lee]

Her uncle's facetious attitude in face of the grave crisis before Nancy, and his vague impractical advice must have brought great discouragement to her. Not one member of her family, not one friend saw that the prolonged torture of thwarted love, the endless complications then attending a young wife's suit for divorce from a wealthy and prominent man, the relentless persecution and ugly, malicious intrigue of her husband, the suspense over her dear child—not one seemed to realize that all of this was having its grave effect on Nancy! She was so young, so pretty, so fond of gaiety! The prevailing opinion seems to have been that when she appeared depressed she was merely "in ye dumps" and could be consoled with a tea party, a new hat, a dance . . . Later however both her mother and father seem to have thought it advisable to side definitely with her husband. Livingston is undoubtedly exaggerating when he writes his brother Edward Livingston of this defense:

I have certainly a Right to know this Woman better than any other person—her Father writes to me he has the fullest confidence in me and commands his Daughter in my presence on her duty to deliver me my Child. . . .

But their attitude towards Nancy comes to the attention of Madam Livingston in New York, for she thinks of herself as Nancy's only defender:

At length my prayers are heard. God hath oppened the hearts of strangers to espouse the cause and interests of my poor dear orphan child, who has been hunted like wild Beast of prey. How singular is her fate, an unnatural Father combined with her Grand parent to exclude her from the common ties of hospitality, even a shelter under their Roof. I dare say no more to you altho their conduct is reprobated by every Body for their

268

sordid interestedness. But with respect to yourself perhaps I have said too much. You as their Daughter must overlook whatever is disagreable. You must forget, and by every means in your power strive to conciliate their affections, which on your mothers part appears to be very sensibly weakned,—I fear with her infirmities. She has by all accounts been severely exercised, and her mind may not have recovered its enervetic powers. It will be in your power to sooth and comfort her when this storm is blown over.

. . . This will be handed to you by my friend the Baron La Rock a gentleman worthy of the esteem of all who have the honor of his acquaintance. His Lady is a person of Letters well acquainted as I am Informed with the Belles Letters, they possess great opulence. He declines his title. His family is a noble one in Germany. He was so obliging as to offer to take our Child under his paternal wing in his own carriage. But upon my having yours of the 3 March handed to me yesterday by Miss Marshal the first I had in many weeks past.—Just now I have another.—I think with you that she must not be removed to me as yet. The Bill must be passed before any steps of that nature can take place. I hope you will give me the earliest account that the Bill is passed. Till then nothing can be said upon the subject, but that I feel an heart overflowing with gratitude for those worthy characters who have interested themselves in supporting oppressed Inocence. I cannot congratulate you as yet. Well do I know that in so large an assembly of different characters some Rubbs may be expected & perhaps his Lawyers may be active against the passing such a Bill and throw in every obstruction. However we will hope the best. I can add no more than to assure you of my Respect and that I am yours

Sincerely,

M L

Remember me in the most affectionate
Manner to my dear child.

Meanwhile Colonel Livingston is taking despicable measures to ruin his wife's reputation,[1] blast Otto's career and injure his child. His mother writes Nancy:

[1] See *Supplementary Records* (6).

My dear Mad^m

At length he [Livingston] is returned but not to stay. He says he will commence Suits against Mrs Cox & Miss Bradford—May heavens best Blessings rest upon them it is the cause of heaven to be the orphan's friend and God will Bless such benevolent hearts. They have my Sincere thanks . . . he desired the Chancellor to intercede with me to give him an order to receive the Child from you that he absolutely refused to do saying the child ought to be with you & that you may be assured I shall never give. I have a letter from your Father stating your appearance at the Judges chambers and says if you had produced the Child it would have terminated agreably to his wish and mine. How could that be seeing his wish & mine are quite different. Had you produced her what security had you y^t [that] she would not have been torn from you. This I have written. I fear he will be displeased, while every body admires your firmness, prudence & maternal affection and applauds your conduct. This I have also written. I sent you some days past a letter by a person to whom I gave my sentiments to delive[r] to you verbaly and inclosed 40 doll^rs to indemnify you for the expense you have been at.

Your Father says it is the Genl opinion and his the Coll^o, [Colonel] that I take the child again. This my friend is impossible. Were I to take her tomorrow he would take her from me the next day till I give up her Estate to him. When that is accomplished I suppose he will never care a straw where she is—in the meantime at my age, being near 69 years, what stability can be expected unless y^t he can command the income of that part of the Estate after my death he may again desire to have her. I am not fit now at this period, to encounter the salleys of his turbulent temper. I must have peace. Y^r father says y^t his conduct has been proper & it may be so. He can be a prosiour when he has a point to carry. He says he knows not what to do both you and Peggy are out of the state. Do not be Secure. Remember who are his friends unless my Letter in which I have stated the whole of the Coll^o [Colonel Livingston] Views makes an alteration. My heart is pained for you; when will your troubles end. He has he says proof of your Infidelity before marriage & after this if I am rightly informed (for him I have not seen) He says he will publish M^r O is named &c &c and he says he will Publish the treatment he has received from his own family. I think that neither will be attempted. I trust that your Reputation is out of his reach. Oh what a malignant heart has he, unhappy man, got. Keep up your Spirits. Pray to God to give you grace and strength for the heavy trials you meet with. Oh may all be sanctifyed to your Soul. Perhaps you may have reason to Rejoyce for those trials in time and Eternity. I insist and so do all the family that Peggy shall be left under your care. That he will not hear of, and then he calls you by hard names. Do not sink under your afflictions. I think if he cant find her he will give up the persuit. Say nothing about what he intends to publish. I have written 5 pages to your father and now my pen is bad and hand tired. I will only add that I inclosed two Letters to Mr Benson our member in Congress directed to you & desired him to give them to Mrs T. Cox himself. Have you received them from Mrs Cox. If you have not he must have sent them to your fathers. God Bless and preserve you and your Dear Child is the pray^r of

> My Dear Mad^m
> Your Sympathizing friend
> M. L.

5 Decem^r
Date your Letters & direct to Mr Peter Schermerhorne

Louis Otto, acutely aware of the depth of Nancy's devotion for her child, had made every possible endeavor to bring about a reconciliation between Nancy and Colonel Livingston. Now that it appeared impossible even in the eyes of Colonel Livingston's mother, one of whose letters Nancy had evidently sent Otto, he wrote her sympathetically:

> March 20th 1789.
> . . . I am at a loss, how to advise you. Even the enclosed letter does not inform me sufficiently of your situation, unless it means that you are to be separated entirely from the ennemy of your tranquillity. This indeed might be considered as a very happy circum-

271

stance if it did not at the same time deprive you of your Child. His determination however seems to imply some tender sentiments in favor of his offspring, it may render him less odious in the Eyes of the World and even in yours. His right seems to me unquestionable unless the Laws of your State have particularly provided for this case. If any thing can rander your situation tollerable, it is the enclosed Letter. To inspire such compassionate sentiments, such regard and esteem to his nearest relations, this supposes the most unexceptionable conduct on your side and the most laudable impartiality on the other. I am sorry to say I am unable to advise you; I have been unsuccessful in my former attempts to promote a reconciliation and I am not sufficiently informed of all the circumstances to give my opinion on this delicate subject. Your relations will be the best Judges of the propriety of your steps in this respect. The passage in the enclosed Letter *concerning his proceedings with you* I do not understand and if you think me worthy of your *entire* confidence I shall perhaps be able to give you some advise. . . .

Your affectionate Friend

M.

That Chancellor Livingston cannot aid Nancy under the New York laws, appears from Madam Livingston's next letter to Nancy, but she gives encouraging news of the interest and the promised aid from friends outside the family:

. . . I find you are misinform'd with respect to the Chancellors power. The Laws of this state confine or limit his power only to orphans. Could this have been done it would have been carried into effect long agoe. I have not yet seen Mr Howel since the first time he was here. I fear he is gone and I do not even know where to direct this so as you may get it. The Baron told me he had been in company with some Ladies who greatly espoused the cause of our poor Inocent. I forbear to mention their names in case of accident—but he assured [me] that their conduct merits the highest praise not only from an heart that feels Gratitude Love and Esteem, but from people of the highest honor in this place. I hope it will not be long before their very friendly cares for my

272

dear girls safety will end, as I expect an answere every day. My heart felt the distressing Situation in which you are at present. I hope the day is not far off when the dreadful fear of incurring expence may be dissapated and your Mother be releved from such tormenting horrors upon that account as to banish into obscurity a sweet child who it ought to have been her pride and Boast to have defended from a father whose only wish it is to see without a shilling of property. This mans word is the pretext, if that which she well knows is not to be depended upon. The covering is too thin to deceive the world. If Peggy is removed without an Idea of her ever returning you then will have peace. . . .

By this time Arthur Lee has been startled into concern over Nancy's difficulties, again refers her to the lawyers Aaron Burr and Jared Ingersoll and writes her frequently:

. . . I feel most strongly for your situation. I would apply to the Attorney Genl & Mr. Ingersol for advice and be governed by them. I can hardly think [Livingston] will venture to solicit legal compulsion, without which I would not suffer him to have her, [Peggy]. What a world we live in! How truly does every day's experience justify Young's satyre that man is to man the surest, the severest ill. . . .

On March 21st he again writes Nancy:

I received your favor, My dear Nancy, when at the board of Treasury & near the time of the post going and I therefore could only write a few lines; & your fair friend will forgive me if most of them were devoted to you & your poor little Peggy. I repeat to you my opinion that nothing but the power of the Law should tear her from you, & that upon all circumstances being stated the Law will defend not destroy her. Try to interest the Ladies— particularly Mrs MaKean & Mrs Judge Shippen. It is the cause of humanity—& in that cause the female voice is irresistible. I do not know any man at your bar, so eloquent as the Attorney general. He will do the cause justice, & supported by the general voice, I am persuaded none but a Butcher of a Judge, who has never had, or wish'd to have a parent's feelings will venture to decide against humanity & you. . . .

Madam Livingston sends this warning note:

You will have a Round of amusement in your Gay Metropolis. The Single and ungaurdined Ladys must now be more prudent than ever. Calumny with her thousand tongues can only be escaped by the wary and wise. By them no male Visitants will be permitted to extend their Visit beyond the hour limited by propriety in its strictest sense, especially if the Lady be alone. Forgive those observations which proceed from a View of the Many Temtations to which the young and ungarded are exposed—and my Sincere wish that you may continue to Steer clear of the Rocks & unseen dangers attending a Contrary Course. . . .

About the same time Louis Otto's next note shows genuine alarm at the scandal Livingston is spreading:

. . . The world you know is a little too malignant—I have a fresh proof of it—They talk rather a little freely of you and a certain future Minister to the European courts—let this hint speak the rest. Prudence is requisite & apearances I think ought to be consulted. . . .

Standing a target for every poisoned shaft directed by her husband toward her and Louis Otto, Nancy hears a disquieting rumour of the French Diplomat's intention to marry again. She must have written him about it for he replies:

February 4th, 1789

It is impossible, my charming Friend, that you should believe the strange report, which you mention in your last Letter; it surprised me the more as I can not conceive upon what it is founded.

I had every reason to hope that the retirement I live in would not permit the public to think of me, but even in this, my Friend, I have been mistaken. In my present situation the report is very malicious and must have injured me in your opinion. Believe me that if ever I am able to take a similar step, you shall be the first informed of it. But really, you could not believe it, you could not think Your Friend weak and inconsistent enough to forget in so short a time, what he owes to you, to himself, to the world. Sometimes indeed strange combinations occupy my mind, I am pleased to indulge dreams which can never be realised, I wish to go to Philadelphia and soon after I think it better not to go. I am endeavouring to persuade myself that I ought to remain where I am, tho' my wishes are constantly at a distance; all this has no connection with the report you mention; no, believe me, my situation can not change unless you and *You only* are acquainted with it. You may now discover the cause of my delais, it is of the greatest importance and you will excuse my irresolution. Your Letter will render me still more cautious in the choice of my acquaintances and I flatter myself that you will be no more troubled with reports on my account, tho' I really do not know who is the *amiable person* you speak of. Let this positive assurance, my dear Friend, be sufficient and if you wish to *partake of my joy* let us wait till I shall see you, for only then I shall be happy.

I am so good natured that I believe every flattering word you tell me, therefore do not write more than you feel. Your affectionate Friendship is now my only ressource and if I could think that you deceive me I should be miserable. You have too much delicacy not to approve the cause of my *jealousy*, tho' the word may appear strange when applied to your Father and me. But there is undoubtedly in Friendship such a feeling as jealousy; it seems to be as nearly allied to it as to Love. We wish to occupy the first place in the bosom of our Friend and to have more than *one* Friend, in the most refined signification of this Word, is impossible. We give our whole affection for an equal return. Perhaps my ideas on this subject are overstrained; perhaps I am mistaken in the nature of my own sentiments, but let this be a mistery [for] you and me. To scrutinize our sensations too minutely may only weaken their energy. Let me [hope] to receive at least every fortnight a Letter from you. I am now so used to this charming correspondence that I expect with anxiety every new testimony of your remembrance. Do not answer the obscure parts of my Letters, I

275

know all you can say on that subject, but I am pleased with my delusion. As most of our pleasures consist in imagination, to deprive me of these would be cruel. I am for ever

Your sincere Friend,

M.

The next letter, February 25, 1789, again reassures her:

Your charming apology, my valuable Friend, would be useless if it did not give me a new proof of the delicacy of your sentiments. I am sorry the mistake you mention should have given you the least uneasiness, tho' I really think that if the report had been true my conduct must have appeared to you very inconsistent. To say the truth I have the greatest obligation to Mr de Chaumont, because he has given me an opportunity to know something more of Julia than I formerly did. I shall not tell what that *something* is, but I really believe I know it. To find out the sentiments of a Lady has been considered by Philosophers as the most difficult task—still I have so much presumption as to think that I have discovered them. My secret shall remain with me untill you guess it, if you take so much trouble, if not I shall perhaps tell it unasked but only—to you.—Indeed, my dear Friend, you could not believe that I was offended. The Lady you mention is my next neighbour; she lives in a family, who is intimately connected with me; it is natural therefore that I should see her very often and as she is fond of retirement, it is natural likewise that I should find her often at home. My former conduct has given me perhaps undeservedly the reputation of a good sort of a husband and as people are very busy in contrieving matches they have considered me as a very good subject. The fact is that if I could ever think of changing my present situation I should be at a loss how to accommodate my humour. I have been treated with so much indulgence by an excellent Woman, whom I shall for ever regret, that I can not now be easily pleased. Implicit submission, a word, which is not to be found in the polite catechism of matrimony, is the very first thing I should expect and probably not meet with. Tho' I am at present not happy I can not say that I am *positively* unhappy. I am in a negative state, neither sick nor well, those moments excepted when I receive a few lines from Julia. Believe me, my good Friend, your Letters are the only enjoyment I can now boast of; they convince me that I am not quite alone in the world and that you take some interest in my situation. If you have well understood my last Letter you will have no farther doubts about my future determinations and when I shall be so happy as to see you they will be entirely removed.

My little Eliza, for whom you seem to feel some affection is perfectly well and in all respects a promising Child. I see her seldom because she lives in the Country and after the disappointment I met with I am really apprehensive of attaching myself too much, lest a second stroke may deprive me of all the comforts of Life.

Receive my tender wishes for your health and happiness and for the success of the excellent education you bestow on your Daughter.

I am yours forever—

"The Lady you mention" of the above letter, was doubtless Mademoiselle Fanny de Crevecœur, daughter of the French consul to New York, New Jersey and Connecticut, the Chevalier St. John de Crevecœur.

II

Although they are in the midst of a storm that is breaking their hearts and lives, Nancy and Madam Livingston place the subject of Peggy's care and education before all other considerations. Peggy is now visiting her mother, and Madam Livingston writes:

[Dec. 5, 1789]

. . . I am very sorry my dear has not yet been put to school as I wished the money she had given her to have been applied to that purpose. . . . Oh why cant I have her with me during the remainder of my life, but at present that is impossible. Tell her I am much obliged and pleased with her Little present. They are very prettily made. I hope she will Improve daily and I have the pleasure to observe both by her Letter and her uncles postscrip that she is a charming girl. But one thing I must Intreat you to guard her against. I mean an artful behaviour of any description. I cannot forgit a Circumstance at which you Laughed not having considered ye matter in the same light as I do. I mean her telling you that nobody saw her take the cake which she had in her pocket. My dear Mrs Livingston these are very serious things. They are only Trifles of which children can be guilty but an artful disguise opens the Door to want of principal which you know is ruin in the fullest extent of the word. I do not appologize as I am actuated by Love and Duty in the advice I give. The greatest external accomplishments can be no counter-ballance to art and deception of any kind. Watch over her heart, her morals. Implant the fear and Love of God in her tender docile mind. So shall her happiness and your comfort be insured.

Be pleased to accept in good part what I have written. I have now relieved my mind, as I hope you will be a mother indeed. Present me to all with you as all here wish to be to you.

I am my dear Mad^m
Yours Sincerely

Decr. 5, 1789. M. Livingston

On another occasion she writes:

. . . I am Sorry you and I differ so widely upon Education. I think Schools properly regulated, open the Mind to emulation. A desire to excell in the different Branches in which the children are Imployed raises a laudable Ambition. It opens the Mind to friendship and affection, to their Little companions by teaching condesention & polite attention and often lays the foundation of friendships which are lasting as Life. These and many other advantages I could name which would never interfere with a Mothers precepts and regulations at home, but as you are upon the spot, and can better judge what effect a school has upon her mind, wether it will prove advantagious or not to one of her disposission, I must Leave intirely to your care. God I hope will preside over her Education and lead you into that way, which shall be most for his Glory and the Dear childs good. . . .

Again she writes:

I am favored with your and Peggys Letter. I am happy that you take so much pains and attention in our dear Girls Education. She has many Advantages [under] your care, and the many young Ladies in the neighbourhood are certainly great advantages which I hope her good sense will enable her to Improve to the best uses. God knows how long she will be permitted to have them. He [Livingston] is quit[e] outrageous. He wrote me such a Letter the day I was at Mr Tillotsons a few hours after the Burial of Caroline as I believe never son wrote, for I have not seen him Since the day after Peggys departure to you. He will sue me and present me to the grand-Jury of Columbia county &c. &c. I believe as soon as his finances will admit of it that he will make another Expedition your way. Therefore it would be proper to have some one in Phil^a to give you notice and provide an assistance for the child in case he should come.

When the time approaches for Peggy to return to her grandmother, Nancy journeys with the child to New York and sends her secretly to Clermont. Every move has to be watched!

On this trip to New York she sees Louis Otto for a few moments. Their meeting is a strained and disappointing experience to them both. Otto writes:

Nothing my amiable Friend, can be more embarrassing than the manner in which I was obliged to behave during your stay in town. So much reserve seems to be incompatible with Friendship and if I was not acquainted with the motive of your sudden departure, I should have attributed it to a change in your sentiments notwithstanding the repeated assurances you have formerly given me of your lasting attachment. No! the Julia, whose letters I can not peruse too often is not the same to whom I spoke and if those letters are the deceiving images of a dream, let them continue to make me happy without ever informing me that I am mistaken. At least, my dearest Friend, I have seen you, I have conversed with your charming little daughter, I have recalled to my remembrance the delightful moments of former times. Perhaps you are dissatisfied; perhaps you think I was wrong in leaving your last letter so long unanswered?—I have verbally explained the cause of my apparent neglect. For several weeks I expected you in town every moment and being apprehensive my answer might fall into other hands I would not expose it. This my good Julia is the true cause of my silence; it is pardonable because it was involuntary. But whatever may be my crime I am certain that Julia was not the same and that probably I shall find her again in her letters: probably?—no there is no doubt, she can not change, she bestows her affection with too much caution to withdraw it ever. Will you kiss your dear little daughter in my name; I am quite in love with her. She seems to have all the sweetness of her Mother and in every respect she belongs to you and not to the cruel man who attempts to tear her from your bosom.

Adieu, may you be half as happy as I wish and as you deserve.

M.

In another few weeks the discordant note seems to have vanished. Their relationship is again harmonious, excepting for a hint between the lines in Otto's letter of August 15th. What is it that he "cannot commit to the paper"?

How can I sufficiently acknowledge your great condecension in writing to me, when my jealous disposition hardly deserved your notice. It is very true, my charming Friend, I was disappointed in your behaviour to me and I was foolish enough to attribute it, not to the very obvious cause you mention, but to some dissatisfaction or even to (forgive it Julia)—to caprice.—You will judge from the enclosed Letter that I wanted very much to write, but even this Letter I defered to send untill I knew the true motives of your conduct. Still I am very much in your debt for this last proof of your sincerity and indulgence. I am proud to confess that I have not deserved either. But to confer even unmerited favours is the work of superior beings and that Julia surpasses all others in magnanimity is too well known to her Friend. If you know the tenderness of my feelings, you will easily judge how much I suf-

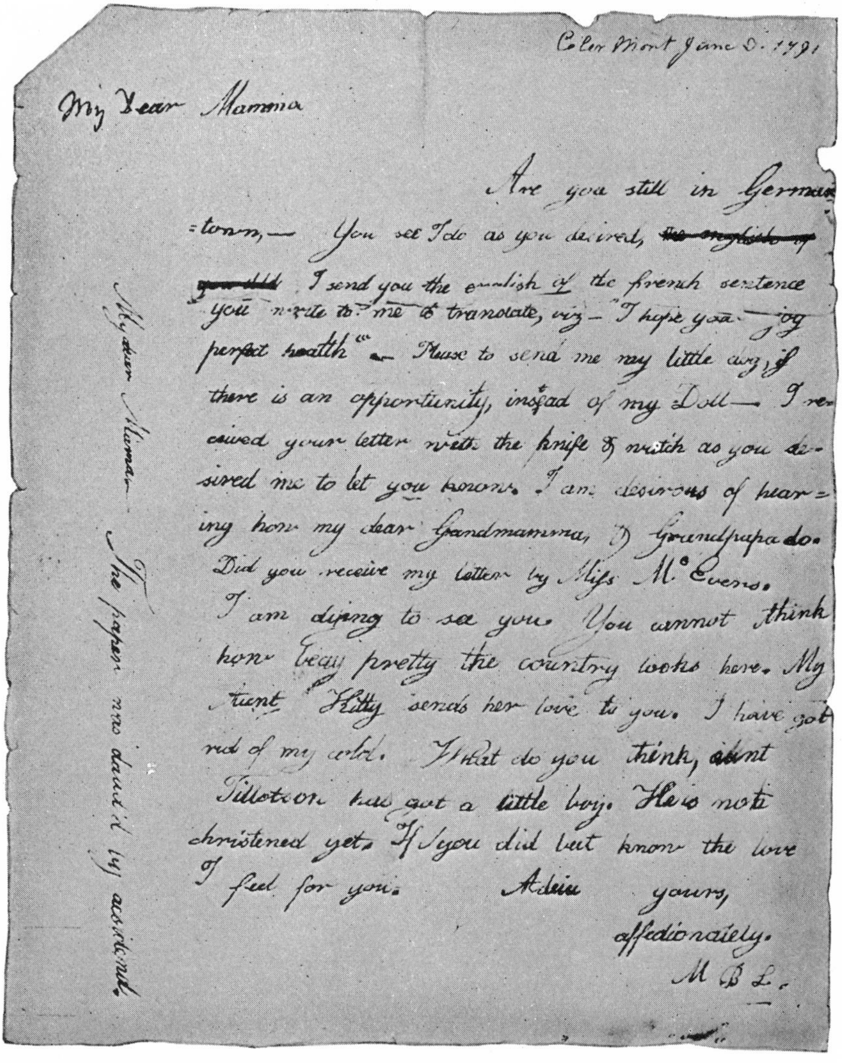

Coler Mont June 2. 1791

My Dear Mamma

Are you still in German-town,— You see I do as you desired, ~~the english of~~ ~~you wrote~~ I send you the english of the french sentence you write to me to translate, viz—"I hope you enjoy perfect health"— Please to send me my little dog, if there is an opportunity, instead of my Doll— I received your letter with the knife & watch as you desired me to let you know. I am desirous of hearing how my dear Grandmamma, & Grandpapa do. Did you receive my letter by Miss McEvens. I am dying to see you. You cannot think how very pretty the country looks here. My Aunt Kitty sends her love to you. I have got rid of my cold. What do you think, Aunt Tillotson has got a little boy. He is not christened yet. If you did but know the love I feel for you. Adieu yours, affectionately. M B L.

My dear Mamma The paper was [illegible] by accident.

LETTER FROM PEGGY LIVINGSTON TO HER MOTHER

fered; how often I wished to break a silence which began to be intollerable. Strange indeed were my suspicions; I thought that during a long absence from your Friend your imagination had framed exaggerated ideas of his amability, that in seeing him you were disappointed and treated him afterwards with that indifference, which a disappointment of this kind must create. In short I was so unhappy as to believe that you had withdrawn all your affection and that I should forever deplore your arrival in this town. Your Letter has entirely cured me and I am more impatient than ever to see whether you are less ceremonious at home than you have been here. Yes, my good Friend, I hope to visit you in about a fortnight and to assure you that nothing in the World can alter an attachment, which time has so fully confirmed. It is now ten years since I first saw you; many circumstances have strengthened a prejudice which I then conceived in your favour and I never hear from you without feeling the warmest emotions of tenderness.—I think I have a great deal to say to you, which I can not committ to the paper; but let us not be disappointed a second time; let us be mutually convinced of our sincerity and take hold of the first opportunity for a complete explanation.—A thousand kisses to your lovely Daughter. She is a most charming little treasure; I am no more surprised of your uncommon affection for her. But I hope she will leave something for the share of

Your very tender Friend
M.

Peggy's letters bring happiness to Nancy while the struggle with Livingston goes on. The child writes from Clermont, first to her mother, and then to her grandmother Shippen:

My Dear Mamma

Are you still in Germantown,— You see I do as you desired. I send you the english of the french sentence you write to me to translate, viz—"I hope you enjoy perfect health"— Please to send me my little dog, if there is an opportunity, instead of my Doll— I received your letter with the knife & watch as you desired me to let you know. I am desirous of hearing how my dear Grandmamma, & Grandpapa do.

Did you receive my letter by Miss McEvens. I am dying to see you. You cannot think how very pretty the country looks here. My Aunt Kitty sends her love to you. I have got rid of my cold. What do you think, aunt Tillotson has got a little boy. He is not christened yet. If you did but know the love I feel for you. Adieu

Yours, affectionately.

M. B. L.

My dear Mama—The paper was daub'd by accident.

My dear Grandmamma,

I have delayed too long to write to you, overlook that fault I pray you; & I will endevour to make up for it by writing often. I have got so many letters to write I hardly know which to write first. I long to see you. How do you do. Write me another letter if you please, & tell me every thing about you & the family. I thank you for your good advice & hope you pray to God to enable me to follow it. I read the chapters you mention in proverbs often but I have not yet learned them. How does Grandpapa & Uncle Thomas do. I must write a letter to them soon. My Grandmamma here sends her compliments to you so does Aunt Joanna. I have been to the Lebanon Springs but we could not stay long enough to do me any good, as Aunt Armstrong went also with us for the ride & we had not been there three days before we found that the air did not agree with Aunt's health. Tell this to my Mamma if you please.

Your most dutiful Grandaugter

Margaret B. Livingston

The changing events in the life at Clermont—now bright, now dark—are given in frequent letters from both Madam Livingston and Peggy. Madam Livingston writes:

. . . I know the feelings of Maternal love not to be conserned for the miscarriage of that which would have consoled you under the Separation from your Beloved Child, and well she deserves to be beloved as she is indeed a sweet child. She at present Labours under many disadvantages with respect to her Music & writing. My Steward who is a very fine penman is absent during the Summer

282

months Surveying Land, so that she has gone far back in her writing, but still she has written four Letters to you which she indited herself refusing any assistance as she said it was your orders to her. I keep her to her french. She writes her fables and translates very prittily but I am sorry to add that it is with great Difficulty that I can keep her to get her different Lessions every day, as she is sometimes very Idle indeed, but in every thing else, she behaves perfectly well. . . .

Yours Sincerely
Marg^t Livingston

Mrs Ann H Livingston
  Philadelphia
To the care of Dr. Shippen

. . . Our Dear Girl grows amazingly tall and behaves very well. I hope her writing will Improve daily. She attends to her French Study under Capt Marceline reputed the first teacher in America. He attends her at 8 'Clock, at 9 she goes to Mrs Hyndshaws Academy. . . .

With respect to Music it is a Science which requires a lifes practice to make a great profficiency in, and a girl of Moderate fortune has many things much more useful to learn. A Little Music at the age of 12 or fourteen [is] Sufficient to entertain herself and friends, occasionally is I think quit[e] Sufficient. I am sorry we differ in this Mode. . . .

Colonel Livingston's attempts to get possession of his daughter grow more and more menacing, as Madam Livingston tells Nancy:

. . . I shall now my Dear Madam let you into a Secret which I hope you will not mention again. Last Summer—he [Col. Livingston] was very attentive to her—One day it happened that all the family were abroad. The Chancellor too. He first went there and would not sit down or give her time to sent to Mrs Defforest and took the Road from the river to my house. I did not dare take her to rinebeck (as Mr Tillotsons children had the whooping Cough). He came in and told the child she must go with him . . . that he had the Phaeton to carry her. She like a child did not seem unwilling to go. M^rs deforest was over ruld and he carried her off. Her aunts took the Coach & said to him that I had sent for the Child. He refused. They wished to see her but were refused except they would go in his house. This Kitty & Joanna did not chuse to do, and came away without her. I then wrote a Letter to her with many instructions and observing to her that as her papa had thought fit to take her Education upon himself, which I had determined to spare no cost to make her an accomplished woman, I advised her to be dutiful and attentive &c. This happened a few days before I left the country. . . . Altho he has no woman in his house but his daughter Hariot, yet the whole family were in the greatest distress. Several very smart Letters passed between the Gent. of our family and him. Coll Lewis at last prevailed to git him to bring her back exacting from me a strict promise not to permit her to go to Philadelphia. What could I do. I was obliged to give my word. I fear whenever he has a mind to extort a promise from me that he will again distress me by taking her out of my house as I have no one Gen^e in it. . . .

I would not suffer her to write this to you well knowing what I had felt to wish you to experience the same. She now sits by me writing a long Letter to her dear Mama, the longest she ever wrote. Present me to your parents, M^r and Mrs Blair and my friend Mr A. Lee. They will all accept of my best wishes for their Happiness.

The mysterious references of Madam Livingston are explained only in part by a letter from Peggy to her mother. Driven to subterfuge by Livingston's continual attempts to make off with his child, her grandmother sends her from Clermont to a hidden retreat. From this hiding place Peggy writes to her mother under the name which she must have been told to use.

My best loved Parent,

This is the second letter I have written to-day, but it is my greatest pleasure to write to my sweet mama. The letter you shall receive from John with this I wrote before I received your second one. You say you must live upon my yesterdays letter, no my sweet mama I will not suffer it, for every day that I am away from you I will send you a letter. I write in a hurry for John is waiting to take this with the other to you. I got so much to say to you I don't know what to put first my paper is gone all to one half sheet. send me [mutilated] to y^r excellent instructions. I will find out a way to see you with out putting myself in danger don't be affraid. You must not make any attempts. I beg you wont. I'll manage it never fear. You must not know where I am. I am safe & comfortable. let note's suffise yet a while, you shall receive one regularly depend on't. I mus[t] now conclude—

Louisa Ann Lewis—

Dear & honour'd Mother

I have at last finished my letter to my Papa, and now I fly to answer the sweet note guided by the hand I love. It is a happ [mutilated] write to my mama. O what a consolation it is for me to think that I have such a good mama such a friend.—I have not written the letter to Papa as well as I could have wished it is true, but indeed mama my pen was so bad: besides my hand was so cold for I wrote it before dinner. Your assurance that nothing has happen'd has encourag'd me. I am as happy my mama as I can be in my situation. I get a pen & ink from the woman whose house I am now in who is very kind to me. she is Mrs Coxe's ser- [mutilated]

Adieu, ever dear mama

Louisa Ann Livingston

P.S. You flatter me too much by saying you love to read my paltry little letters.—

My dearest Mother,

How shall I thank you sufficiently for this instance of your love and care for me. I have been very well. After my morning task was over, I employed myself at the new shifts, & finish'd marking the other. I had not enough work, I therefore read 2 or 3 sections in E. of Critticism. I have not been idle I assure you. I finish'd what you left me, last night before I went to bed, and B—— slept with me as you desir'd. I have been very anxious to see you indeed my dear Mama. I hope to-morrow you will be able to dine with us at least. B—— did not clean the room the day being so very bad. I'm very sorry last night it was such a charming night you did not take advantage of it for we are quite lost without you.

The head looks much better than I expected—Adieu my beloved M—— Your dutiful & affectionate Daughter

M B Livingston

I have a thousand things to tell you but I can't think of keeping Miss McClenagan's man so long. I have written this so fast I'm quite ashamed to send it you.

Mrs. Livingston writes Nancy that Colonel Livingston threatens to sell all his estate and remove to Georgia, take Peggy from Clermont and educate her himself, but that she has a plan

. . . which if I can bring it to bear will Secure the child and Establish her Education. I have not yet got an answere. If I succeed, you will have timely notice to get the child with you so as she can be conveyed to me. This you will remember is to be an inviolable Secret to all but those Dear friends, who have taken part with us. Therefore I think it best that P[eggy] shall remain where she is as by her Letter she appears to be with decent Industrious people. Let the dear girl amuse herself as she likes for the present. Her trunk you can take off when you go. I have her baby and some little trinkets which with some Lanning & new Stockings, I have defered sending till her abode was fixed. . . .

Soon Madam Livingston writes Nancy in anguish:

Dear Mad^m

My Pen is Bad, my heart is Sore, very, very Sore. I write upon paper ruled for my dear childs use to you. My fears are strong he is gone yesterday to N York to see Lawyers to bring a Suit against me in the Feadral Court. From me he vows to seek redress. I know the Man, this may be pretence to put you off your Gaurd. Will your Father, your B^r your 2 Hon^d uncles, will none interfere. In our State he is the only Gaurdian. As your Lawyers this Question which has been suggested by one of our Lawyers, Viz a devorse has taken place, you are now *feme sule*. Are you not as much intitled to be her Gaurdian as he—or rather her Sole gaurdian. She is a Citizen of Philad^a. Can she be forcibly taken from you—I cannot tell you what my feelings were when cruel necessity compelled me to order that my poor child should be exposed at this Season to ride in the night as I never suffered her to be out in the night air. Well did I know she would have been persued had he had any Idea of the rout she [one line cut out here] next day it would have been too late—Y^e next day I wished to avoid him and left home. I used a strategim which succeeded beyond my expectation. He was certain she went out with me and came to Genl Armstrongs in the morning Saying he came to fetch P[eggy] but heard she was there and expected to see her & asked me where she was. I was Silent, and he remained there till night. I had then gained a whole day & a night. He left us at dark expecting to get intelligence from ye Chancellor & family, but in vain. My Servants were then asked. Money was offered but not one of the number could be tempted to betray the trust. He then returned to G. A. expecting I suppose to find her, but not seeing her he attacked me most violently affecting [illegible] passion Spoke of his feelings, his heart torn &c but as I knew he had many times disowned her to be his child and that it was all Duplicity I remained silent & left the Room. I promised the next morning that I would consider of his proposal y^t he should keep her at his House 3 weeks, & y^t she should spend the winter with me in town. On the fourth day after peggy left me I informed him that I was under engagement of Honor with you—that I held a promise Sacred & that I had made to keep the Child myself & not to suffer her to live with him—that it was Impossible to permit a child of one of the first families in the United States to be in a family without a white woman in it—that by the time he would receive the letter his Daughter was safe in the embraces of her Mother & friends in Philad⁰ This produced a Letter to the Cllʳ and me. He tells me again that from me he will have [her] He looks to none else & I shall answer for the Breach of trust, that all his family shall go with him to Georgia &c, which I answered with the old adage I fear God & I have no other fear—Thus I have given you a detail of an affair which has indeed been very painfull. When I arrive at N York I shall make you a remittance for her Education &c, her baby shells, &c and shoes, shifts have been left but the occasion will I hope excuse it for he had told me if he found her I should never see her more and yᵗ she should not be independant of him. This is the foundation upon which he would have her in order to bring me to make no provision for her in case of my dis[decease] I hope time and reflection will bring him to a sense of reason. Mʳ Cox is not yet returned. I am very anxious to hear how her health is and how she bore the Journey. The Suddeness of her departure, prevented my saying many things which I ought to have said. Assure her of my truest affection and give her a kiss for me. Excuse the many faults and ascribe it to its true cause, anxiety.

I am Yours Sincerely

[Unsigned]

Clermont
Monday 29 Octʳ

P.S. I have written in confidence, Remember he is still my son & yr childs father.

Still more alarmed by the threats of her son, Madam Livingston at last gives orders to send the child under her new name secretly to Philadelphia, and writes to Nancy in agitation:

May she arrive in Safety. I own I have my fears on that head. Should he send tomorrow and miss her I well know he will persue. I tremble at the Idea of her being conveyed to the Southern States where her relatives will never see or hear of her as he is determined she shall never be independant of him. Poor child, I fear for her health, as Mʳ Cox the Genˡ who acts for my Estate has orders to ride all this night. I shall order Blankets &c to keep her warm. Sara, one of my Maids goes with her to take care of her by the way. Cherish the tender plant if it shall please God to permit her to arrive in Safety. Implant every Sentiment of Piety Virtue and Goodness. I Leave her w[ith] you. Pray my dear Madam for Grace to enable you to fulfill the Charge committed to your care. Be watchful of her person that alass—why must—I only fear her removal to such a distance. I can no more—farewell

Y^{rs}

M L

A few days later Madam Livingston hurriedly writes to Nancy:

I Snatch a moment my dear Madam to inform you to be on your Guard. He declares the Moment he is in cash he will go in persuit of —— He says he has heard that there is one at Beth^m of her name. He has purchased a new Saddle & I believe that he will take that Rout and I know y^t he has sold for a term of years Lotts in his fine woods. Every body flocks to buy, so that he cant be out of cash at present. He declares that he will never see me while he exists &c &c.

I hope you have £30 from Mr Kean which he has for Peggys use. £30 more shall be sent in Jany by some good hand. . . .

At length Colonel Livingston, having secured a writ of habeas corpus for Peggy, approaches his wife for a conference.

My Dear Madam

Let me entreat you to an interview of a Moment. I have no other View but to Convince you of an Error that begins already to Operate much to Your Prejudice. The writ is still in force & your Lawyer has by this time given in your answer so that the Cause is at issue & you & your Father will each forfeit the Penalty if you refuse I promise you on my word & Honor not to Terrify you by any Measures or improper words if you will see me. We may reason on the Business untill your Papa comes if you please. You will ease an anxious Heart.

Yours

H. B. L.

Upon Nancy's refusal to see her husband he replies:

Dear Madam,

I was last Evening Honourd with your fav[t]: and have taken the Night to reflect on your proposal.

I am indeed sorry to inform you that the proposition you have made me is not such as I can with Honor Agree to. And even if this insurmountable Barrier was out of the Question & such a Place as you mention could be found & agreed on which perhaps would not be—unless you had your Election who in this Case is to Act for me and place her there a Person appointed by you, or by me, if the latter, do you not (as you want confidence in my Honor) place her as much in my Power as if you had complied with my first Proposition? & even were all this to be got over what is to become of her when her education is compleat. Must she still go to school or must the Question of her being with either of us again be Agitated to the injury of the Child and the disgrace of one of us—Is it not better that you should embrace the Certainty of seeing her when you please, than to reduce the Business to a Possibility a Bare possibility (which you must admit may happen) of your being deprived of her forever. I will not endeavour to inspire you with Confidence in the Rectitude of my intentions farther than to request of you to lay your Hand on your own Heart & ask yourself if your Confidence in me has ever injured you and if most of the Serious Evils that has happened to us has not in a great Measure had its Rise in a want of it. This being the Case will you persist in the Same Conduct to the injury of our dear Child. I hope you will not—for be assured if in this instance I take any Measures disagreable to you it will be with extreme reluctance. I shall certainly leave Town on Monday Morning for N.Y. & in the Interim will make no attempts to recover Peggy other than by Negotiation with you & your Family in which your consent will be presumed. I only Chuse to say to you at present that I am sustained by the dictates of Honor and propriety from entering into any Obligations but that I believe the line of conduct I shall pursue in case you meet my wishes

will please [you] & that it will be dictated by my Ideas of Justice
& propriety.

I have the Honor to Subscribe my[self]
   Madam Your Most Ob⁺ & very [Humble]
    Serv⁺
        Henry B. Livingston

The veiled threat in her husband's letter . . . "a Possibility
a Bare possibility of your being deprived of her forever . . ."
must have struck cold terror to Nancy's soul. She continued to
keep Peggy in hiding and left the city herself for a period of
two weeks so that the writ would expire before Colonel Livingston could lay hands on the child. Nancy's attorney, Jared
Ingersoll, writes her:

I do myself the pleasure to inform you that yesterday a Motion
was made in the Court of Common pleas for an Attachment against
you as having been guilty of a Contempt in not producing your
Daughter, at the time you made a return of the Habeas Corpus—
The Court were of opinion that the Writ was extinct, & that nothing could be done upon it. You may therefore with safety return
to town as soon as you please. Suspicions are entertained (on what
foundation I know not) that Col. Livingston means to seize the
Child whenever he can find it—I have given the hint to your
friends.

III

The litigation ended in defeat for Nancy. The record at this
point is incomplete and more or less incoherent, but it appears
that a divorce could have been given Nancy on condition that
Colonel Livingston have the custody of their child. In this
event he could legally take Peggy to the far South, or any-
where, and do with her what he would. Nancy might never
again lay eyes upon her child. The alternative was that the
existing situation, miserable and unfair to Nancy, Louis Otto

and Peggy as it was, would remain the same. Nancy would no
be given her freedom so that she and Otto could marry; bu
she could at least hope to visit her daughter in New York anc
have her with her a few months of every year. Furthermore, i
would be possible for her to continue to have a voice in the
child's care, training and education. If there was any financia
settlement, it is not mentioned.

Thus Nancy Shippen was faced with a choice where there
was no choice. Otto always knew there was none that she could
make. If she took her freedom and married him she would
throw her child to the wolves. Knowing this, and knowing
Nancy, he did not urge her divorce to make possible a marriage
with him.

The date of the last letter Nancy received from Otto wa
August 15, 1789, in which he wrote:

"I have a great deal to say to you which I cannot comitt to the
paper."

This may have meant that he wished to tell Nancy of hi
intention to re-marry; that he expected to ask the Chevalier de
Crevecœur for the hand of his daughter, or that they were
even then engaged. Undoubtedly he must have written Nancy
of his decision, and talked over the matter with her in ful
detail. Not to have done so would have been unlike him, un
like his honest heart, his honorable nature. If such a lette
had come to Nancy, obviously it would be the only one of hi
she would destroy.

The fall and the long winter pass without further word
from Otto. Then, as the first year of Washington's presidency
was drawing to a close in April, 1790, the marriage of Loui
Otto and Mlle. de Crevecœur took place in New York City
Those present were: The Most Honourable Mr. Thomas Jef

erson, Secretary of State of the United States; the Honourable Jeremiah Wadsworth and Honourable Jonathan Trumbull, members of the Congress of the United States; the Honourable Richard Morris, Judge of the Superior Court of New York; the Honourable Antoine R. C. M. Delaforest, Vice-Consul General of France in the United States, and Catherina Delaforest, his wife; the Honourable John Kean, member of the Treasury Commission of the United States, and Susannah Kean, his wife; Christopher Mantel Duchoquetez, Esq., St. Jean de Crevecœur, Beau manoir Delaforest; William Seton, Esq., and John Trumbull, Esq.[2]

What did Nancy think? With the passing of the numbness that undoubtedly followed the shock, she must have reminded herself that there was no other course for Louis Otto to take. He had a motherless child. He had waited for Nancy eight years. He had risked his career through the constant linking of his name with hers in dishonoring gossip. Furthermore, in his new office in the diplomatic service of his country, he would have in the lovely Fanny de Crevecœur, daughter of the distinguished scholar and French officer, St. John de Crevecœur, a wife who had high standing in both American and French society.

Nancy may have read again that line in Louis' letter of the preceding year: "I was born for the peaceable enjoyments of domestic Life. . . ."

Perhaps she made herself think that this was the one reasonable course for her former lover to take. Her former lover —how bitter the adjective must have been! But of this she writes not a syllable. Leander's name never again appears in her journals.

No longer did she find occupation and solace in recording

[2] See *Supplementary Records* (7).

the daily events of her life in the little books that were onc
like friends and confidants. Undoubtedly, life itself was to
severe for speech, as she came squarely face to face with it
horrible realities and summoned all her forces to withstan
them. Then and in the long years after, for her daughter's sak
and her own, how she must have struggled for the strength t
bear her grief!

For the year 1791 there is but a single paragraph, the fina
entry of her *Journal Book*. It is written on Christmas Day
nearly two years after Louis Otto's marriage to Fanny d
Crevecœur:

I have consider'd my life so uninteresting hitherto as t
prevent me from continuing my journal & so I shall fill up th
remainder with transcriptions—It is certain that when the min
bleeds with some wound of recent misfortune nothing is o
equal efficacy with religious comfort. It is of power to enlighte
the darkest hour, & to assuage the severest woe, by the relie
of divine favor, & the prospect of a blessed immortality. I
such hopes the mind expatiates with joy, & when bereaved o
its earthly friends, solaces itself with the thoughts of one friend
who will never forsake it.

In that bitter darkness, there was one heart beating close t
hers—the heart of her child. But the days were long anc
lonely, and the fight was hard. Silence covers the next tw
years. As Christmas of 1793 is approaching with its glad ex
pectation for Nancy of a visit from Peggy, the child writes:

My dear Mama, December ^{the} 11th 1793—

How slow and tedious the time is in coming that will bring m
once more to the arms of my Mother.—Dr Todd is not come from
town yet with the fine paper, or I would have enclosed the tw
letters to my dear Grandmama & to Mrs Cramond. The poo

294

womans shift is now finished. As I knew you would like to hear from your girl the first opportunity that offered I would not wait for the arrival of the paper to let you know that I am well.

Your discription of your journey to town was truly very diverting, 'tho not so much so as the poor taylor's to see Cousin Snip. Dr Batchelor has been here but I would not have my tooth drawn, because in your letter to Mrs Erwin you desired that nothing might be done to my teeth except in your presence. That little sore place in my heel has proved to be a chilblane.—I don't know whether I have spelt the word right or not having never met with it before as I remember; But the Doctor has given me something to put upon it. Mr Erwin is going to town some time next week and will send this by him. It's the first safe opportunity I have had to write. Please my Mama to give my best love to Grandpapa and Grandmama, to my Uncle and Aunt, and to my sweet little Cousin William. What does the dear little rogue thinks of the *Tuskorora ice* that I sent him?—But, stop, its almost four o'clock. I must finish my exercises, for it will soon be dark. . . .

I am, dearest Mama, your ever-affectionate,

Ma. A. B. Livingston.

Wednesday.

P.S. Its quite unfashionable I'm told now, to put post-scripts but I forgot to tell you Mrs Erwin sends her love to you. But she will write herself by this opportunity I expect. This letter Mama is intended for nobodys eye but your own. I'll try my very best hand 'tho when I get the other paper. Adieu. M A B L. . . .

Four years more—heavily laden with sorrow for Nancy—dragged by. At length in the early spring of 1797, when Peggy had reached the age of sixteen, she took affairs into her own hands, gave up the comforts and luxuries of Manor Clermont and all prospect of her expected fortune, left her adoring grandmother and aunts, and came to her mother, never again to leave her in life or in death.

All this is told in three letters and in epitaph.

295

Peggy's Aunt Janet wrote to Nancy:

Dr Madam

We part with your little girl with the less regret as she is to b
with a Mother so well calculated to form, and compleat her edu
cation—& most certainly you could not have a better subject t
work upon, since she has a fine understanding with a tast[e] fo
books. The graces she will doubtless acquire in your circle. I pra
for her happiness and hope to hear that she is safely arrived a
Philadelphia and in the arms of a family on whom she has doubl
claims, and to whom I request my Compliments. You also wil
accept my best wishes. I am ever

Your Most Obedient Servt

Janet Montgomery

When Eliza Coxe learned the news she wrote:

. . . How happy am I to have it in power to congratulate you o
the return of your charming Daughter—she has I dare say mad
great progress in her improvements as well as in her person—
Maria joins me in begging you will present our love to her & as
sure her we have not yet forgotten her tho' it is almost three yea
since I have seen her. . . .

From Williamsburgh came a gay letter from Tommy, date
April 20, 1797, which is among the last he lived to write:

My dear Sister

. . . Yesterday's post brought me the letter which I am thu
early doing myself the pleasure to answer, and I assure you tha
I have very great pleasure in answering it. First, because it is fro
you, and then because it is so well written, and full of such agree
able topics. . . .

You astonish me by saying that my grandfather has not ye
made his intended visit—Shall I then never see him again? If h
has no objection to it, I really think we will make a large part
this Summer to visit him in Sussex—What say you to it—you an
Peggy—Shall we fill the Coaches & all go up together? Who know

296

but we may make such a trip—but I fear most from your natural repugnance to *Parties*—Perhaps Peggy may for once overcome it by her entreaties—Ha! Peggy!

(On verso of this sheet is the following):

To Miss M. B. Livingston—

I would with great pleasure do more than you ask me, my dear Niece, for instead of a postscript, I would write you a letter, had I not already written both to your Mamma and Grandmamma this morning, and if I were not fatigued by doing so. Besides that, I am this moment informed of an opportunity of writing to a place where I have urgent business, and for which an oppr^y seldom offers.

Your letter gave me great pleasure & I could not but applaud that overbalancing love for your dear Mamma which is so natural and does you so much honor, and which induced you to forego all the advantages your grand Mamma Livingston offered you by a residence in her family. When you write to her next, do not forget my dear, to assure her of my respect and constant regard— So—your cousin Lewis is the Belle of N. York—Well you must try to be if not the Belle (which by the bye I cannot think the most honorable or desirable distinction) the most accomplished and the most amiable young lady in Phil^a Nothing could give more heart felt pleasure to your and your Mammas

Most affectionate friend
Th. L. Shippen

But this happiness for which she had so yearned came too late for Nancy Shippen. Anxieties, persecution and grief had encompassed her from the day she was forced to break her troth to Louis Otto. Her marriage and the years following it had been beset with dangers, and with dread that her child would be taken from her. Her brother, at the age of thirty-two years, was dead of consumption. Her feeling for her parents had changed. She had come to a full realization of their part in wrecking her life by making her marry Livingston and, at a critical point of the divorce proceedings, defending him against her. The man she loved, her Louis Otto, was estranged from her and gone forever across the seas. Never again would she see or hear from him.

All the sorrows of her life must have gathered in strange and menacing shadows, crouching to spring upon her. Against them her daughter flung her brave spirit, her undying love for her beautiful mother. But even her sacrifice was too late.

Nancy's bright faculties dimmed and faded out.

. . . .

As the eighteenth century came to an end, the blinds of Shippen House were closed, its hospitable hearths cold, the rooms empty, and the gardens untended. Passing into the ownership of the Wistar family, a new stage of its history began, and even its name was obliterated. Dr. and Mrs. Shippen, stricken by the premature deaths of their son and the elder grandson, and by the estrangement from their afflicted daughter, moved to Germantown with their one surviving grandson, William Shippen. Dr. Shippen died at Germantown July 11, 1808. Nancy remained in Philadelphia under the care of physicians and occupied chambers of her own with her devoted child always in attendance. Occasionally they had a semblance of social intercourse with friends and neighbors: ghosts of old "gaieties," parties and dances to which Peggy was invited, and over which perhaps her mother hovered. But eventually mother and daughter went into a seclusion from which, so far as record can be found, they never emerged. Nancy's former spirit and zest for life blurred into a form of religious melancholia.

The papers and letters extant show that at intervals Nancy was sufficiently normal to feel a responsibility for the financial aspect of her child's welfare, for she wrote several times to her husband's brother, Honorable Edward Livingston, in reference to Peggy's estate. Now and then she expressed an interest in her nephew's affairs and exchanged letters with him and with some of her old friends. There were days when she recognized her daughter's presence beside her and took comfort from it.

The letters of Louis Otto were always in her possession until they passed into her daughter's cherishing hands. After Peggy's death they went, with all her mother's other letters and documents, to Tommy's son, William Shippen, who without knowledge of their authorship and possibly not even of their contents, left them to his descendants. There may have been moments when Nancy read them again, when, perhaps, she told Peggy of the Louis whom she loved and who was lost to her.

Her own mother, Alice Lee, lonely and blind in her old age, was the last survivor of the Stratford Lees. Nancy did not see her, even in death. Her five beloved uncles and her aunt, Hannah Ludwell Corbin, all died long before the year 1817 when her mother passed away. Nancy's "dear Virginia" beckoned her no more.

When Madam Livingston died she left to her namesake and favorite grandchild, Peggy, so long a member of the Clermont household, the fortune which the young girl had renounced for her mother's sake.

In a letter dated February 6, 1801, Nancy's old friend Maria Burrows wrote to her:

I am highly pleased that Peggy's Grandmama has provided so well for her I always thought she w^d as she has been spoken of as a very fine and good old Lady—and as she well knew the persecution you have endured on account of your marriage she no doubt had a feeling for your Child.

In Dr. Shippen's will some provision was made for Nancy, and in Tommy's will were the characteristic bequests:

I give to my dear sister Anne Home Livingston an hundred pounds to be laid out in Tea & Coffee urns cream pot & sugar dish made of silver & engraved with my coat of arms. . . . I give to my niece Margaret Beekman Livingston two hundred dollars to be laid out in a harpsichord or a wedding bed & bed curtains as she may chuse.

But for Nancy's daughter there was never a thought of harpsichord or wedding bed, nor of use for the Livingston fortune save as it ministered to her mother's needs.

After the turn of the century, as the black-hooded years trod slowly, mournfully on, the mother and daughter lived to see even the memories of their kinspeople and early friends fallen like dead leaves. Their own lives were like candles blown out.

The end of Nancy's long death-in-life came in the summer of 1841. For the greater part of forty years she had been immersed in hopeless melancholy, roused occasionally by the passing of relatives and friends. She took a morbid interest in composing epitaphs and hymns and in writing long confused letters of condolence, which are chiefly accounts of her dreams of the dead.

Her daughter lived after her for twenty-three years. Of these long years the only record is a letter from a Philadelphia attorney to Peggy's cousin William Shippen. The attorney makes it clear that, like her mother and her grandmother before her, Peggy too became a religious fanatic. Swindlers posing as clergymen made away with their portion of the Livingston fortune. Except for her physician and the men who victimized her and her mother, Peggy Livingston was literally buried alive. She who was the accomplished daughter of one of the

rst families of the United States, the most historic figure
mong American children in the days of the nation's making—
he pet of President Washington, of her uncle Chancellor Liv-
igston, of her great-uncle, Richard Henry Lee, and of other
tatesmen of the First Congress—this gifted child strangely,
erribly, dropped from sight.

Peggy died in the closing year of the Civil War and was
lso buried in the cemetery of Woodlands, that ancient estate
f the Hamilton family, friends of Shippens, Lees and Liv-
igstons in every generation for more than a century.

So, in the end Nancy and her daughter are together in sweet
nd friendly soil,—they are buried in one grave. They sleep
ear the path leading from Mansion Avenue, close to the
arred old stone house. A red rose bush blooms all summer
ong within their burial plot, and sometimes the petals drift
lown upon the low white marble slab with its few carved lines:

Here lie the remains of
Mrs. Anne Hume Livingston
Daughter of Dr. William Shippen,
who died Aug. 23, 1841, in the 78th
year of her age

The remains of
Miss Margaret Beekman Livingston
Died July 1, 1864, in the 82nd year of her age

Supplementary Records

Shippen

SUPPLEMENTARY RECORDS

TOM SHIPPEN'S DESCRIPTION OF WESTOVER, 1783

When Nancy Shippen's brother Tom was studying law at Williamsburg in 1783 and 1784, he spent part of the Christmas holidays at Westover. His letter describing the historic mansion and its grounds was found by the editor in the Shippen Papers in the Library of Congress and given its initial publicity.

Westover Decr 30 11 oclock at night.

My very dear Papa and Mamma,

I am just now retiring to rest after having spent a most delightful day with the lovely inhabitants of this place; they are charming indeed: Mrs B. seated at the head of her table, with her four amiable and accomplished daughters around her exhibits the most engaging scene, and inspires the most exalted idea of human nature: But their portraits I will draw for you at another time, as they deserve each of them a particular one, at present I will only give you a short account of my chamber in which I am writing, and in the morning endeavor to make you acquainted with Westover itself.

Imagine then a room of 20 feet square, and 12 feet high, wainscoted to the cieling, hung with a number of elegant gilt framed pictures of English noblemen and two of the most beautiful women I have ever seen (one of whom opposite to the bed where I lay) and commanding a view of a prettily falling grass plat varrigated with pedestals of many different kinds, about 300 by 100 yards in extent an extensive prospect of James River and of all the Country and some gentlemen's seats on the other side; the river is banked up by a wall of four feet high, and about 300 yards in length, and above this wall there is as you may suppose the most enchanting walk in ye world Nor are the prettiest trees wanting to compleat the beauty of the Scene. I must tell you too as I am now only introducing you to my chamber, that on the floor is seen a rich scotch carpet, and that the Curtains and Chair covers are of the finest crimson silk damask, my bottle and bason of thick & beautiful china, and my toilet which stands under a gilt framed looking glass, is covered with a finely worked muslin. Taking together the different parts of this incoherent account you will have a pretty just idea of my chamber. And now my dear friends I wish you a good night, the first hour of ye morning shall be devoted to you, for from you not even the many charms of Westover can divert a moments attention. A fine fire smiling in my chimney seems almost to tempt me to proceed, but it is late, and Sleep begins to enforce her claims.

Decr 31. 83. A fine snow has fallen last night, and adds very much to the beauty of my prospect; the contrast between the trees and the whiteness of the ground is pleasing; But to my promise, which I must endeavor to fulfil, tho' I shou'd fall very short of my desire. I will begin then with the entrance to this favored seat of Grace and Beauty. You leave the main road from Williamsburg to Richmond about two miles from Westover and ride a mile and a half thro' a most charming Wood which has ever been the hobby horse of its possessor on account of its beauty, and has always belonged to Westover. You pass thro' two gates, and from the second, which leads you into the improved grounds, may be seen a village of quarters as they are called for the negroes. The road you get into upon opening this gate is spacious and very level bounded on either side by a handsome ditch & fence which divide the road from fine meadows whose extent is greater than the eye can reach; and on one side you see the river through trees of different sorts. These meadows well watered with canals, which communicate with each other across the road give occasion every 50 yards for a bridge; and between every two bridges are two gates one on each side the road. You cannot easily conceive how fine an effect this has, but I must not omit mentioning the trees which tho thinly planted on both sides the road are a considerable accession. This road so beautiful that I can never go slow enough thro it, does not run in a straight line to the house it goes on the right of it for a little more than a quarter and a ½ quarter of a mile, you then turn to the left thro a very magnificent gate into the farm yard, where are the most commodious stables for the stock that I ever saw, You pass thro the extreme edge of it on the left, leaving it on the left. The road now becomes circular, & the remaining ½ quarter of a mile conducts you to the house itself. I do not know how to give you a better idea of the building themselves than by the assistance of a simple figure whose unseemliness you must excuse, as you know I am no draughtsman* from this figure you can form but a very imperfect idea of the buildings indeed, but it is

* Unfortunately the faded condition of the sketch prevents its reproduction here.

as good a one as I can give you, as such I am sure you will be satisfied with it. I only mean to describe the ground floor of any of the houses. The circular dotted line marked L. may represent the road which leads to the house the middle J, the gate opposite to the house which you ride up to, it is made of iron curiously wrought, and is exceedingly high, wide and handsome. The letter N which is put there for North is also the front door, which leads thro' a very wide entry, beautifully adorned with pictures and furniture of different sorts, and an elegant staircase, is very high and Stocoed at the top. The 1st room on the left after you enter the N. door marked d, is the common dining room, with fourteen black & gilt framed pictures, wainscoated (as all the rooms are) to the cieling, with windows as you see described on the paper. The room marked c is the drawing room of the same size of the last mentioned and both of the dimensions of my chamber. The furniture here is more rich, being silk damask and in the other room a yellow stuff with red and white cases to the chairs, but has a handsome marble slab, which the drawing room has not. The pictures too are better than in the dining room, and it commands the view which I told you I enjoyed from my chamber, which is the room above it. The rooms e, f, g, & h are you see of a less size and not equal to one another as the rooms on the other side of the entry are. Of their particular uses I am ignorant.

The house is only two story high but the garrets are commodious and clever. The house marked T. was the library, and appears very well suited to the purpose, as it is large and very light having (tho' 'tis not so on the paper) two windows on each side of the door, which is in the middle This is the room where they used to dance too. The others are large and ornamental, but now uninhabited, and I cannot conceive what were the uses of all of them. The kitchen is somewhere between L & O. The houses marked P are Temples of Cloacina. Q R & S have been Stables, Coach houses &c The crooked line marked x shows you where the garden is which is very large and exceedingly beautiful indeed. The one opposite to it &c is the place where there is a pretty grove neatly kept, from which the walk thro' one of the pretty gates marked g^1 leads you to the improved grounds before the house. The letters, a, a, & a, are put where the River flows beautifully along, carrying with it, or rather giving birth to Commerce Riches & Happiness I have markd some little crooked ugly figures for Gentlemen's seats, which tho' they do not beautify indeed the picture, add much to the prospect, about as many Seats are to be seen on the other side.

307

There are some pot hooks and hangers, which I have intended to make personate tall & stately trees, which least you should mistake them I write under, as the painter did under his sign "These are Trees. One principal fault of my draught is that the circle of which you see the segments, ought to be much larger, so that the periphrasis of it should come much nearer to the buildings K & I &c. Thus much for what is inanimate,(?) the rest I must reserve to another letter, as I dare say you are hear[tily] tired and I am sure my arm is. If you derive a moments entertainment from this essay, I shall be more than paid for my trouble, which tho' 'tis not very trifling, I fancy will not prove so great, as yours has been to read what I have wrote. A post is just arrived and brings no letter, what a dissappointment! No letter yet from Mama, Nancy, Grandpapa, Washington or any but my dear Papa who is very good indeed and obliges me exceedingly by writing as often as he does, I hope my sweet Mamma thinks of her son often, tho' she finds it troublesome to write. My next letter must be a long one as I have a great deal to say. Adieu. THOMAS LEE SHIPPEN

My Uncle William desires to be remembered to you, and wishes to know what you would advise him to do for his eyes which he finds are beginning to grow exceedingly weak insomuch that he can't read at all by candle light. You do not mention any thing about my hat.
N. B. Bank notes pass without difficulty or loss in Williamsburg. Jany 6

Addressed:
Dr William Shippen Junr
   Philadelphia

[Endorsed]: Description of Westover
   1783

Shippen Papers, Library of Congress.

BARBE DE MARBOIS, FIRST SECRETARY OF THE FRENCH LEGATION IN PHILADELPHIA

Monsieur Marbois was a social lion among the Philadelphia ladies, as evidenced by this letter from Nancy's friend M. Coxe, inviting her to a country party:

Mr. H. takes Sophia Francis under his care, & T. Footman is to go with the Hamiltons, but in what carriage is not determined. Mr. Bache will be with us, & I hope Mr Franklin who is expected in Town before Tuesday. Mr Marbois, who I have also asked, has a very gentle horse, & if you have a Chair, I think the best way will be to make a pair of you at once, by putting you under his protection. We shall see him this evening, when I will mention the plan, which I am sure will give him pleasure; but if you do not like it, I trust we have other resources left. I am happy to find that the party anticipate a good deal of pleasure in this country frolic, & hope their expectations will be answered.

GENERAL FRANCISCO DE MIRANDA

General Francisco de Miranda was another of the famous guests of Shippen House during 1783 and 1784. A native of Venezuela, he dedicated his life to liberating the Spanish colonies from the rule of Spain. He is designated by South American writers as "The Precursor of Spanish-American Independence." During his service in the American Revolution he conceived the idea of liberating South America from Spain.

NOTES ON ELIZABETH WILLING POWEL, WIFE OF THE MAYOR OF PHILADELPHIA. BY THE MARQUIS DE CHASTELLUX

"I have already mentioned Mr. Powel, at present I must speak of his wife; and indeed it would be difficult to separate from each other, two persons, who for twenty years have lived together in the strictest union; I shall not say as man and wife, which would not convey the idea of perfect equality in America, but as two friends, happily matched in point of understanding, taste, and information. Mr. Powel, as I have before said, has travelled in Europe, and returned with a taste for the fine arts; his house is adorned with the most valuable prints, and good copies of several of the Italian masters. Mrs. Powel has not travelled, but she has read a great deal, and profitably: it would be unjust perhaps, to say, that in this she differs from the greatest part of the American ladies; but what distinguishes her the most is, her taste for conversation, and the truly European use she knows how to make of her understanding and information."

LETTER FROM BUSHROD WASHINGTON

This letter from Bushrod Washington in the Shippen Papers without the name of the person to whom it was addressed, was identified

*by the editor as having been written to Nancy. One wonders whether
Bushrod Washington still cherished a hope that circumstances might
bring him into closer relations with Nancy, or whether the following
letter in the stately yet intimate style of the day was purely one of loyal
friendship.*

Bushfield Westmoreland County
April 28th 1784

Dr Madam

Had I not a great deal of fortitude to leave Philadelphia on Good
Friday, although so much happiness was promised me if I had staid?
I certainly should have felt myself incapable of resisting the pleasing
prospect, had I not considered, that the succeeding Day might Appear
with equal attraction, and might render me equally desirous of being
attracted—In short, my regret on parting with you and my other
Friends was not the effusion of a moment or from the peculiar happiness *of a Day*, but it was produced by a sincere and lasting attachment
which dreaded a seperation—I have often wished that Philadelphia had
fewer charms for me, or that Fortune had fixed me there for Life—
Added to the reluctance with which I was about to bid adieu, the
Moment of my departure was attended with very inauspicious circumstances, and had I been superstitious, I wou'd certainly have postponed
my design until things should wear a more propitious face—My Horse,
than whom a more peaceable, good natured animal lives not, Sancho's
Dapple not excepted, appeared to be infected with feelings somewhat
congenial with my own, and either refused to move a step, or if he did,
it was retrogade—In this manner did he for some time give a loose to
his inclination, until by reiterated strokes of the whip, he thought me
too much in earnest and humbly submitted his will to mine—Whilst I
am mentioning the ill boding Signs which attended my departure, I
will just observe that a most violent and chilling Snow escorted me
eight miles from the City to allay I imagine that warm attachment
which so often tempted me "To cast one longing, lingering look behind"—No other accident attended me, nor no adventure occurred
worth relating—I arrived home in Nine Days, and thank Heaven
found my Parents in good health and happy to see me—

May I congratulate you on the happy interview with your lovely,
and endearing little Baby? I hope Mr Willing did not disappoint you—
After so long a seperation, (for to you it must have appeared so) I can
fancy nothing more exquisitely tuned than your feelings on the occasion
—I most sincerely hope that you found her in good health, fare ad-

vanced in the improvements of her little mind, and if possible in beauty . . .

Be pleased to Remember me in the most friendly manner to my female acquaintances, particularly to the Miss Shippens Miss Coxes & Miss Delainy—Assure your own family of my attachment—

I thank you sincerely for allowing me the pleasure of writing to you, and of assuring you of my Friendship—Although to hear from you by letter, would be a very high gratification, yet I leave you perfectly unrestrained; I should consider it as a favor for which I could never be sufficiently grateful, but I will not stipulate for it as a right— I only lament that illiberal Custom should in this Country alone discountenance a correspondence between the Sexes—

That you & yours may enjoy the most perfect health and the most uninterrupted happiness is amongst the sincerest wishes of
your friend and very humble Servant

B Washington

P.S. The family beg to be remembered to yours—My sister's compliments to you and will be much indebted to you for the Ballad of "One fond Kiss" &c.

CHRISTIAN'S COMMENTARY ON BLACKSTONE

That Nancy had no legal protection from any slander Colonel Livingston might put in circulation is shown by the following:

Female virtue, by the temporal law, is perfectly exposed to the slanders of malignity and falsehood; for any one may proclaim in conversation, that the purest maid or the chastest matron is the most meretricious and incontinent of women, with impunity, or free from animadversions of the temporal courts. Thus female honour, which is dearer to the sex than their lives, is left by the common law to be the sport of an abandoned calumniator. [Blackstone] 3 Vol. 125

From this impartial statement of the account, I fear there is little reason to pay a compliment to our laws for their respect and favour to the female sex.—Notes by Christian (early editor of Blackstone's "Commentaries") following Blackstone's chapter on "Husband and Wife."

Commentaries on the Laws of England, in Four Books by Sir William Blackstone. 13th ed. with notes and additions by Edward Christian. London, for A. Strahan, 1800. Volume I, Book I, Chap. 15, p. 445[c].

COPY OF RECORD OF THE MARRIAGE OF M. OTTO AND
MLLE. DE CREVECŒUR, 13 APRIL 1790

Received by the editor from Comte Louis de Crevecœur

To each and all, greeting in God's name

I, the undersigned, Catholic and apostolic pastor of the church of
St. Peter, "Novæ Eboracentis" commonly called *New-York*, by these
presents give notice and certify to all and sundry whom it may concern that I have united in marriage, according to the rites of the Holy
Roman Church,

M. Louis Guillaume Otto, knight of the Most Christian King, *chargé
d'affaires* in the United States (which he discharged to the approval
of all) by his own right and Miss America Francisca de St. Jean de
Crevecœur (by father of the bride) Michaele Guillaume Joanne de
St. Jean de Crevecœur, knight, Consenting on the thirteenth day of
April A.D. 1790.

Witnesses present were: The Most Honorable Mr. Thomas Jefferson
secretary of State of the United States, the Honorable Jeremiah Wadsworth and Hon. Jonathan Trumbull members of the Congress of the
United States, Hon. Richard Morris Judge of the Superior Court of the
state of New York, Hon. Antoine R.C.M. Delaforest, Vice-Consul
General of France in the United States and Catherina Delaforest his
wife; Hon. John Kean member of the Treasury Commission of the
United States and Susanna Kean his wife; William Seton Esquire,
John Trumbull esquire; Christopher Mantel Duchoquetez esquire; in
proof whéreof I have signed with my own hand

Done at "novi Eboraci," commonly New York on the above day of
this month of April A.D. 1790

(Autograph signatures) Louis Guillaume Otto   A. Francis de
Crevecœur St Jean de Crevecœur Th Jefferson Jere Wadsworth—
Jonᵃ Trumbull Ri Morris Antoine and C. M. de la Forest—Beau-
manoir De la Forest John Kean S. Livingston Kean—Ph. Living-
ston—Wᵐ Seton—Juᵃ Trumbull Mantel Duchoquetez—Nicolaus de
St Thoma Burke Pastor ut supra

We, Vice Consul General of France in the United States of America
residing at the seat of the general government at New York, certify
to all concerned that Monsieur Nicolaus de S Thoma Burke, who
signed the certificate of the celebration of marriage in preceding part

is in fact the curate and priest of the Catholic parish of St. Peter in this city, and that every certificate signed by him in this capacity is entitled to credence in law as elsewhere; in testimony whereof we have signed these presents and have had affixed the royal seal of the Consulate of New York.

Given at our Consular residence in New York the fourteenth of April 1790

de la Forest

DESCENDANTS OF DR. WILLIAM SHIPPEN.

COMPILED BY CHAS. R. HILDEBURN.

On page cxxxv of "Letters and Papers relating chiefly to the Provincial History of Pennsylvania, with some Notices of the Writers," the editor, Mr. Balch, after referring to a preceding page on which he gives only the parentage and date of birth, remarks: "Of Dr. William Shippen I have no further information than such as is already in print." The following table of Dr. Shippen's descendants has been prepared to supply the omission, and to correct the confusion which has arisen from Lauman (Dictionary of Congress), Alexander (History of Princeton College), and others having confounded the elder Dr. Wm. Shippen with his son Dr. Wm. Shippen, Jr.

AUTHORITIES.

1 Named in father's will.
2 Named in grandfather's will.
3 Records of the First Presbyterian Church.
4 Records of the Second Presbyterian Ch.
5 Records of Presb. Church, Germantown.
6 Records Presbyterian Church, Abington.
7 Newspaper of the period.
8 MSS in the possession of Ed. Shippen, M.D.
9 Tombstone.
10 Thacher's Medical Biography.
11 Wood's History of the Univ. of Penna.
12 Wood's Centennial Address, Penn. Hosp.
13 Journal Continental Congress.
14 Colonial Records, Vols. XI–XII
15 Cat. Colleg. Nova Cæsaris.
16 Hodge's Obstetrics.
17 Carson, Hist. Med. Dept. Univ. Penna.
18 Charter, By Laws, etc., Coll. Physicians.
19 N. E. Gen. and Hist. Mag., XXI.
20 Sprague's Annals Am. Pulpit, Vol. III.
21 Deeds.

William Shippen,
of Hilham, Yorkshire, England.
=
Edward Shippen, == Elizabeth Lybrand,
first wife.
emigrated to Boston, Mass., 1669, and
removed to Philadelphia, 1693.

Joseph Shippen == Abigail Gross,
first wife.

Dr. William Shippen,[1] == Susannah, eldest daughter
of Joseph Harrison, of Philadelphia,
by his wife Katherine Noble, born
Philadelphia, June 30, 1711; died
between June 4, 1774, and Jan. 10,
1775.[21]

youngest son born Philadelphia, Oct. 1, 1712, married Sept. 19, 1733,[4] died Germantown, Nov. 4, 1801.[9] He early applied himself to medicine, and soon attained eminence in his profession.[10] He was one of the founders of the Second Presbyterian Church, 1742; a member of the first Board of Trustees of the College and Academy of Philadelphia, 1749; one of the founders and many years a Trustee of the College of New Jersey; Physician to the Pennsylvania Hospital, 1753–78;[12] elected member of the Continental Congress, Nov. 16, 1778,[13] and re-elected Nov. 13, 1779,[14] and throughout both terms was most constant in his attendance.[13]

Alice, youngest == Prof. William Shippen,[1] M.D. ==
daughter of Col.
Thomas Lee,
Gov. of the Pro-
vince of Vir-
ginia, by his
wife Hannah
Ludwell, and
sister of Richard
Henry, Francis
Lightfoot, and
Arthur Lee, born
in Virginia,
June 4, 1736,[9]
died in Phila-
delphia, March
25, 1817.[7]

born Philadelphia, Oct. 21, 1736;[3] married in London[8] circa 1760; died Germantown, July 11, 1808.[7][9] Graduated at College of New Jersey, 1754,[15] delivering the Valedictory for that year. Studied with his father till 1758, when he went to England and studied anatomy under Dr. John Hunter, and midwifery under Drs. Wm. Hunter and McKenzie.[16] Graduated M.D. of the University of Edinburgh, 1761, and after a short visit to France returned to Philadelphia in May, 1762.[10] On Nov. 16, 1762,[7] he commenced the first course of lectures on anatomy delivered in America. The introductory was given at the State House.[6] He con-tinued to lecture on Anatomy and Midwifery until Sept. 23, 1762, he was elected Prof. of Anatomy and Surgery in the Medical School of the Col-lege of Philadelphia,[17] of which he was the founder. On July 15, 1776, he was appointed "Chief Physician for the Flying Camp."[13] In March, 1777, he laid before Congress a plan for the organization of a Hospital Department, which, with some modifications, was adopted,[13] and on April 11, 1777, he was unanimously elected "Director General of all the Military Hospitals for the Armies of the United States;" he resigned Jan. 3, 1781.[13] On the reorganization of the College of Phila-delphia as the University of Pennsylvania, he was elected May 11, 1780, Prof. of Anatomy, Surgery, and Midwifery; he resigned in 1806.[11] He was one of the originators of the College of Physicians, 1787, and President 1805, till his death.[18]

Joseph W. == John Shippen,[1] == Susanna,[1]
Shippen,[1] M.D., born born Phila-
born Phil- Philadelphia, delphia,
adelphia, Jan. 23, 1740,[3] Oct. 23,
Oct. 17, o.s.; graduated 1743, mar-
1737;[9] at Coll. N. J., ried at Ab-
died, un- 1758,[15] studied ington, Ct.,
married, at under his fa- Sept. 24,
Oxford, ther, and after- 1768;[8] died
Sussex Co. wards at the German-
N. J., Sept. University of town, Oct.
13, 1795.[7] Rheims,[17] Fr., 12, 1821.[7]
where he re-
ceived his de-
gree of M.D.
Soon after his
return he com-
menced, April
5, 1770, a course
of lectures on
Fossils, etc.
married, Baltimore, Md.,
Nov. 26, 1770.[1]   He died un-

+Francis Lykfapart

Rev. Samuel Blair, D.D., son
of the Rev. Samuel Blair, by
his wife Frances Van Hook,
born in Chester Co., Penna.,
1741, died in Germantown,
Sept. 23, 1818. Graduated at
the College of New Jersey,
1760, and was a tutor there
1761–4; licensed to preach
1764; installed Pastor of the
Old South Church, Boston,
Mass., September, 1766; resigned Oct. 10, 1769. Elected
President of the College of
New Jersey, but declined in
order to secure the election of
Dr. Witherspoon, 1767. Resided in Germantown, 1769,
till his death.[20]

See page 111.

1763

Ann Hume,[1] &[2] m. March 11, 1781, d. Philadelphia, Aug. 2, 1841, aged 78.

Henry Beekman Livingston, son of Robert R. Livingston, Sr., of Clermont, and brother of Chancellor Livingston, b. 1750. He was a colonel in the Continental Army.

Thomas Lee Shippen,[1] &[2] = of Farley, Bucks Co., Pa., b. 1761, m. at "Nesting," Va., March 10, 1791, d. near Charleston, S.C., Feb. 4, 1798. Educated at Booth's Academy, Md., Honorary M.A. Princeton 1788[2] studied law under James Madison, Williamsburg, Va., and afterwards, 1786, at the Inner Temple, London.

Elizabeth Carter, daughter of Maj. James Parke Farley, of Antigua, W.I., by his wife Elizabeth, daughter of Col. Wm Byrd, 3d of Westover, Va., by his first wife Elizabeth Carter. She m. 1st, John Banister, Jr., Esq., of Va., and after the death of Mr. Shippen m., 3d July, Gen. George Izard,[3] U.S.A. She d. Philadelphia, June 24, 1827, aged 32 years.[3]

William Arthur Lee Shippen, b. Philadelphia, Aug. 21, 1775,[4] who, with five others of whom I can find no information, died young.

Margaret Beekman,[5] b. Philadelphia, Dec. 28, 1781,[6] d. Philadelphia, July 1, 1864.[9]

Thomas Lee Shippen, b. at "Farley," d. at "Farley," Aug. 2, 1810, aged 1?[1]

William Shippen,[1] &[2] M.D., b. at "Farley," Jan. 19, 1792, m. Petersburg, Va., Feb. 14, 1817, d. Philadelphia, June 5, 1817: studied medicine under Dr. Wistar, University of Pennsylvania M.D., Demonstrator of Anatomy, University of Pennsylvania, Trustee of Princeton, 1841-67.

Mary Louise, daughter of Thomas Shore of Petersburg, Va., by his wife Jane Gray Wall, b. Petersburg, Va., March 17, 1798, living in Philadelphia.

Jane Gray, b. Violet Bank near Petersburg, Va., Feb. 23, 1818, m. Philadelphia, Oct 1843.

Edward Wharton, son of Fishbourne Wharton by his 1st wife Susan Shoemaker, b. Philada. Jan. 25, 1819, d. Baltimore, Md., Jan. 17, 1868.

Emma Manigault, b. Farley, Aug. 27, 1819, d. May 3, 1820.

Alice Lee, b. "Violet Bank," Va., March 5, 1821, m. June 1?, 1847, d. Bristol, Jan. 27, 1862

Joshua Maddox Wallace, M.D., son of Joshua M. Wallace, Jr., by his wife Rebecca, dau. of Dr. William McIlvaine, by his first wife Mary Coxe, b. Burlington, N. J., Jan. 13, 1815, d. Philadelphia, Nov. 1?, 1851.

Thomas Lee Shippen, of Petersburg, Va., b. "Violet Bank," Nov. 27, 1824, m. Petersburg, Jan. 11, 1860.

Jane Gray, daughter of Dr. John Gilliam by his wife Elizabeth S. Shore, b. Petersburg, Dec. 11, 1823, d. Petersburg, Aug. 1874.

William Shippen, b. "Farley," May 21, 1823, m. Baltimore, Md., Nov. 1, 1855, d. Philadelphia, April 3, 1858. Graduated, Princeton, 1844.

Achsah Ridgley, daughter of Chas. R. Carroll, of Baltimore, by his wife Rebecca Ann Pue, b. Jan 1833.

Joseph Shippen, b. July 18, 1829, d. May 18, 1830.

Edward Shippen, M.D., of Philadelphia, b. Farley, June 23, 1827, graduated Univ. Penna. M.D. Apr. 25, 1848.

James Parke Farley Shippen, b. Farley, Aug. 9, 1831, d. unm.

Mary Louisa, b. Burlington, N. J., April 19, 1833

Richard Henry Lee Shippen, b. Philadelphia, Jan. 12, 1836. d. Jan. 23, 1836.

Mary Louisa, b. Arrowfield, near Petersburg, Va., April 7, 1845, d. unm. Baltimore, Jan. 16, 1868.

Mary Coxe, b. Oct. 25, 1851, d. Bristol, Aug. 27, 1853.

Laura Christina, daughter of John O'Conner Barclay M.D., U.S.N., by his wife Ann Wilkes Collet, b. Nov. 10, 1831, d. Burlington, N. J., Nov. 13, 1874.

Shippen Wallace, b. Philadelphia, Feb. 26, 1850, m. Burlington, N. J., June 16, 1871.

William McIlvaine Wallace, b. Philadelphia, Aug. 28, 1848, d. Violet Bank in Va., Feb. 21, 1854.

Charles Carroll Shippen, b. Philadelphia, Oct. 2, 1856.

William Shippen, b. "Arrowfield," Va., May 21, 1861.

Violet Lee, b. Berlin, Germany, July 11, 1872.

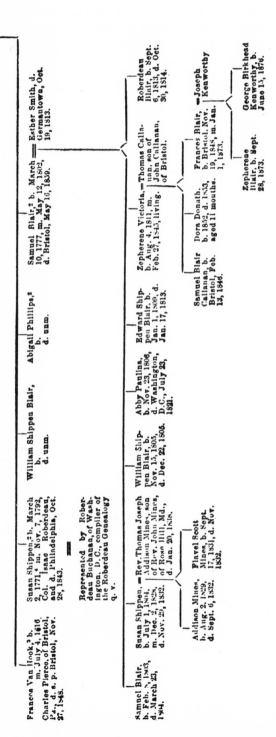

Frances Van Hook, b. July 4, 1818, m. Charles Pierce, of Bristol, Pa., d. s. p. Bristol, Nov. 27, 1848.

Susan Shippen, b. March 2, 1771, m. Nov. 7, 1792, Col. Isaac Roberdeau, and d. Philadelphia, Oct. 28, 1843.

Represented by Roberdeau Buchanan, of Washington, D. C., compiler of the Roberdeau Genealogy q. v.

William Shippen Blair, b., d. unm.

Abigail Phillips, b., d. unm.

Samuel Blair, b. March 10, 1777, m. May 12, 1802, d. Bristol, May 16, 1839.

Esther Smith, d. Germantown, Oct. 19, 1813.

Samuel Blair, b. Feb. 5, 1803, d. March 23, 1844.

Susan Shippen, b. July 1, 1804, m. Dec. 2, 1828, d. Nov. 20, 1832.

Rev. Thomas Joseph Addison Mines, son of Rev. John Mines, of Rose Hill, Md., d. Jan. 20, 1838.

William Shippen Blair, b. Nov. 13, 1805, d. Dec. 22, 1806.

Abby Paulina, b. Nov. 23, 1806, d. Washington, D.C., July 23, 1821.

Edward Shippen Blair, b. Jan. 1, 1809, d. Jan. 17, 1813.

Zepherene Victoria, b. Aug. 4, 1811, m. Feb. 27, 1845, living.

Thomas Callanan, son of John Callanan, of Bristol.

Roberdean Blair, b. Sept. 6, 1813, d. Oct. 30, 1814.

Addison Mines, b. Aug. 2, 1829, d. Sept. 6, 1832.

Flavel Scott Mines, b. Sept. 17, 1831, d. Nov. 1832.

Samuel Blair Callanan, b. Bristol, Feb. 13, 1846.

Dora Donath, b. 1852, d. 1853, aged 11 months.

Frances Blair, b. Bristol, Nov. 19, 1848, m. Jan. 1, 1873.

Joseph Kenworthy.

Zepherene Blair, b. Sept. 28, 1873.

George Birkhead Kenworthy, b. June 13, 1876.

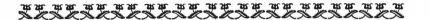

BIBLIOGRAPHY

BOOKS

Abbatt, William, Ed. "The Life and Career of Major John André, Adjutant-General of the British Army in America." By Winthrop Sargent. New edition with notes and illustrations. New York, William Abbatt, 1902.

Archambault, Anna Margaretta, Ed. "A Guide Book of Art, Architecture, and Historic Interests in Pennsylvania," Phila., The John C. Winston Co., 1924.

Beverley, Robert. "The History of Virginia," Richmond, J. W. Randolph, 1855.

Biddle, Henry D., Ed. "Extracts from the Journal of Elizabeth Drinker from 1759 to 1807," Phila., J. B. Lippincott Co., 1889.

Bowers, Claude G. "Jefferson and Hamilton; the Struggle for Democracy in America," Boston and New York, Houghton Mifflin Co., 1925.

Brissot de Warville, Jacques Pierre. "New Travels in the United States of America, Performed in 1788," Tr. from the French. Boston, J. Bumstead, 1797.

Brown, Alexander. "The Genesis of the United States," with 100 Portraits, Maps, and Plans . . . Lond., W. Heinemann, 1890.

Campbell, Charles. "History of the Colony and Ancient Domain of Virginia," Phila., J. B. Lippincott & Co., 1860.

Carson, Hampton L. "The Supreme Court of the United States: its History and its Centennial Celebration, February 4th, 1890," Phila., A. R. Keller Co., 1892.

Chase, Eugene Parker, Ed. and Tr. "Our Revolutionary Forefathers; the Letters of François, Marquis de Barbé-Marbois during his residence in the United States as Secretary of the French Legation, 1779-1785," N. Y., Duffield & Co., 1929.

Chastellux, François Jean, Marquis de. "Travels in North-America in the Years 1780, 1781, and 1782, Tr. from the French by an English Gentleman," Lond., G. G. J. and J. Robinson, 1787, 2 vols.

Cluny, Alexander. "The American Traveller," By an Old and Experienced Trader, Lond., E. and C. Dilly, etc., 1769.

Cousins, Frank, and Phil M. Riley. "The Colonial Architecture of Philadelphia," Boston, Little, Brown and Co., 1920.

Crèvecœur, Michel Guillaume St. Jean de. "Sketches of Eighteenth Century America," Ed. by Henri L. Bourdin, Ralph H. Gabriel and Stanley T. Williams. New Haven, Yale University Press, 1925.

Davies, Benjamin. "Some Account of the City of Philadelphia, the Capital of Pennsylvania, and Seat of the Federal Congress," Phila., Printed by Richard Folwell, 1794.

Dumas, Mathieu, Comte. "Memoirs of his Own Time; Including the Revolution, the Empire, and the Restoration," Phila., Lea & Blanchard, 1839, 2 vols.

Earle, Alice Morse. "Stage-Coach and Tavern Days," N. Y., The Macmillan Co., 1900.

—— "Home Life in Colonial Days," N. Y., The Macmillan Co., 1898.

Eberlein, Harold Donaldson, and Horace Mather Lippincott. "The Colonial Homes of Philadelphia and its Neighbourhood," Phila. and Lond., J. B. Lippincott Co., 1912.

Ellis, Annie Raine, Ed. "The Early Diary of Frances Burney (d'Arblay) 1768-1778," Lond., G. Bell and Sons, Ltd., 1913, Vol. I.

Glenn, Thomas Allen. "Some Colonial Mansions and those who Lived in them," Phila., H. T. Coates & Co., 1900.

Grant, Mrs. Anne (Macvicar). "Memoirs of an American Lady, with Sketches of Manners and Scenes in America as they Existed Previous to the Revolution," N. Y., Dodd, Mead and Co., 1901.

318

Griswold, Rufus Wilmot. "The Republican Court, or American Society in the Days of Washington," N. Y., D. Appleton & Co., 1867.

Hayden, Horace Edwin. "Virginia Genealogies," Wilkesbarre, Pa., 1891.

Humphreys, Mary Gay. "Catherine Schuyler," N. Y., C. Scribner's Sons, 1897.

Jefferson, Thomas. "Notes on the State of Virginia," Boston, 1801.

Keith, Sir William. "The History of the British Plantations in America," Lond., S. Richardson, 1738.

Lee, Edmund Jennings. "Lees of Virginia, 1642-1892," Phila., Franklin Printing Co., 1895.

Maclay, William. "The Journal of William Maclay, United States Senator from Pennsylvania, 1789-1791," N. Y., A. & C. Boni, 1927.

McClellan, Elizabeth. "Historic Dress in America, 1607-1800," with an introductory chapter . . . illustrations by Sophie B. Steel, Philadelphia, G. W. Jacobs & Company, 1904.

"Magazine of the Society of the Lees of Virginia," Vol. IX, No. 1, Mar. 1933.

Mease, James. "Picture of Philadelphia, Giving an Account of its Origin, Increase and Improvements in Arts, Sciences, Manufactures, Commerce and Revenue," Phila., R. Desilver, 1831.

Mereness, Newton D., Ed. "Travels in the American Colonies," N. Y., The Macmillan Co., 1916.

Monaghan, Frank. "French Travellers in the United States, 1765-1932; a bibliography," N. Y., The New York Public Library, 1933.

Myers, Albert Cook, Ed. "Sally Wister's Journal; Being a Quaker Maiden's Account of her Experiences with Officers of the Continental Army, 1777-1778," Phila., Ferris & Leach, c1902.

Parsons, Jacob Cox, Ed. "Extracts from the Diary of Jacob Hiltzheimer of Philadelphia, 1765-1798," Phila., W. F. Fell & Co., 1893.

Parton, James. "Life and Times of Benjamin Franklin," Boston and New York, Houghton Mifflin Co., 1892.

Paxton, John Adems. "The Stranger's Guide. An Alphabetical List of all the Wards, Streets, Roads . . . Wharves, Ship Yards, Public Buildings, &c. in the City and Suburbs of Philadelphia," Phila. 1810.

Robertson, William Spence, Ed. "The Diary of Francisco de Miranda tour of the United States, 1783-1784," N. Y., The Hispanic Society of America, 1928.

Robin, Claude C. "New Travels Through North-America," Phila. Robert Bell, 1783.

Schaw, Janet. "Journal of a Lady of Quality; Being the Narrative of Journey from Scotland to the West Indies, North Carolina, and Portugal, in the years 1774 to 1776," Ed. by E. W. & C. M. Andrews. New Haven, Yale University Press, 1934.

Sélincourt, Ernest de, Ed. Spenser's Minor Poems. Oxford, Clarendon Press, 1910.

Sherrill, Charles Hitchcock. "French Memories of Eighteenth Century America," N. Y., C. Scribner's Sons, 1915.

Smith (Mrs. William Stephens [Abigail Adams]). "Journal and correspondence," Ed. by her daughter, N. Y., Wiley & Putnam 1841.

Tillotson, Harry Stanton. "The Exquisite Exile, The Life and Fortunes of Mrs. Benedict Arnold," Boston, Lothrop, Lee & Shepard Co., 1932.

Tower, Charlemagne. "The Marquis de La Fayette in the American Revolution," Philadelphia, J. B. Lippincott Company, 1895, vols.

Twining, Thomas. "Travels in America 100 Years Ago," N. Y. Harper & Brothers, 1894.

Washington, George. "Diaries," Ed. by John C. Fitzpatrick, Boston & N. Y., Houghton Mifflin Co., 1925, 4 vols.

Watson, John F. "Annals of Philadelphia," Phila., Carey & Hart, 1830

320

Weddell, Alexander Wilbourne, Ed. "A Memorial Volume of Virginia Historical Portraiture, 1585-1830," Richmond, The William Byrd Press, 1930.

Wharton, Anne Hollingsworth. "Salons Colonial and Republican," Phila., J. B. Lippincott Co., 1900.

Wood, Anna Wharton. "The Robinson Family," [With letters of Vicomte de Noailles] In Rhode Island Historical Society Bulletin, No. 42.

MANUSCRIPT COLLECTIONS

Shippen Papers. (Library of Congress)

Richard Bland Lee Papers. (Library of Congress)

The Lee Collection of Original Letters and Documents of the Robert E. Lee Memorial Foundation, Inc.

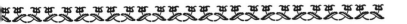

Index

INDEX

THIS INDEX HAS BEEN PREPARED BY MARION H. ADDINGTON AND K. L. TREVER
WITH A VIEW TO MAKING MORE READILY AVAILABLE, BOTH TO GENERAL READER
AND SPECIAL STUDENT, THOSE FEATURES OF EIGHTEENTH CENTURY COLONIAL LIFE
AND CUSTOM SO REMARKABLY SET FORTH IN NANCY SHIPPEN'S JOURNAL BOOK.—
EDITOR'S NOTE.